Industrial Innovation and Public Policy:
Preparing for the 1980s and the 1990s

Recent Titles in
Contributions in Economics and Economic History
Series Editor: Robert Sobel

Industrial Innovation and Public Policy:
Preparing for the 1980s and the 1990s

Roy Rothwell

and

Walter Zegveld

CONTRIBUTIONS IN ECONOMICS AND ECONOMIC HISTORY, NUMBER 42

Greenwood Press Westport, Connecticut

Published in the United States and Canada by
Greenwood Press, a division of Congressional
Information Service, Inc., Westport, Connecticut

English language edition, except the United States and Canada,
published by Frances Pinter (Publishers) Limited

First published in 1981

Library of Congress Cataloging in Publication Data

Rothwell, Roy.
    Industrial innovation and public policy

    (Contributions in economics and economic history; no. 42
ISSN 0084-9235)
    1.   Technological innovations.   2.   Technology and
state.   3.   Industry and state.   I.   Zegveld, Walter,
joint author.   II.   Title.
HC79.T4R68   303.4'83   81-493
ISBN 0-313-22989-9   AACR1

© SPRU, Sussex University and TNO, The Netherlands

Library of Congress Catalog Card Number: 81-493
ISBN: 0-313-22989-9

Typeset by Anne Joshua Associates, Oxford, England
Printed in the United States of America

CONTENTS

ACKNOWLEDGEMENTS

The authors wish to thank those of their colleagues who have contributed to this book by providing both useful information and critical and informed comment on previous drafts. Thanks in this respect are due to Professor Christopher Freeman, Mr Keith Pavitt, Dr Tom Whiston, Mr Peter Senker, Dr John Clark, Mr Paul Gardiner and Dr Ian Miles of the Science Policy Research Unit and Dr Frits Prakke of TNO. Thanks are due also to those authors who kindly gave permission for the use of their work in the book, notably Professor Jim Utterback, Dr Fred Steward and Professor Gerhard Mensch.

Special thanks are due to Dr Ben Martin of SPRU who prepared Chapter 5 (in consultation with Roy Rothwell). He has, we believe, made a useful and original contribution to this book and brought together a diverse body of data in a logical and well-structured manner.

Dr Rothwell would like to thank in particular, the Leverhulme Trust Fund for their financial support during the preparation of this book.

Finally, thanks are due to Simone Sharp of SPRU and Jeanine van de Vort of TNO for their patience and help in preparing the manuscript.

1. INTRODUCTION

Following the so-called 'energy crisis' of 1973–74, with the rapid four-fold increase in the price of oil, there has been a marked reduction in the rate of growth in the world economy. Oil is now not only expensive, but is also seen as a finite, and increasingly scarce, resource. The recessionary trend since 1974 is leading to a decline in the quality of social and health care services in some countries along with a probable future decrease in the availability of higher education. Further, certainly within Western Europe, there now exist high levels of structural unemployment with lowered expectations for graduates.

There is a growing belief among western governments that one means of at least partially overcoming the effects of high oil prices, and of stagnating markets for many major product groups, and therefore of breaking out of the current recessionary cycle, is the stimulation of industrial innovation. Indeed, evidence will be presented in this book which suggests that the roots of the current world economic crisis go back further than 1973 and are very much bound to the rate and nature of technological innovation. The energy crisis merely accelerated and exacerbated previously established trends.

As a result, governments have become increasingly involved in the formulation and implementation of measures to assist, and to instigate, innovations in industry. Certainly with high levels of unemployment, low rates of industrial expansion and increasing competition from newly industrializing countries in traditional areas, high rates of innovation would seem to be essential to the maintenance of competitiveness, quality of services and high living standards in the advanced nations.

A crucial question to ask here is 'what is innovation policy'? The answer, for the purposes of this book, is that it is essentially a fusion of science and technology policy and industrial policy. Science and technology policy has been in existence for many years and has traditionally consisted of the patent system, technical education and the promotion of basic science and applied research within the scientific and technological infrastructure. Public policy for industry is also of long standing, being better expressed in some countries than in others. It consists of such measures as industrial restructuring, tariff policy, tax policy and investment grants. Today it seems obvious that the two should be closely related.

Innovation policy, in contrast to the other two, is quite new and built on a theoretical basis that is, as yet, rather weak. Fortunately, however, it is now possible to formulate innovation policy on a rapidly growing foundation of empirical work. This book does not, therefore, pretend to offer a theoretical analysis or basis for innovation policy, but adopts instead a rather pragmatic approach. It describes in detail a number of innovation policies currently being pursued in the advanced market economies.

During a period when there is a call, in some countries at least, for less government involvement (interference) in industry it is becoming increasingly evident that consideration of the threats and opportunities posed by radical innovations need to be an important component of government policy. Since this implies greater government involvement with industry, this could pose a dilemma. Involvement of industry in the policy formulation and implementation processes might go some way towards resolving this dilemma; it should also result in policies of greater relevance to the needs of industry.

Belief that the current world economic crisis is structural, and bound to a significant extent with the mode of evolution of industries and of technologies, implies that the changes necessary to overcome this crisis are difficult and rather long-term in perspective. This means that policies being developed and introduced today will probably not begin to have a significant impact for five to ten years. Governments should thus be prepared to adopt a strategic, long-term approach to innovation policy, which should be largely divorced from the short-term, and often rather cynical, dictates of party politics. To achieve this means that policies should be based on a consensus between government, industry and society regarding long-term economic aims. There is little doubt that in all the countries of the west these aims would consist largely of the maintenance of relatively high standards of living and the provision of reasonable social, health care and educational services. Outside the natural resource-rich countries, this can only be achieved through a healthy industry competing successfully in world markets.·

While we are not, in this book, discussing social policy and the need − or otherwise − for social change, we do recognize that considerations of economic growth, and the values and structure of society, are interwoven. Indeed, it might be that during an era of structural change in the world economy, some social change is necessary to accommodate the requirements of innovation policy, in order to avoid social strife. Certainly, the very rigidity of society might, in itself, slow down the application of necessary technical change and thereby deepen the economic − and ultimately social − crisis in a number of countries. In this respect the opposition of unions in some countries to the adoption of new technology − to the detriment of those countries' competitiveness and economic wellbeing − is well known.

Some of the measures described in this book are, in a sense, social measures − government regulations, for example. This is also at least partially true of policies towards small and medium-sized firms which are important for social policy, as well as for innovation policy reasons. It is true also of employment policies.

The bulk of the measures described in this book are, however, strictly related to innovation policy and designed to improve the innovative − and thereby economic and competitive − performance of industry. These include government subsidies to private firms, innovation-oriented procurement, and the scientific and technological infrastructure.

Certainly the rationale underlying this book is that innovation is crucial to industrial efficiency and competitiveness, and to economic growth, and, ultimately, to the benefit − in the long-term at least − of society at large. This leads to a belief in the necessity for carefully thought-out, strategic, long-term innovation policies based on an assessment of current and future technological, economic and social needs and problems, and on an awareness of technological trends and associated commercial opportunities. We believe that such policies are both necessary and possible.

2. THE INTERNATIONAL ECONOMIC, SOCIAL, AND POLITICAL BACKGROUND TO GROWTH AND WELFARE

The quarter century from 1948 to 1973 was one of exceptional prosperity and worldwide economic growth. Although long-term historical comparisons are hazardous, it is probably safe to say that the average Gross National Product growth rates of 4 to 5 per cent that were achieved in the OECD area throughout this period had never previously been attained for so long in so many countries. The developing countries also shared in this expansion, although in most cases high population growth rates and inequitable distribution of incomes meant that the relative 'gap' in per capita incomes increased, and for vast numbers of people extreme deprivation persisted. The communist countries mostly attained or surpassed the high per capita income growth rates achieved in Western Europe and North America, but fell below the exceptionally high Japanese growth rate.

It is generally agreed that technical innovation was an extremely important factor in the prosperity of the 1948–73 period. High rates of technical change were attained both in the new, rapidly expanding industries, such as electronics, drugs and synthetic materials, and in some of the older industries such as coal-mining and, of course, agriculture. The steady improvement in output per man-hour in most sectors of the economy, together with redistributive social policies in many European countries, meant that standards of living were probably rising more rapidly for more people than in any comparable period in the history of the world.

The prosperity of the 1948–73 quarter century may be illustrated by comparison with the interwar period from 1919 to 1939. Average rates of economic growth were more than twice as high, perhaps three times as high. Whereas the interwar period was marked by the deepest depression (1929–33) ever experienced by the world economy, and by two other severe recessions in 1921 and 1937, the recessions during the period 1948–73 were relatively mild and of short duration, although slightly more frequent. Whereas unemployment was a severe problem throughout the interwar period, the third quarter of the twentieth century could be fairly described as an era of full employment.

In the 1930s unemployment rates of between 10 and 20 per cent were commonplace and it was not until the Second World War that the unemployment rate in the United States fell below this level. Yet most European countries had unemployment rates below 2 per cent almost constantly during the 1950s and 1960s.

Perhaps the sharpest contrast was in the growth of the volume of international trade. At the end of the interwar period (1938) the volume of trade was actually less than it had been in 1913. In the period 1948–73 international trade grew even more rapidly than the volume of world production — at a rate of about 7 per cent per annum. The 1930s were a period of intense economic nationalism and rising trade barriers; the 1950s and 1960s witnessed remarkable advances in trade liberalization, and the promotion of successful free trade areas such as the European Economic Community.

Another sharp contrast was in the relative stability of agricultural incomes and prices since the Korean War. During the interwar period agricultural incomes and farm prices were very depressed and while falling prices in the 1930s had of course some benefits for consumers, the poverty in rural areas was a major cause of social unrest and instability.

One result of the economic development and of the full employment experienced since the Second World War associated with the general availability of cheap household consumer durables, has been a marked rise in female participation in the labour force. Between 1960 and 1974 the female participation rate (proportion of all females between 25 and 64 at work or actively seeking work) increased from 40 per cent to 59 per cent in the United States, from 35 per cent to 68 per cent in Sweden, from 42 per cent to 53 per cent in the United Kingdom, and by rather smaller amounts in other countries of the European Community (OECD, 1977).

The attainment of a more equal status for women in the labour force was only one of a number of significant social changes associated with rising prosperity. Other major changes were the worldwide expansion of secondary and higher education and far greater access to medical care.

Although some improvements in living standards did occur during the 1920s and even during the 1930s for those who were in regular employment, the general insecurity, the severity of the 1929–33 world crisis and the ruin of many farmers and businessmen meant that the interwar period is generally regarded as one of economic failure and frustration. Both in the industrialized countries and in their colonial possessions, nationalism became widespread and the 1930s saw the collapse of the League of Nations and many other idealistic attempts at international collaboration. It would be unwise to forget that mass unemployment and insecurity can lead to frightening and explosive social catastrophes and international tensions.

While it would be naïve to equate changes in per capita GNP with equivalent improvements in the 'quality of life', or perceived 'welfare', there is little doubt that for most people there is some connection between rising real incomes and life satisfaction. For what they are worth, worldwide attitude surveys do confirm that there is a fairly strong association between unhappiness and low incomes, both within and between countries. It is also true, however, that this correspondence diminishes at higher levels of per capita income. 'Happiness' or 'life satisfaction' was apparently greater in several European countries than in the United States, even though they still had slightly lower per capita incomes. At the higher income levels, further increments are not desired so strongly as at lower levels.

It is gratifying to have this confirmation of the continuing validity of the common-sense view of poverty from recent sociological survey findings. It is, incidentally, also an interesting justification for marginal analysis and its relevance for income redistribution. However, it would be naïve to build too much on the strength of this association between real income, quality of life and satisfaction. As is known, the latter concepts are hard to define and even more difficult to measure. Political and environmental circumstances can hardly be left out. Nor can such extremely difficult issues as family structure, crime rates, neighbourliness and security. It is far beyond the scope of this book to embark on such a discussion.

For our purpose, then, it is sufficient to make a few relatively simple generalizations which, although they will not command universal assent, would probably get fairly wide acceptance and help to structure further discussion on the objectives of public policy and the rationale for various government measures in relation to technical innovation:

— at low levels of per capita incomes, such as those which are almost universal in developing countries today and were widespread in Europe and Japan in the 1930s, there is a very strong popular belief that a significant improvement in the quality of life can only come about through a major and sustained increase in real incomes;

— such an improvement in the quality of life was experienced by large numbers of people in the industrialized world in the prosperous quarter-century 1948–73. It was generally welcomed by them and was envied by the less fortunate majority in the 'third world' who would mostly like to emulate this achievement and are now exerting considerable political pressure to this end;

— as per capita incomes rise, there is increasing concern with those aspects of the quality of life which are less easily satisfied through simple increases in private consumption. Issues such as urban amenity, leisure facilities, work experience, political participation, and various social services become more important for large numbers of people.

The prospect that progress towards a more widely shared world prosperity might slow down or cease altogether is an extremely unwelcome one to the vast majority of the world's inhabitants. The problems of growth are difficult enough; the problems of stagnation are acute but the problems of deep world depression are incalculable.

Public awareness of a drastic change in the economic climate usually dates from the OPEC crisis — the quadrupling of oil prices at the end of 1973. However, most economists have recognized that a number of important changes had already occurred before the OPEC crisis.

Among these changes were:

— an acceleration of the rate of inflation in the early 1970s, associated with a steep rise in food and other primary commodity prices;

— the breakdown of the international exchange-rate system between 1970 and 1973 and the shift from an 'adjustable peg' system to 'managed floating' by countries or blocks of countries;

— a fall in the share of non-residential construction in total investment since the early or mid-1960s, indicating a shift from expansion of capacity through construction of new factories to rationalization investment based on scrapping and replacement of equipment in existing plants;

— an increase in the concentration of industry and a fall in the number of small firms and of their share of output throughout the 1960s;

— a fall in the rate of profit in several leading industrialized countries from the mid or late 1960s;

— a continuous rise in the capital investment per employee and a decline in the rate of increase in capital productivity over the same period and in some cases a negative trend in the productivity of capital.

Although drawing attention to most of these factors in its analysis of 'What went wrong?', the McCracken Report of the OECD (1977) drew the relatively optimistic conclusions that:

the most important feature was an unusual bunching of unfortunate events unlikely to be repeated on the same scale, the impact of which was compounded by some avoidable errors in economic policy. In other words, the first half of this decade saw an upheaval in the economic affairs of the western industrialized nations that is unlikely to be repeated. Though it has left a legacy of uncertainty and unstable expectations which will contribute to very difficult policy problems in the years ahead, this upheaval is not necessarily a sign of a permanent change to an inevitably more unstable and inflationary world.

Other commentators were less optimistic about the situation confronting the OECD countries. Those who believe that the problems of revival of the world economy may be severe generally point to factors such as these:

- private investment is not likely to be so buoyant in the fourth quarter of this century as in the third quarter, for a variety of reasons, including the profit rate, the general climate of economic and political uncertainty and the apparent 'saturation' of some important markets which were a major source of expansion in the 1950s and the 1960s.
- unemployment is not likely to return to the low levels of the 1960s. If, as most people expect, growth rates are a good deal lower than the 5.5 per cent envisaged in the McCracken Report, well over 5 per cent unemployment could persist into the 1980s.
- 'wage push' may continue to be a source of inflationary pressures and social conflict despite the prevalence of higher levels of unemployment;
- monetary policies may be more restrictive and the freedom of governments to finance public sector deficits more severely limited, partly because of the difficulties of curbing inflation;
- the growth of international trade may slow down and both protectionism and non-tariff barriers to trade may become more widespread as international competition becomes more severe;
- some of the older traditional industries, such as shipbuilding, steel, cotton and wool textiles, clothing, mechanical equipment, and metal products, will suffer severe competition not only from Japan and the communist countries but increasingly from the industrializing Third World countries, such as Korea, Brazil, Mexico and some OPEC countries. This competition is also expected to become more intense in newer branches of industry such as motor vehicles, chemicals and electronic equipment;
- the process of concentration in manufacturing and service industries may continue, so that a relatively small number of multinational corporations will control an increasingly large share of production and trade in the industrialized countries. This may increase international investment decisions;
- energy supplies may become even more expensive as a result of the very high capital intensity of new energy sources and of the failure of governments to apply effective energy conservation policies;
- rates of technical change may continue to slow down providing fewer opportunities for new investment and thereby contributing to the lack of buoyancy in private investment (see Chapter 3).

The fears of economic stagnation, large-scale unemployment and deep world depression underlie public reactions to the slowdown in economic growth, to the first severe recession of the postwar period and to the continuing higher levels of unemployment in the 1970s and 1980s. It is a matter of central concern of policy-makers at all levels to prevent a return to the conditions of the 1930s. It is this concern that found expression in the preparation of the OECD McCracken report

(1977), which analysed what went wrong in the early 1970s and set out the objective of a return to such high growth rates as 5.5 per cent through the 1980s.

The McCracken report can be considered an extremely competent piece of analysis but it pays little attention to the problems of technical innovation. The capacity to manage technical change efficiently has now become a vital factor in international trade competition, just as important or even more important than wage levels. Technical change is also of critical importance in relation to future investment and employment prospects. Following an initiative by the government of Japan, therefore, a major research project was established within the framework of the OECD in 1976, to study 'the future development of advanced industrial societies in harmony with that of developing countries'. The project, referred to as *Interfutures* (OECD, 1979a), ran for a period of three years. The primary purpose of the project was to provide OECD member countries with an assessment of alternative patterns of longer-term world economic development in order to clarify their implications for the strategic policy choices open to them in the management of their own economies, in relationships between them, and in their relationships with developing countries.

Parallel in time with the OECD *Interfutures* work, a number of other studies were undertaken. All of them dealt with the future ten to twenty years ahead of us and stressed the role that science and technology could and should play in future development. The reports to which we make special reference in this respect are EEC–FAST (1980), Business International (1979), Danzin (1979), OECD (1979b), Hall (1978), EEC (1979a), European Industrial Research Management Association (1978). All these studies agree that there are many political, economic and social problems ahead. The most obvious elements of the present crisis are lower economic growth, increasing unemployment and growing inflation. The recent economic recession has also led to political tensions, such as the North–South dialogue and international competition, and has brought to the surface important value changes in the industrialized world. These value changes especially, and the differences in values of important segments of the population make planning for the future more difficult than before and consequently the tone of most outlooks is set by insecurity about both the goals and the means of the 'post-industrial' society. These goals are increasingly questioned under the influence of 'post-materialist' values that alter, for instance, the work ethic, the trust in technology, in the welfare state and the acceptance of hierarchy.

Ian Miles, of the Science Policy Research Unit of the University of Sussex, in a paper presented at the Futuribles Meeting at Arc-et-Senans in September 1979 (published as Miles, 1980) presented the following scheme of value change in advanced industrial countries (Table 2.1).

As to the means of achieving growth, they are put to question as tools of the past since they seem to be less useful for the future; different structures are required for the solution of our present-day and future problems. The best-known example is in the field of economic planning. Economic theories no longer seem to have the answer to present problems of stagflation, meaning inflation and unemployment at the same time. The problems of our present industrialized society used to be described primarily in macroeconomic terms, but most recent studies also focus on the behavioural changes, and consequently often speak about 'post-materialist' society instead of 'post-industrial'.

There is nothing to indicate that the pressures on advanced industrial societies will be any stronger in the future than in the past, but their nature will change and,

Table 2.1 Economic growth

Economic growth: more job security,
political stability, goods for consumption,
social welfare

↓

Satisfaction of 'lower' needs of wider
sections of society: less motivation
directed by fear of insecurity, lack of
basic good, largely as result of childhood
experience

↓

Emergence of more individuals motivated
by 'higher' needs, especially in more
affluent, more educated social groups.
For example: demand for improved
work conditions, more opportunities
for women, etc.

→

Growing tendencies to:
value leisure above additional income,
rethink the work ethic, seek participation
in work and politics,
engage in voluntary and informal sector
activities, prioritize environmental concerns
and distrust big technology

↓

Fragmentation of society as
groups diverge in social values between
post-materialist minority and the
majority.
Divisions along lines of new sectional
interests, new struggles over distribution

→

↓

Demands for more government intervention
but for more participation and less bureaucracy.
New conflicts over public expenditure,
industrial control

Result

Growth is as necessary as ever, to satisfy demands in a non-zero-sum way. But its content
is changed by environmental and technological controls and these, together with rigidities
prompted by the organization of sectional interests, may make it less feasible.

---

above all, they will be exerted in a context of slower growth that will make adjustment more difficult. The resistance to this adjustment is manifold, but four sources
are essential: population, final demand, the cost of exchanges with the physical
environment, and the competitive positions of economies. In their different guises
the origins of these pressures are: population growth marked by the ageing of
the population and by changes in participation rates and the size of the labour
force; changes in final demand under the combined influence of population, values,
income levels, price structures and the sizes of significant social groups; an increase
in the cost of exchanges with the physical environment (higher prices for energy
and certain raw materials, and the influence of environmental protection policies);
and changes in the competitive position of the developed countries' economies,
both as between one another and *vis-à-vis* the Third World, and at the global as
well as the sectoral level.

    Given the perceived uncertainties within the forecasting horizons (up to the
year 2000) and the widespread scepticism towards integrated forecasts, most
studies are seeking at least practical solutions through the use of multiple scenarios
and contingency planning. The question is then what plausible scenario will all
the pressures and trends add up to. No one can answer this question, as there is
simply not one plausible scenario for any country, for Europe, for the OECD or

the world. Forecasting studies like OECD's *Interfutures* (1979a) or the European Economic Community *Project 1990* (EEC, 1979a) end up with several scenarios. These scenarios represent the probable boundaries within which the future state of the economy and international relations are likely to lie. The future could ultimately have components of each scenario. The mixture which currently seems plausible, or even possible, is most undesirable for the next decade and would require major changes in policy to prevent its realization. The elements of this mixture are (Norse, 1979):

- slow and moderate growth in most OECD countries for the next ten to fifteen years, with continuing structural unemployment;
- inadequate coordination of short-term economic policies, and continuing haphazard structural adjustment, of variable effectiveness;
- protectionism aimed at imports from other industrialized countries and from the Third World;
- higher growth in productivity with problems caused by the more rapid and effective adjustment of some countries, such as Japan and West Germany, generating friction between these countries and the less successful industrialized countries; and
- governments facing problems of arbitrating between a majority with rather traditional demands and active minorities pressing new demands.

It may be clear that the world is entering a transition period and that several countries will have a hard time to maintain their competitiveness. The world market is not growing as fast as it used to and there are more competitors. The less developed countries (LDCs) are eager to industrialize. Japan and the United States need to export more for reasons of trade balance. The rise of several 'new Japans' (Korea, Taiwan, Brazil, Singapore) is spectacular from the viewpoint of the international trade relations. Countries should find their way in a world of growing competition, while at the same time their domestic markets will be more difficult to protect.

The major asset of the industrialized country is the skill and ingenuity of its people which can compensate for its relative poverty in materials and energy. It should therefore set out to use the resource that is relatively most abundant: its technological and scientific knowledge, which has to be translated into effective innovation of products, processes and services. Given this situation both the EEC and the OECD recently commissioned studies on the function of science and technology in present-day society (Danzin, 1979; OECD 1979b). From these studies it can be concluded that there are several reasons for giving urgent attention to the potential of science and technology. In the next few decades the industrial countries will be confronted with many complicated problems and must increase their efforts to find new solutions to control structural change. Science and technology can play an important but differing role in the structural adaptation of these societies (OECD, 1979c):

- the first is a *science and technology-adjusted* structural adaptation. This is a situation where science and technology are developing in response to the needs of society to adapt to the rapidly changing socioeconomic and cultural environment;
- the second is a *science and technology-led* structural adaptation. Here science

and technology play an important role as a driving force for structural change by establishing or rapidly increasing certain activities in societies (such as the development and introduction of microelectronics, biotechnologies, new energy technologies).

Consequently, it will be critical for industrialized societies to stress more the role of R & D and innovation. But confidence in scientific progress as a major vehicle of economic growth and consequently the welfare of society is no longer undisputed. Increasingly, the question is not, and will not, be *how much* R & D and innovation, but *what kind*.

We have pointed out that value changes are a key concept in the explanation of the structural changes confronting us. Several studies point out that next to economic and political forces, individual motivations will increasingly shape the future. One study (Hall 1978) coins alienation of the individual as one of the central problems of present and future society. Science and technology are often at the heart of the controversy on the present state of our society and, consequently, views on the future contribution of science and technology may vary widely. It is quite clear to many, however, that potentially this contribution is large. The direction of future scientific development is open for debate and ever more actors and factors are influencing the outcome of this debate.

An important element of the debate is the future industrial structure and the role science and technology could play here. This is all the more true if one reflects on the maturity and the likely decline of the industrial sectors which traditionally were the locomotives of economic growth and still now account for a relatively high share of industrial employment. This necessitates a structural adaptation of industry under such tight constraints of lower economic growth, high unemployment levels, inflation and the tightening of government financial resources.

Under these conditions much creativity is needed to control the structural changes with which the industrial countries are faced. A major study like *Interfutures* (OECD, 1979a) concludes that our future will be limited by the quality of our social and political resources rather than by energy availability or physical resources. In all analyses (like *Interfutures* and *Europe under Change*) one can read that innovation will increasingly have a non-technological component. The report of the FAST-group of the European Economic Community (EEC-FAST, 1980) points to the fact that 'it is necessary to become adapted to a lower rate of growth by modifying the qualitative content of technological, economic and industrial development, by the way of social innovation (education, organization and finality (ethics) of work, life and leisure styles). In some countries this is called the 'qualitative' or 'selective' growth of the economy. We realize the vast amount of discussion going on about the subject of innovation. Most countries have recently brought out studies or policy papers on the subject. Brief summaries of these efforts are given in Chapter 5.

Analysts and studies have pointed out that many of the present problems are rooted in changes in the western world which preceded the oil crisis of 1973. The relations and trends analysed cannot be accounted for by conjuncture alone; they underline the specific and deep structural nature of the present problem as compared to the 1950s and the 1960s.

We consider that it is better to prepare for the problems of the future by assuming that the changes of the 1970s contribute to a new economic and social context for science and technology. The tone was already set by the OECD (1971) Brooks report:

> Thus, science policy is in disarray because society itself is in disarray, partly for the very reason that the power of modern science has enabled society to reach goals that were formerly only vague aspirations, but whose achievement has revealed their shallowness or has created expectations that outrun even the possibilities of modern technology or the economic resources available from growth. It is against this background that the limitations and relative failures of science policies during the last decade can be understood most clearly. A crisis of growth and a crisis of the linkage of science policy to social aspirations seem to be two closely related aspects of the same problem.

Only by looking to the future can the industrial countries select goals and objectives that they should strive to achieve, and by which they should be guided in setting priorities. Innovation is definitely such a priority. The aim of the innovation, however, is not so much a growing economy, but a society that responds to change and challenge.

The authors feel that the industrial countries should take the change and challenge of the 1980s seriously and work actively towards a restructuring of their industrial and technological potential. This will take time, but the 1980s should be used as a transition period toward the 1990s when this restructuring will bear fruit in a new, but ever-challenging, socioeconomic context of an independent world society.

INNOVATION OPPORTUNITIES AND CONSTRAINTS

According to the *Interfutures* study (OECD, 1979a) there will be important changes that will affect the growth, organization and worldwide distribution of industrial production and trade. These changes will be different from those in the past in four ways:

(1) Interaction between industry and scientific research, and complementarity between industry and many service activities are gradually making the concept of industrial activity lose its precise shape. As a corollary industry as a whole is no longer playing the essential role of a creator of employment that it has had over the past twenty years.

(2) A new generation of key industries is gradually taking the place of those which brought about postwar growth. In the first rank is what may be called the 'electronics complex', covering automation, data processing and telecommunications, whose development will increasingly affect the very nature of economic activity, whether in terms of production processes in industry and services, styles of consumption or the role of communications.

(3) The above changes will be taking place in a context of slower growth, mainly for reasons of rigidities within societies and pressures on these societies.

(4) This context of slower growth has arisen at the very time that the system of worldwide industrial relations is subject to pressures of many kinds. The interaction between the industrial forces in North America, Western Europe and Japan is changing. In addition, there is broader interaction superimposed involving the industries of Southern Europe, the Third World and Eastern Europe.

Change in Factors and Actors

Empirical research shows that the rate and direction of innovation is influenced by four factors: costs, demand, competition, and technological capabilities. We would like to add a fifth factor that is often regarded as obvious, but will become increasingly important: the influences from the actors in the innovation process. By this we do not mean the managers or the entrepreneurs who influence innovation directly, but the growing number of actors who either directly or indirectly influence technological and industrial developments. The changing pattern of innovation shows the dynamic character of the process that through the interaction with socioeconomic and cultural developments no longer remains predominantly technical, but ever more social and organizational involving a larger number of factors and actors. The role of governments in promoting and guiding innovation is already important. The role of other actors, like trade unions, organized consumer groups and social interest groups, are still rather marginal, but might become more important in the future. In the United States *Domestic Policy Review on Industrial Innovation* (White House, 1979) special sub-committees were formed on public interest aspects and with trade-union representatives. Their recommendations called not for more, but for different, innovation. This aspect will involve changes in both structures and in the diffusion of technology.

In Europe, trade unions are increasingly taking an interest in technological changes. In the United Kingdom a TUC report on employment and technology (TUC, 1979) concludes: 'we have to maximise the benefits and minimise the cost of the new technology. We have to ensure that the benefits are distributed equitably. Reliance on market forces alone will not be enough to enable us to meet the challenge of rapid industrial change.' A recent report by the European Trade Union Institute (ETUI, 1979) remarks: 'A central requirement for a satisfactory resolution of the problems associated with new technology is that trade unions should be involved at the earliest opportunity at all levels of policy-making – the enterprise, company or industry level, the national level and the European and international level.'

For the European consumer the gradual strengthening of the Common Market has produced a source of influence over how industrial producers perform. The EEC was created to eliminate trade barriers among its member countries and has increasingly harmonized the conditions under which companies operate – on the theory that any advantages or disadvantages among these nations would distort the trade among the members.

The result has been to open the door to shaping social policy throughout the nine member states. Issues such as the environment, youth and female employment, and worker participation, have come to the fore. Perhaps no issue, however, has as much potential for revising the regulatory environment for business as consumer protection.

Changing Costs

The OECD report on science and technology (OECD, 1979b) discusses at some length the issue of changing costs:

> Some of the most obvious opportunities and constraints relating to innovation came from the changing pattern of costs in the 1970s. In the 1950s and 1960s,

the key components of costs to which technical change was directed were those of labour. Whilst this remains a major concern of industry, there has been the abrupt, and probably irreversible, shift upward in real energy prices, resulting in an increased search for alternatives to crude oil, and for methods of conserving energy. This in turn has influenced innovative activities in all the major sectors of the economy (consumers, producers, public and private services). Simultaneously, major increases in the costs of other raw materials have occurred or are anticipated.

In the past few years, the rate and direction of innovative activities have also been strongly influenced by the new social awareness of the negative side-effects of science and technology, and the corresponding regulations to protect environment, safety and health. These concerns are expressed in new legislation, or in much stricter enforcement of old legislation. Such regulation is not even-handed in its effect on different industrial sectors; it has had a greater impact on the processing and automobile industries, and on mining, than on others. Regulations have sometimes been cumbersome instruments of control. While they increase the range of values and costs considered by decision-makers, they are often crude, with some dimensions of pollution, safety or work hazard being prescribed and others not, and sometimes with scant regard for the effects of regulation on costs and social utility.

These problems have been illustrated very clearly in studies of pharmaceutical products and pesticides. For some groups, particularly in the USA, the reduction in the frequency, and increase in the cost, of innovation are matters for concern. They argue that indiscriminate regulation has stifled or slowed down innovation; such products as penicillin and aspirin would not be able to meet today's requirements. They argue further that there is no longer much incentive for the support of longer-term, more speculative R & D. [For a detailed discussion of the 'regulation/innovation issue' see Chapter 8.] However, other groups argue to the contrary; the rate of introduction of major innovations had hardly slowed down at all, even if they take longer to produce; only minor improvements have been discouraged; further basic research is needed to open up new possibilities for major innovations; in the meantime, innovations will be less hazardous.

The relative merits of these two lines of argument cannot be evaluated in isolation from the national context in which they are developed. Regulatory requirements have changed very rapidly over the past ten to fifteen years, and have evolved at different rates in different countries. For example, four times more medicines were introduced into the UK between 1968 and 1971 than into the USA. This may reflect differences between the two countries in the preference for innovation or safety. But it may also reflect the fact that a great deal of regulatory action results from political initiative, and that its scientific and social base is shaky.

The effectiveness of the new regulations will depend on the technologies that they generate. This in turn will depend on how the regulations are designed. Efforts to encourage less pollution and safer technologies should involve some kind of a private–public mix of R & D funding and responsibility. Enough government-financed R & D needs to be done to ensure that regulatory standards are established on a strong factual basis, and that the claims of private parties about what they can and cannot do and at what cost are reasonably evaluated.

The effects of properly devised regulations on innovation can be very positive. In the pulp and paper industry, for instance, regulations and higher energy prices have eliminated old plant, and stimulated the introduction of more efficient and less polluting equipment and processes. There is evidence in other sectors of efficient innovations having been stimulated by the new constraints.

Changing Patterns of Demand

The last ten to twenty years have shown considerable shifts in patterns of demand, which have influenced the rate and direction of innovative activities. Consumers have been shifting their preferences partly due to higher living standards and partly to changing patterns of relative costs. There is now a greater emphasis in existing product ranges on reliability, on quality and on new products and services related to health, education, amenity and energy-saving.

At the same time there has been increasing interest in harnessing technology more effectively to areas of growing public expenditure such as health, education, housing, public transportation and general administration.

Professor Emma Rothschild (1979) commented on the OECD report as follows:

Two changes are important. In the first place, those industries which are consumers or producers of research now seem to contribute less to economic well-being. Several such industries (chemicals, metals, electricity supply) are among those where productivity growth rates have fallen most sharply. Others, including transport equipment, are important sources of inflation. In the second place, activities such as collective services and government, whose use of research has been modest or directed to other than economic objectives, have increased in relative importance. In several countries, employment has shifted substantially into these sectors. [Policies to increase overall demand are indeed likely to increase demand for low productivity services, as was conspicuously the case during the United States recovery of the mid–1970s.]

One explanation for these changes, very briefly, is that there is an asymmetry between innovation and the demands of societies. Consumption and production are out of joint; on one hand, consumption is increasingly 'socialised', as demand grows for environmental goods and for collective services; on the other hand, the system of production has changed more slowly, and research is still concentrated in resource-intensive industries.

Opportunities from New Markets

The pressures of international competition have been among the most powerful motives for industrial innovation. This had led in the 1960s and 1970s to a general trend to increase innovative capabilities throughout the industrial world. But competition is now also felt from the newly industrializing countries which are competing with the western countries on the basis of cost over a wider range of products. This has further stimulated innovative activities in the western industrialized world in three directions: towards more capital-intensive laboursaving technologies, in order to offset higher wages compared to the newly industrializing countries; towards products and materials that are competitive in quality (including technological quality) rather than price; and towards products and services that meet the needs of the growing markets of the newly industrializing countries.

In determining market opportunities of the future one should not stick to geographical markets only. We have already pointed at the demand changes in the direction of more social services. Innovation could become quite important for the development of such sectors as education, recreation activities, medical services, etc. Due to the population and employment trends there will also be an increasing quantitative demand for services for elderly people, which in itself seems to be a neglected 'market'.

Opportunities from New Technologies

The velocity and cost with which innovations are developed in response to opportunities and constraints depend on the state of development of science and technology. It now seems probable that we are only just beginning to see the results of the past patterns of R & D funding. Developments on the horizon already suggest that conditions exist for a second industrial revolution, with economic and human prospects probably as deep and as far-reaching as those of the first.

New lines of advance are many:

- new energy resources, nuclear and renewables, but also coal (provided it can be used in a clean and dependable way), and new technologies for a much improved energy management;
- new manmade materials, which will gradually substitute for traditional ones that become scarce or whose energy costs are exceedingly high;
- new ways to exploit the oceans (aquaculture, mineral resources from the sea) and the space (telecommunication and observation satellites, orbiting stations for production of energy);
- new developments in electronics and information technologies, which will dramatically change production and services through extensive automation and the diffusion of the microprocessor and computer techniques;
- new ways of communicating, which will change the sector of transport by progressively substituting the flow of information to that of people and merchandise;
- new developments in biotechnologies, streaming from the progress in microbiology, biochemistry, and genetic engineering, will profoundly change such sectors as agriculture, health, the chemical and food industries and will give rise to a new stream of innovations in the related sectors.

It is quite clear that all the industrial countries, and many firms, have already discovered these opportunities and are actively exploring them.

The EEC–FAST (1979) examination of the changes confronting Europe concluded by showing that:

- employment and energy are currently, and undoubtedly for the next ten years, the principal points of focus and application for most of the other problems;
- two changes could fundamentally transform society during the following decades; namely, the 'informatization' of society (that is, its pervasion by new information technologies), and then in the longer term, the biological revolution.

Since the energy constraint is already the object of numerous other research activities (both at European Commission level and in member states), the distinctive feature of the FAST programme could be its adoption of a framework of analysis which considers a plurality of time horizons, and hence reviews in certain priority areas the R & D actions which can, directly or indirectly:

- impinge upon work and employment (the major problem of the next ten years);
- Prepare for the 'information society' (the major change of the next twenty years);
- seize the opportunities presented by the 'biosociety' (the major change of the next thirty years).

The Largest Influence: People and Their Motivation

Ideas alone are not enough; one must find people who have the feeling and the mentality to implement them. One of the greatest dangers to innovation is the fact that both in the short and the long term there is a defensive attitude to risk-taking and entrepreneurship. In the short term one sees a defensive attitude toward future opportunities, because of the economic recession and the heavy pressures from the socioeconomic environment, like government regulation and industrial democracy issues.

Even in the United States venture capital investment in new, innovative business has greatly declined. There is no question that the emphasis in industrial R & D has shifted away from major product and process innovation to shorter-term evolutionary product improvement and cost reduction.

Except in a few companies, industrial investment in basic and long-term research has shrunk. At the same time some people believe that scientific and technological development will slow down because of the societal discussion on acceptability and on the requirements set by government regulation. This could lead to a situation where the need for restructuring of European industry is broadly acknowledged from a macroeconomic viewpoint, while at the microeconomic level change and innovation are resisted.

The longer-term problem for innovation is that the 1980s will show substantial lack of training opportunities for (future) entrepreneurs, because of the scarcity of challenging jobs in existing firms. For the coming years no industrialized country will be capable of generating as many challenging jobs as there are bright educated people.

The whole issue of employment has rightly been singled out by the FAST group as being the principal issue (next to energy) for the 1980s (see Chapter 11).

According to the report *A Blueprint for Europe* (EEC, 1979b) there is a structural tendency for unemployment to increase under the combined impact of several factors, which may be divided into two groups:

(1)   Causes affecting labour demand:
- the end of a major cycle of 'autonomous' investment brought about by the large-scale technological innovations of the postwar period;
- the rise in productivity due to laboursaving techniques;
- the tendency towards saturation of certain markets.

(2)   Causes affecting labour supply:
- the increase in the female participation rate. Until recently, only women belonging to the least favoured sections of the population worked, whereas now women from all social categories work. Society has adapted very badly to this trend;
- changes in attitude to work. There is a growing qualitative discrepancy between the kind of jobs offered and the kind of jobs people want.

This is particularly true of young people who, because of a higher level of education, look for better quality jobs;
— demographic trends. Until 1990 labour supply will continue to increase while population growth rates in Europe will fall gradually between now and 1990. This will result in a more limited supply by about the year 2000; the structure of the labour market will be considerably changed.

The above causes will in many ways have considerable impact on innovation, as the heated discussions on the microelectronics revolution have shown. There are many opposing trends in this field. While on the one hand there is an increasing lack of mobility because of fewer career opportunities, at the same time the explosive growth of automation could increase job and even career mobility. In fact some sectors of industry are already running into trouble because they cannot train their employees fast enough to cope with technological innovations. Training and education can therefore be seen as a major growth sector in the future. From these developments, it is quite clear that an issue like job satisfaction will become increasingly important in relation to technological change. Consequently the social and therefore the political aspect of industrial innovation can also be expected to become a stronger element than it has been up to the present time.

SOME POLITICAL ASPECTS OF INNOVATION*

A discussion of technical change and the involvement of government to both advance and direct this process of change has to be accompanied by a discussion of the political process by which the necessary decisions are taken. Since our contemporary socioeconomic system ought to be regarded as being in transition because of such facts as changing values, the changing international division of labour, the problems of energy and of other resources, our concern for safety and the environment, and by productivity-induced employment problems, we also ought to investigate the matter of political transition as well as its direction.

To speak of political transition is a deliberate choice. Not all of the topics discussed in this chapter have political dimensions. It is, however, also true that various elements of the socioeconomic system as described, call for profound changes in the institutions and balances which served to support the economic expansion of the postwar period, and which are now buckling under the weight of uneven development that they made possible. The form of the new structures which will replace the older ones is unpredictable. These structures, however, are not socially neutral and are thus potential sites of political conflict. As well as political conflict arising around such issues as, for example, industrial restructuring, there are also forces towards a restructuring of political institutions themselves.

Previous periods of structural crisis in the economies of the industrial countries have been associated with transformation of the role of the state. From securing the ground-rules of generalized commodity production, to introducing control over banks and factory legislation, to creating public education and welfare systems,

*This part of Chapter 2 is largely based on a paper by Ian Miles of the Science Policy Research Unit, University of Sussex, presented at a meeting of Futuribles, France, September 1979. (Published as Miles 1980.)

to the support of collapsing industries, the state has taken a more and more dominant position. Although it would obviously go against the initiatives of 'new right' governments with their desire to cut back the state apparatus, and against the demands for participation and control from the 'new left', an extrapolation of these trends would suggest that the next area for the state to become involved in would be that of profitable industry.

Extrapolations are of limited value, but in this case there are both analyses and empirical observations which support this thesis. Given the failure of Keynesian instruments to cope with stagflation, the increased near-zero-sum competition for shares of the world market, and problems around access to resources, the state is driven to play an important role in the restructuring of productive capital — in rationalization, coordinating different sectors, redistributing profits and limiting wages, and so on. The present round of technological innovation — especially microelectronics — has almost met with a stampede of governments seeking to support the generation of national capabilities in the new technologies. States are moving to co-determine what companies will specialize in what aspects of the technologies, and to set up mixed private–public firms, as in the United Kingdom.

Needless to say that if these are lasting developments — whether or not they are effective in creating profitability — they do nothing to resolve the legitimation problem. And here it is worth noting a possible transition in the form of the state — that towards corporatism. The ideology of corporatism is that decisions over social and economic affairs are taken by round-tables consisting of representatives of major interest groups. Consensus-reaching structures in Japan seem close to this situation.

The possibility of a corporate society is one that needs to be taken seriously. The utmost type of this development would be a policy in which parliamentary decision-making was even more radically delimited than at present, and popular legitimacy for public policies was won through a combination of the claims for rational decision-making and discipline within the institutions articulating the interest groups whose representatives are involved in corporatist policy-making. For example, the unions would have to be in a position to persuade their members to accept income policies, changing workplace technologies, accept regional and sectoral development plans, and the like.

It should be noted in this respect that already many of the political proponents of such a programme — trilateral commission authors, for example — have begun to make noises about the 'excesses of democracy' and the 'overloading of the political system' that go rather further than criticizing parliamentarianism. Does a liberal corporatism, however necessary it may seem to be, harmonize with other developments in the future of the west?

The Strong State, the Informal Economy and the Alternatives

The detailed answer to the question that was posed above will vary according to the existing political situation and to the economic leeway of different industrial societies. However, certain important areas of harmony and discord should be noted. Far from representing a more democratic or more rational form of politics, corporatism still subordinates social policy and economic planning to the logic of capital accumulation, even if it is state capital. A number of immediate political problems are also becoming apparent. The disciplining of workers by their union leadership may run, as before, into grassroots resistance. Also, some union leaders would be likely to oppose the sorts of sectoral restructuring of unions that corporatism might demand. Similar conflicts would arise in other social movements where allegiance to a corporatist strategy was sought.

In terms of pressures exerted by the grassroots on the leadership it seems likely that a corporatist ideology has a limited ability to keep demands for more popular control off the agenda, unless it could plead a state of national emergency.

In fact, it is not too fanciful to suggest that some of the 'value changes' discussed in the *Interfutures* (OECD, 1979a) report are responses to existing developments of corporatist structures. The demands for greater participation in work and political decision-making, the distrust of corporate élites, the emancipation movement, may reflect changes in the power structures of society. If this is the case, it is not surprising that these 'new values' appear among groups who find that their training for positions where they can exercise creative decision-making fail to correspond to their actual life-situations.

The problems indicated above may mean that a smoothly functioning, conflict-free corporate society along the lines of the ideal type is a mirage. But if there are strong underlying tendencies towards more corporatist structures in European societies, then various more-or-less adequate, more-or-less short-term, solutions to these problems may be attempted. The two possible solutions discussed below — the strong state and the informal economy — are based on existing tendencies and political movements in European countries. Although they are analytically isolated here, they are by no means incompatible.

The strong state would represent the culmination of tendencies towards political repression, introduced not in the form of fascism nor that of military rule, but as a gradual restructuring of the existing state apparatus. The disciplinary mechanisms and systems of control needed to bring labour and grassroots movements into line with corporatist strategy — the political institutions — would be introduced in a series of steps. Each step would appear as a temporary essential response; for example, to immediate emergencies, to particularly damaging consequences of specific strikes for the general public, to terrorist threats and scares. But these responses would not be seen as essential to the emerging form of the state. The state would appear as a benign organization legitimately founded on consent, whose coercive systems are a justifiable and transient effect of external hostilities, rather than a real basis of its power.

The routine and automated monitoring of public activities — telephone calls, movements across local boundaries, opinions expressed in public — could be regarded as one more of these effects. To extrapolate further, legitimation of the social order might additionally be obtained through highly selective presentation of political information to different social groups; through 'bread and circuses' for the masses based on elementary welfare services, and electronic mass entertainment; and some increased channels for public participation in decision-making over a limited range of local affairs. To locate the strong state as a real possibility is not to claim that this sort of development is free of contradictions itself. There is neither any guarantee that it will be able to carry through an appropriate economic restructuring, nor that it will be able to permanently suppress internal or external political challenges.

What of the informal economy *model?* For *Interfutures* (OECD, 1979a):

there might be a development within households of an informal sector transforming goods into services and substituting for purchased private services. The existence of this informal sector may provide individuals with the source of satisfaction that will make up for the relatively lower incomes due to the reduction of time worked in the formal sector. Similarly, this future might see the tentative emergence of a third system of social organisation additional to the market and administrative systems and characterised by non-market forms of private self-organisation.

In the more elaborate designs for a redirection of western society along these lines, stimulation is proposed of both formal economic activity involving high productivity, innovation and competitiveness, and informal initiatives to satisfy the material needs of depressed areas and the social and cultural needs of the population at large. At one stroke the problems of unemployment, of wasteful consumption, of alienating work, and of a bureaucratic and overgrown welfare state can be ended.

Certainly this appears a preferable image to the strong state. A problem, however, is that the development of informal economies and third systems can be quite compatible with the growth of a strong state, as long as adequate checks are placed on the degree of self-management sought in these sectors. Indeed, given the degree of economic and political restructuring called for, and the problems that this would pose for numerous sectional interests, it may be that a strong state would be necessary to realize it in more than a marginal form. Just as the strong state may find some popular support through its reduction of what are perceived as cushioning welfare services and feather-bedded work relations, so the informal strategy may gain some approval through offering more control of social services to their providers and recipients.

But whether or not it is associated with a strong state, there are a number of problems with the informal model that have a bearing on political transitions. They are all basically issues of power and inequality, factors overlooked by the more enthusiastic proponents of the model.

The first group of problems relate to what might be called the internal dynamics of the informal economy and third system. Even if the ideal type could be realized, there are questions of inequality to consider. Local self-reliance is likely to amplify existing differences in access to skills, resources, capital, etc. — which means the possibility of new regional/cultural hierarchies and divisions of labour. Only some sort of active centralized control system could cope with such inequalities.

The second group of problems are probably more immediately relevant, stemming as they do from the relationship between the new social sector and the whole social order. First, there is the matter of economic power: what guarantees are there that the high-technology, transnational, formal economy, will cooperate with the new sectors? Why should it consent to provide profits to support informal activities, to producing so-called 'household capital' instead of export goods? The likelihood is that the threat of investment strikes and relocation elsewhere in the world would be used to limit the demands of the new social sectors: that the informal economy could be pushed into the position of providing cheap labour-power and repair and maintenance services for the high technology sector. Now, this colonization of the informal sector by capital might be lessened if the state and industry were closely fused in a corporatism. Would this transition do more than moderate the subordination of the informal sector to the requirements of the monopoly sector? This would be its first determinant, with community needs being processed only within terms of reference already established.

While there are possibilities for resolving the present fiscal crises of governments through withdrawing from any welfare services — these could be transferred to voluntary neighbourhood agencies — this would not be implemented in terms of a socially neutral rationality. As in past attempts to create participatory structures from above, the encouragement given to third-system initiatives by the state is likely to tend towards creating hierarchical forms, open to manipulation from central agencies, individualizing their 'clients' and bureaucratizing their more committed workers, imposing quasi-legal rules and coercions, and privatizing and pacifying communities.

Basically, a mixture of elements might be anticipated: formal economy and state sectors run on repressive lines with corporatist ideology; parts of an informal third system organized around the principles of private profit, reduced state expenditure and public order; other 'underground' economic activity involving low wage labour-intensive services; and some growth of activities seeking to escape taxation or undercut corporate prices.

Of course, attempts should and will be made to obtain concessions or even help from the state in developing new services, new means of meeting collective needs — not to mention protecting existing services. But while it may welcome cheapened social and welfare services, a lessening of its administrative burden in planning transport, housing and urban development and the like, it will place strict limits on any real transfer of power to organs of community self-management.

To achieve progress in the face of increasing corporate power requires more than devotion to the 'higher needs' that may be satisfied through alternative ways of life, and more than the struggle to achieve a commanding position from which corporate structures may be redirected toward different social needs. Beyond this there is the possibility that movements to defend the structures of liberal democracy may well find themselves posing questions concerning how to achieve higher forms of democratic society. The possibilities of heterogeneous groups in European societies mobilizing around such political movements are therefore important, if alternative futures are to be discussed. The absence of consideration of potential democratic movements from most 'futures' reports is more likely a function of the audience and frameworks around which these forecasts are constructed than the absence of such possibilities in Europe's political transitions.

What tendencies can put these possibilities on the agenda? The increasing role of the state can mean a fusion of economic and political conflicts: with a deepening economic crisis, and the increase of struggles over income, employment, social services and public investment, there is simultaneously the possibility of delegitimation of existing decision-making processes and that of the coalition of workers and consumers, of technical and manual labourers, around common projects.

We will not, however, go deeply into these issues: what matters is that they should be included in a discussion of the direction towards West Europe's industrial societies could and should be in transition. The political transitions of Europe's states need not involve corporatist or repressive destinations; but new relationships between state and civil society will need to be forged if alternatives are to be created. Coordinated action, and the development of alternative plans could serve to create new centres of power prefiguring a decentralized society in which production and consumption are integrated according to social need. This would go along with more conventional political action to influence government policies with intriguing questions concerning how far existing state structures could be used to promote greater decentralization of power.

As with other possible political futures, there are significant obstacles confronting the realization of such tendencies. These obstacles are certainly great enough to forestall any great optimism concerning the future.

An antidemocratic outcome for a movement rooted on democracy is not historically unknown, and various factors that might increase its possibility in Europe may be cited. Among these are popular support for strong leadership in the event of disruption of economic and social institutions in the wake of power struggles. The crucial indicator regarding the likelihood of such a development is the condition of democracy within popular movements themselves.

In conclusion, it can be stated that the future period of economic development will be accompanied by substantial changes in our economic, social and political institutions.

References

Business International (1979), *Europe in the 1980s, Corporate Forecasts and Strategies*.
Danzin, A. (1979), *Science and the Second Renaissance of Europe*, Oxford, Pergamon Press.
EEC (1979a), *Project 1990*, Brussels.
EEC (1979b), *A Blueprint for Europe, EEC Study-Group on New Characteristics of Socio-economic Development*, Brussels, December.
EEC–FAST (Group Future Assessment of Science and Technology) (1979), *Workprogramme*, December.
EEC–FAST (1980), *Europe Under Change*, April.
ETUI (1979), *The Impact of Micro-electronics on Employment in Western Europe in the 1980s*, Brussels, October.
European Industrial Research Management Association (EIRMA) (1978), *Technology '88*.
Hall, P. (1978), *Europe 2000*, London, Duckworth.
Miles, I. (1980), 'Effacing the Political Future: Some Comments on the Interfutures Analysis', *Futures*, December.
Norse, D. (1979), 'Scenario Analysis in Interfutures', *Futures*, **11**, 5, October.
OECD (1971), *Science, Growth and Society*, Report of the Secretary General's *ad hoc* group on new concepts of science policy, Paris.
OECD (1977), *Towards Full Employment and Price Stability* (McCracken Report), Main Report and Annex, Paris.
OECD (1979a), *Interfutures, Facing the Future: Mastering the Probable and Managing the Unpredictable*, Paris.
OECD (1979b), *Science and Technology in the New Socio-economic Context*. Paris.
OECD (1979c), *Technology and the Structural Adaptation of Industry*, Paris, September.
Rothschild, Emma (1979), Comment to OECD Report, Paris, September.
TUC (1979), *Employment and Technology*, interim report.
White House (1979), *The President's Industrial Innovation Initiatives* (fact sheet), Washington, DC, October.

3. TECHNICAL INNOVATION AND ECONOMIC DEVELOPMENT

It has long been regarded by economists as almost self-evident that expansion over time of aggregate per capita output was directly related to net investment. More recently, though, this view has been challenged and it has become increasingly accepted that scientific advance and technical change are necessary prerequisites for the growth of the economy. But just what role does technical change play in economic growth? How important is technical change in relation to increases in labour, capital, or education and to economies of scale, as a determinant in the growth of the national economy? This chapter will address this question, the answer to which is clearly important to the determination of national science and technology policy.

During the postwar years the volume of world trade has increased significantly, and a greater interdependency has grown up among the major trading nations. Because of this, considerations of international competitiveness have become an increasingly important factor in government industrial policy formulation. In the context of national innovation policy, it is of extreme importance to ask the question 'how important a factor is technical change in the export competitiveness of manufactured goods?' Data will be presented below which suggest that, in many areas of manufacturing, technical change (technical sophistication, design excellence) is a *sine qua non* in determining export competitiveness.

Finally, governments are becoming increasingly concerned that the current world trade recession is not just a temporary aberration from previous postwar expansionary trends, but rather reflects a fundamental structural change in the world economy. Moreover, it is increasingly being mooted that this structural change is a result of underlying changes in the nature of technical change. This chapter will offer evidence which supports a structuralist interpretation of the current world economic crisis.

TECHNICAL CHANGE AND ECONOMIC GROWTH

A number of analytical techniques have been employed to calculate the contribution of technical change to economic growth in the US economy during several periods of the twentieth century. Several of the more widely accepted of these techniques, and their results, are described below.

Technical Change and the Aggregate Production Function

In this section, the method used by Solow (1957) to estimate the contribution of technical change to the growth of output is outlined.

Solow uses the following expression to relate aggregate output Q to the inputs of capital K and labour L, for a level of technology A at various time periods t:

$$Q = A\,(t) \cdot F\,(K,L) \tag{1}$$

Using various assumptions, and taking discrete time intervals, Solow derives the following relationship between the level of technology and output and capital *per man-hour.*

$$\left(\frac{\Delta A}{A}\right) = \left(\frac{\Delta(Q/L)}{Q/L}\right) - \left(\frac{b\Delta(K/L)}{K/L}\right) \tag{2}$$

where b represents the value of capital as a proportion of the value of output.

Hence, it is possible to obtain an estimate each year for $\Delta A/A$ which measures that part of the annual percentage increase in GNP per man-hour which can be attributed to all causes other than changes over time in capital per man-hour. The contribution of technical change each year is computed as the difference between the actual percentage changes in output per man-hour and that part of these changes attributable to capital per man-hour. The final step is to compute the cumulation over the period under consideration of the total increase in output per man-hour (as distinct from percentage changes) which can be ascribed to technical change.

By arbitrarily setting A (year 1909) to unity, Solow used the following expression to derive an entire series:

$$A\,(t+1) = (t)\left\{1 + \frac{\Delta A(t)}{A(t)}\right\}. \tag{3}$$

For the private, non-agricultural sector of the US economy during the period 1909–49, Solow found A (year 1949) to equal 1.809: the cumulative annual percentage changes in output per man-hour due to technical change amounts to 80.9 per cent. Solow calculated that 87.5 per cent of the total increase in output per man-hour over the same period is due to technical change, the rest being due to increased capital per man-hour.

Massel (1960), applying the above method to US manufacturing over the period 1919–55, ascribes 90 per cent of the observed increase in output per man-hour to technical advance.

It must be noted here that the statement that 10 to 15 per cent of change in output per man-hour due to increased capital input refers to a special kind of investment, that is, an investment in plant and equipment which does not change 'inform, quality or composition'. Obviously, if technical change requires investment in plant and equipment, it is difficult to argue that technical change *by itself* or investment *by itself* can account for certain increases in productivity, since both together would be responsible. Hence, the contribution of capital to economic growth is understated while that of technical change is consequently exaggerated.

Total Factor Productivity

A second method of calculating the contribution of technical change to economic growth is that of *total factor productivity*, where indexes of labour and capital are combined to form an index of total resources. Weighting the inputs by their respective earnings in the base period, the contribution of each unit of input to output at its base-period level of efficiency is frozen, and an index of total input is obtained. This index is then taken to show how output would have changed if only the *quantities* of the inputs changed. This method assumes:

- constant returns to scale, that is, an *x* per cent increase in all inputs result in an *x* per cent increase in output;
- no changes in the *quality* of the inputs with time (for example, the quality of labour is constant);
- technical change is neutral — is affected equally by changes in capital and labour — otherwise the relative marginal productivities will vary as a result of technical change.

The *actual* ratio of output to input provides an index of *total productivity* — here, *all* influences in efficiency are included. Thus, the difference between the economic growth calculated above, using the base-period efficiency, and the growth which has, in fact, occurred, with both the *quantity and efficiency* of the input changing, gives a measure of the amount of growth attributable to technical change.

Kendrick (1961), using the method of total factor productivity, and empirical data concerning the growth in real net national product in the United States over the period 1889–1953, found that the per capita growth due to increased capital was 16 per cent of the total per capita growth: 'productivity' improvement accounted for 75 per cent of the per capita growth: 9 per cent is due to change in 'labour' per capita.

The Residual

The term 'technical change', as employed above, is a catchall for all those factors which contribute to economic growth other than increases in capital and labour. This includes increasing scientific, technological and managerial knowledge, changes in efficiency of the economy, and economies of scale. The term generally used to describe this catchall is *the residual*. A definition of 'technical change' in the narrower sense is 'the introduction or the spread of cost-reducing changes in technique'. Another definition is 'the advance of technology, such advance often taking the form of new methods of producing existing products, new designs which enable the production of products with important new characteristics, and new techniques of organization, marketing and management' (Mansfield, 1968). A number of workers have attempted to break down the residual into its component parts.

Some Results

Denison (1960), in his study of the growth in real national income during the period 1929–57 in the United States, found, using the method of total factor productivity, that 32 per cent of growth was the result of increased output per unit of input (that is, increased efficiency) and 68 per cent of growth was the result of growth in the combined inputs. The contribution from 'advance of knowledge' (technical change) was 20 per cent and the contribution from 'economies of scale' was 11 per cent. The difference between Denison's results and those of other workers lies mainly in his novel procedure for the classification of outputs.

Table 3.1 shows the results of several studies concerning the various contributions to percentage growth in gross national product, during the period 1949–59, in a variety of countries. It can be seen that in all cases, technical progress made a major contribution to economic growth.

More recently, a number of economists have voiced reservations concerning the

Table 3.1 Contributions to per cent growth in GNP during 1949–59

Country	Increased labour	Increased capital	Technical progress	Total
United Kingdom	0.4	0.9	1.1	2.4
Sweden	0.3	0.6	2.5	3.4
France	0.1	1.0	3.4	4.5
Italy	0.8	1.0	4.1	5.9
West Germany (1950–59)	1.1	1.8	4.5	7.4
Japan (1952–58)	1.7	3.2	3.0	7.9

Sources: UN Report (1962), and Aukrust (1959)

use of total factor productivity to measure the economic impact of technical change. Specifically, it is said that the technique treats labour, capital and technical change as simply 'add-on' functions, that is, as if they enjoy a simple arithmetical relationship. In fact, the relationship between these quantities is complex and highly interactive. A second objection is that the technique cannot take into account major discontinuities in economic progress. There are also serious problems in measuring inputs, especially capital inputs, and combining them in a measure of total factor productivity, as well as problems in measuring output when the quality and nature of products produced is changing (for a detailed discussion of this issue see Griliches, 1979).

R & D Expenditure and Economic Growth

Most technical change that contributes to economic growth might be expected to arise as a result of organized R & D effort (although some technical progress does occur through the efforts of individuals involving little R & D expenditure (Jewkes, Sawers and Stillerman, 1970) and many improvements in plant and equipment derive from users' experience rather than from R & D), therefore it seems reasonable to suppose that a relationship might exist between national R & D expenditure and GNP, or between R & D expenditure and growth in GNP. In fact, no clear relationship appears to exist between these quantities and, given that 'economically motivated' R & D is only a part, and not always the greatest part, of national R & D expenditures (the rest being defence, space, nuclear, academic, welfare and other miscellaneous R & D), lack of any such correlation is perhaps not surprising.

Table 3.2 presents data showing the ratio of R & D expenditure to GNP for a number of advanced western economies; it also shows the ratio of *defence* R & D expenditure to GNP. Table 3.3 (a) and (b) show indicators of the economic performance of a number of advanced market economies, notably growth in GNP and industrial productivity growth. Comparison of Tables 3.2 and 3.3 shows that it is those countries that have spent proportionally less of their national R & D resources on defence that have enjoyed the greatest GNP and productivity growth rates. This suggests that the opportunity costs to economic growth of defence (non-economic) R & D might be high. Although there have been a number of notable spinoffs from defence-related R & D, this would appear to be a rather inefficient way to achieve commercial ends.

Table 3.2 Trends in expenditure on R & D as a percentage of GDP in selected countries, total, defence and other

	1963*	1967	1971	1975
France				
total	1.60	2.20	1.90	1.80
defence	0.43	0.55	0.33	0.35
other	1.17	1.65	1.57	1.45
Germany				
total	1.40	1.70	2.10	2.10
defence	0.14	0.21	0.16	0.14
other	1.26	1.49	1.94	1.96
Japan				
total	1.30	1.30	1.60	1.70
defence	0.01	0.02	–	0.01
other	1.29	1.28	–	1.69
United Kingdom				
total	2.30	2.30	2.10[a]	2.10
defence	0.79	0.61	0.53	0.62
other	1.51	1.69	(1.57)	1.48
United States				
total	2.90	2.90	2.60	2.30
defence	1.37	1.10	0.80	0.64
other	1.53	1.80	1.80	1.66
Netherlands				
total	1.90	2.20	2.00	1.90
defence	–	–	0.04[a]	0.03
other	–	–	(1.96)	1.87
Sweden				
total	1.30	1.30	1.50	1.80
defence	0.40	0.43	0.23[b]	–
other	0.90	0.87	(1.27)	–
Canada				
total	1.00	1.20	1.20	1.00
defence	0.09	0.09	0.06	0.04
other	0.91	1.11	1.14	0.96
Italy				
total	0.60	0.70	0.90	0.90
defence	0.01	0.02	0.02	0.02
other	0.59	0.68	0.88	0.88

*Germany, Netherlands, Sweden, United Kingdom: 1964.
[a]1972.
[b]1970.
Source: OECD (1979), *Science and Technology in the New Socio-Economic Context.*

Taking now economically motivated R & D, Black (1968), calculated the co-efficients of correlation between funds for R & D advanced *by industry*, and GNP, during the period 1958–63 in the United States. For the sample of industries he chose,* he found a consistently high positive correlation. This, of course, does not of itself necessarily indicate causality, although logically one might expect the relationship to be causal.

*Chemicals (0.99), scientific and measuring instruments (0.99), machinery (0.99), aircraft and missiles (0.96), motor vehicles (0.97), electrical equipment (0.94), fabricated metals (0.77), petroleum (0.95), non-ferrous metals (0.82), primary ferrous metals (0.85), rubber products (0.97), industrial chemicals (0.98).

Table 3.3(a) Global economic trends

	1960-65	1965-70	1970-75	1975-80	1980-85
GDP:					
World	5.0	5.5	3.8	3.9	4.5
Developed countries[a]	5.1	5.5	3.3	3.3	(4)
of which:					
Canada	5.7	4.8	5.0	3.9	7.0
United States	4.6	3.1	2.4	2.7	4.1
Japan	10.1	11.6	5.5	5.0	5.9
France	5.8	5.4	4.0	2.8	4.4
Germany	5.0	4.5	2.0	3.4	3.7
Italy	5.1	6.0	2.5	3.4	4.8
United Kingdom	3.1	2.5	2.1	1.4	3.4
Trade					
World[b]		6.8	9.2	5.7	5.6	5.8
Inflation					
World[b]		4.0	5.0	10.0	11.4	7.5
Current account					
OECD (end of period − $ Bill)	3.8	6.7	−0.3	−24.4	−90.0

[a]13 major industrialized OECD countries.   [b]Excluding centrally planned economies.
Source: OECD (1980), *Newsletter*.

Table 3.3(b) Industrial labour productivity growth (output per person employed)

	1960-64	1964-69	1969-73	1973-77
United States	3.7	1.9	2.2	1.3
France	5.5	6.0	4.2	2.1
Germany	5.2	5.7	4.7	3.5
Italy	4.9	7.1	4.1	0.8*
United Kingdom	3.1	3.4	3.9	0.2

*1973-76 only.   Source: Jones (1976).

So far we have discussed the role aggregated R & D expenditure and technical change play in the growth of GNP. A number of researchers have adopted a more disaggregated view and looked at the relationship between productivity growth and R & D expenditure in firms and industries. Mansfield (1965) studied data regarding ten large chemical and petroleum firms and ten manufacturing industries in the United States during the postwar period. For both the firms and the industries, the measured rate of growth in productivity was related in a statistically significant way to the rate of growth of cumulated R & D expenditures made by the firm or industry. The particular form of the relationship depended on whether technical change was disembodied (better methods and organization that improve the efficiency of both old capital and new) or capital embodied (innovations that must be embodied in new equipment if they are to be utilized). If technical change was disembodied, the average effect of a 1 per cent increase in the rate of growth of cumulated R & D expenditure was a 0.1 per cent increase in the rate of productivity increase. If technical change was capital embodied, the effect was a 0.7 per cent increase in the rate of productivity increase.

Minasian (1969), in the United States, studied the relationship between value added, and labour, capital and cumulated R & D expenditure in seventeen firms in the chemical industry during 1948–57. He found that a firm's cumulative R & D expenditure is related in a statistically significant way to the firm's value added, holding its labour and capital inputs constant. Finally, Brown and Conrad (1967) studied the relationship between R & D expenditure and productivity increase in a number of US manufacturing industries in the postwar period. They also found that R & D expenditure has a statistically significant effect on the rate of productivity increase.

It appears then, at least for the 1950s and 1960s, that there exists a relationship between a firm's R & D expenditure and its productivity change. Since individual organizations will vary in their ability to capitalize on the results of R & D endeavours however, the relationship will vary from firm to firm. Further, since the nature, rate and direction of technical change vary between different industry sectors, the R & D-productivity change relationship will also vary sectorally.

More recent work has suggested that the relationship between R & D and productivity growth has changed during the last decade or so. Griliches (1980) found, when looking at the effects of R & D on productivity in US manufacturing, that while positive results appear for the period 1959–68, the results for the period 1969–77 indicate essentially no effect. Other US researchers have also found a lack of correlation between R & D and productivity change in US industry during the 1970s (for a review of these results see Thomas, 1980).

A number of explanations have been offered for this changed relationship between R & D and US manufacturing productivity growth. Among the most important of these are:

— a change in the character of R & D due to regulatory constraints;
— a slowdown in investment in new capital equipment in which the beneficial effects of past R & D are embodied;
— economic uncertainties caused by the shock of massive energy cost increases have meant that firms are operating within existing production frontiers and have not taken advantage of R & D-led outward shifts in these frontiers.

Recent research has indicated that the rate of productivity growth in US firms is related more strongly to expenditure on basic research, rather than to applied research expenditure (Link, 1980). Taken with the fact that industrial basic research expenditure as a proportion of the total has declined in the United States during the 1970s (Nason, Steger and Manners, 1978), and that this is due to a great extent to regulatory compliance costs, the first explanation offered above would appear to have a great deal of validity. There is, however, an alternative 'structural' interpretation for the changed relationship between R & D and productivity growth. This is discussed briefly in the note at the end of this chapter.

TECHNICAL CHANGE AND COMPETITIVENESS

Perhaps the greatest difficulty in attempting to determine the role of embodied technical change in the export competitiveness of manufactured goods lies in obtaining a precise measure for this quality and, short of studying all competing goods in great detail, precise measurement is impossible. It is possible, however, to employ a number of proxy measures for technical sophistication, the two most useful being *patent activity* and *unit value*. In the first case the assumption is that the level of patenting activity undertaken by a firm or nation is an indication of the amount of technical activity being undertaken which will in turn be reflected in the technical quality of the goods that nation or firm produces. In the second case the assumption is that if a customer is willing to pay significantly more for a particular good than for its chief competitors, then this is an indication of that good's superior technical sophistication and performance.

Taking, first, patent activity, Figure 3.1 presents data at a highly aggregated level. It plots patents registered in the United State by five advanced European countries for five years between 1899 and 1975 against those countries' shares of manufacturing exports during the same five years.* It can be seen that, generally speaking, there is a close relationship between patent share and world market share, which in turn suggests that a relationship exists between national technical activity — as a proxy for technical sophistication — and national trade share.

The 1913 data for the United Kingdom are interesting since they suggest that the United Kingdom had a significantly larger share of world manufacturing exports than her patent share would appear to justify. In 1913, however, 37 per cent of UK exports were in textiles and 21 per cent were in raw materials and agricultural produce, that is, areas of low technical activity. Even in the 'new' industries (machinery, transport equipment and chemicals), 78 per cent of UK exports went to markets outside the industrial bloc (the eight leading industrial nations), in other words, to areas where the demand for the technically more advanced products was relatively low. In short, Britain's exports were mainly in traditional goods which involved relatively little technical — hence patent — activity and orientated towards imperial markets.† Much of Britain's subsequent decline in manufacturing competitiveness can be traced to this earlier tradition of trading in technically less demanding markets (for a detailed discussion of this point see Walker, 1980).

Soete (1979) has used US patent statistics rather more rigorously to investigate the importance of technical change on export performance in manufactured goods. He regressed exports per head of 40 industries in 1974 against cumulative US-registered patents per head for the period 1963–76 for all OECD countries (excluding Iceland, New Zealand and, of necessity, the United States). The results of this analysis are shown in Table 3.4. It can be seen that, for most capital goods industries, where technical change is relatively strong, significant results are obtained. For most consumer goods and intermediate goods, where technical change is weaker and often based on the diffusion of innovations that have occurred in the capital goods sector, non-significant results are obtained. Thus, according to this analysis, in a large number of industries, international competitiveness is based to a large extent on technical change.

Taking, second, unit value, interesting data are available linking unit value to trade performance in engineering goods, and the relationship can best be illustrated using a bilateral comparison of the performance of the British and West German industries in OECD markets. Table 3.5 gives OECD export shares, export–import

---

*It is assumed that since the United States is a large market and major competitor for the five countries, as well as the leading innovative activity country, then firms registering important patents abroad will almost certainly register them in the United States.

†There are, of course, a number of objections to the use of patents in this way. For example, not all patented inventions carry the same weight in terms of their potential commercial impact (radical versus incremental innovations). Nor are all the patents subsequently commercialized. Nor do the aggregate data allow for national industrial specialization. Nevertheless, rigorous use of these data has indicated their validity.

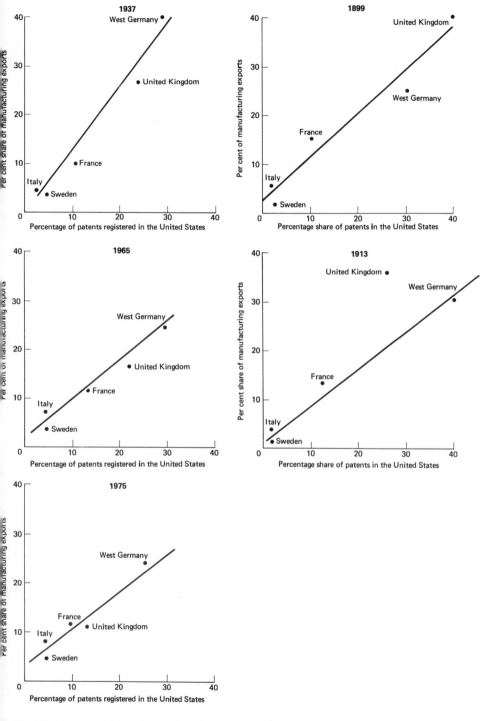

Fig. 3.1 Percentage share of manufacturing exports versus share of patents registered in the United States in 1899, 1913, 1937, 1965 and 1975

Table 3.4 Inter-country regression results for 40 SIC industries (1974)

Industry	United States SIC	t-value b coefficient	R^2	(United States) Applied R & D/value added
(1) Significant results*				
Drugs	283	12.12	0.89	9.05
Special industrial machinery	355	12.13	0.89	1.33[a]
Metalworking machinery	354	11.99	0.88	1.00
Engines and turbines	351	8.40	0.79	11.07
Instruments	88	8.24	0.78	7.65
Electrical transmission and distribution equipment	361, 3825	7.88	0.77	8.23
Ordnance, guided missiles	348, 376, 3745	7.50	0.76	43.48
Electrical industrial apparatus	362	7.30	0.74	6.18
Industrial inorganic chemicals	286	5.86	0.65	3.08[b]
Office and computing machinery	357	5.42	0.61	18.79
Communications and electronics equipment	366, 367	4.49	0.52	22.45
Aircraft	372	4.34	0.51	19.13
Electrical lighting, electrical equipment	364	4.17	0.48	3.70[c]
Soaps, cleaning products, etc.	284	4.07	0.48	3.12[d]
Construction machinery	353	4.13	0.47	3.12
Miscellaneous chemical products	289	3.68	0.42	3.12[d]
Fabricated metal products	34	3.48	0.41	2.73
General industrial machinery	356	3.52	0.40	1.33[a]
Industrial organic chemicals	281	2.92	0.31	3.08[b]
Petroleum products	13, 29	2.79	0.30	2.53[e]
Miscellaneous machinery	359	2.67	0.30	1.33[a]
Motor vehicles	371	2.81	0.30	8.43
Railroad equipment	374	2.71	0.28	3.83[e]
Refrigeration and service machinery	358	2.51	0.25	1.33

(2) Non-significant results

Radio and TV receiving equipment	365	2.20	0.23	2.44
Plastic materials	282	2.21	0.22	7.92
Miscellaneous electrical equipment	369	2.24	0.22	3.70[c]
Electrical household appliances	363	2.16	0.21	3.70[c]
Rubber products	30	1.82	0.18	2.09
Textiles	22	1.59	0.15	0.7
Farm machinery	352	1.62	0.12	3.08
Miscellaneous transportation equipment	379	1.53	0.12	3.83[e]
Stone, clay, glass products	32	1.32	0.11	1.13
Non-ferrous metal products	3336, 3398, 3463	1.33	0.11	0.87
Ferrous metal products	331, 332, 3399, 3462	1.30	0.10	0.61
Food	20	0.99	0.08	0.58
Agricultural chemicals	287	1.08	0.07	3.51
Motor and bicycles	375	0.61	0.06	3.83[e]
Paints and allied products	285	0.52	0.03	3.12[d]
Ship and boat building	373	0.47	0.03	3.83[e]

*Significant at the 1 per cent level.
[a] R & D/value added figures were only available for the group of SIC 355, 356, 358, and 359.
[b] R & D/value added figures were only available for the group of SIC 281 and 286.
[c] R & D/value added figures were only available for the group of SIC 363, 364, and 369.
[d] R & D/value added figures were only available for the group of SIC 284, 285, and 289.
[e] Estimated.
[f] R & D/value added figures were only available for the group of Standard Industrial Classifications.

Table 3.5 OECD export shares, export--import ratio and index of effective
exchange rates, United Kingdom and West Germany 1971 and 1975 (all
engineering)

		United Kingdom	West Germany
Share of OECD engineering exports	1971	10.9 per cent	22 per cent
	1975	9.2 per cent	22 per cent
Export–import ratio	1971	2.7	3.7
	1975	2.1	5.0
Unit value, exports	1975	5.71	8.16
Index of effective exchange rates			
(1971 = 100)		78	123

ratios and index of effective exchange rates for both United Kingdom and West
German engineering exports in 1971 and 1975. It can be seen that, despite a
22 per cent devaluation in the value of sterling between 1971 and 1975, and
a 23 per cent revaluation of the DM, Britain's share of OECD exports declined
while the share enjoyed by West Germany remained constant at more than double
the UK share in 1975. During the same period Britain's imports increased more
than did her exports, while West Germany's exports increased significantly more
than her imports. These data, taken with the fact that in 1975 the unit value of
West German exports was more than 40 per cent greater than the British, suggest
that non-price factors − technical change − are rather more important than is
price in determining export competitiveness.

The data presented in Table 3.6 further show that the export unit value of
British and West German engineering goods is diverging, which suggests that the
disparity in technical quality between the two countries' exports is increasing,
and the United Kingdom is progressively specializing at the bottom end of the
range, while the West German product mix is increasingly towards the more sophisticated end of the range. The export–import unit value data in the table support this
view and show that the United Kingdom has a clear tendency to 'export cheap' and
to 'import dear', while the more successful West German industry has the reverse
tendency.

Table 3.6 Value per tonne of engineering exports and import–export unit value,
United Kingdom and West Germany, 1963, 1971 and 1975 (21 product
groups)

		United Kingdom	West Germany
Value/tonne of exports	1963	$2300	$2600
	1971	$3100	$4100
	1975	$4800	$7600
Export–import unit	1963	0.65	1.06
Value ratios	1971	0.71	1.20
	1975	0.77	1.24

Source: Saunders (1978).

In a detailed study of a single sector of engineering — agricultural implements — Rothwell (1981) has used both patent and unit value data to show that technical quality is a prime determinant of export competitiveness. The unit value data are shown in Table 3.7.

Table 3.7 UK imports, exports and unit value: soil preparation and cultivation machinery and harvesting machinery, 1964 and 1974

	Soil preparation and cultivation machinery (whole machines)		*Harvesting machinery (whole machines)*	
	1965	*1974*	*1965*	*1974*
Imports ——— (per cent) Exports	35.5	55	75	172
Unit value imports ————————— Unit value exports	0.82	0.93	1.01	1.47

It can be seen that in both soil preparation and cultivation machinery and in harvesting machinery, as the ratio unit value imports : unit value exports increased, so did the import : export ratio. Hence, increased import penetration is associated with increased unit value, that is, increasing technical quality of imports. Significantly, this is particularly the case with the generally rather more sophisticated harvesting machinery.

Probably the person best qualified to decide which factors — price, quality, service, etc. — are most important in determining competitiveness, is the customer. It is he, after all, who has to weigh one factor off against the other when making his purchasing decision. Table 3.8 shows the results of a survey of British farmers concerning the reason underlying their decisions to buy British-made and foreign-made agricultural machinery. It can be seen that with respect to the purchase of British machinery, price and convenience are dominant in the farmer's purchasing decision; in the case of foreign-built machinery, factors relating to technical quality predominate. Given the increased import penetration of the UK market by foreign suppliers (from 20.3 per cent of the UK market in 1964 to 46.5 per cent in 1974) this clearly suggests that technical quality is a more important factor in competitiveness in agricultural engineering goods than is price. This contention is borne out in the opinions of the British farmers who further stated that in most machinery areas they 'bought British' when they wanted smaller, more conventional items, and 'bought foreign' when they required sophisticated, high production-rate machines.

A previous study of the world textile machinery industry by Rothwell (1977) yielded similar results. Indeed, since much of the technical change that has taken place in the textile machinery area during the postwar years has been of a quite radical nature (as opposed to agricultural engineering where it has been largely 'incremental') its importance in international competitiveness was, if anything, greater.

Finally, study of world trading patterns in manufactured goods shows that import penetration in the advanced economies has been due mainly to goods from other advanced nations, and that the 'technical change' imports have increased more rapidly than 'low cost' imports from developing countries. This is illustrated below in Table 3.9.

Table 3.8 Reasons given by 150 UK farmers for buying foreign-built and British-built agricultural machinery between 1972 and 1977

	Foreign machinery		British machinery	
	Number	Percentage	Number	Percentage
Performance factors (better overall performance superior overall design, more reliable, more efficient, more advanced design)	146	54.9	26	16.0
Price factors (machinery cheaper, better value for money, i.e. equivalent performance at lower cost)	25	9.4	46	28.4
Convenience factors (convenience of local manufacturers, local dealers, local source of spare parts)	–	–	52	32.1
Better service provided	31	11.6	13	8.0
Availability (off the shelf)	21	8.0	6	3.7
No UK equivalent	31	11.6	–	–
Other factors	12	4.5	19	11.8
Total	266*	100	162*	100

*A number of farmers gave more than one reason for their purchasing decision.
Source: Rothwell, R. (1979), *Technical Change and Competitiveness in Agricultural Engineering Products: The Performance of the UK Industry*, Science Policy Reseach Unit, Occasional Paper Series No. 9, September.

Thus, there exists a great deal of convincing evidence to suggest that technical change is a prime factor — albeit not the only one — in determining the export competitiveness of a wide range of manufactured goods. A growing realization of this fact is causing governments in all the advanced market economies increasingly to become involved in instigating measures to stimulate, and assist with, technological innovation in manufacturing industry.

TECHNOLOGY AND STRUCTURAL CHANGE IN THE WORLD ECONOMY

While it is generally accepted that the shock to the world economy of the fourfold increase in the price of OPEC oil in 1974 contributed to the current world recession, it is increasingly being mooted that this simply accelerated an already established trend; that the current world economic crisis is the result of fundamental structural changes taking place in the world economy in which technical change plays a central role; that the fourth quarter of the twentieth century will be rather more similar to the second rather than to the third quarter of this century.

These conjectures have led to a resurgence of interest in the possibility of long waves occurring in the development of the world economy. Probably the earliest

Table 3.9 International trade as a percentage of domestic consumption, total manufacture

Trade as a percentage domestic apparent consumption	United Kingdom		EEC-6		United States		Japan	
	1959–60	*1973–74*	*1959–60*	*1973–74*	*1959–60*	*1973–74*	*1959–60*	*1973–74*
External imports	17.05	29.03	7.56	10.12	3.28	7.95	6.02	7.09
from LDCs	3.64	3.35	1.46	1.62	0.73	1.93	1.16	1.80
from DCs	12.41	24.42	5.53	7.53	2.53	5.66	4.74	4.61
External exports	20.78	27.74	15.96	18.56	5.08	8.39	14.10	16.71

detailed formulation of long-wave theory was that of a Russian economist Kondratiev (1935), who in the 1920s analysed the development of long-term trends in selected economic indicators. He discovered a number of long waves in the world economy of between 50 and 60 years' duration. While Kondratiev did not explicitly include the role of technical change in long-wave formation, he did suggest that when a major wave of expansion was under way, inventions that had remained dormant would find application.

The notion of long waves was later taken up by Schumpeter (1939) who ascribed a central role to technical change in long-wave formation. He introduced the idea of *technological revolutions* as the driving force of the Kondratiev cycles, and pointed in particular to the role of steam power in the first Kondratiev (1818–42), railroads in the second (1843–97) and of electric power and the automobile in the third (1898 to about 1949). Schumpeter related these major changes primarily to bursts of innovative activity by entrepreneurs.

Kuznets (1940) later pointed out that there appears to be no special reason to expect that the intensity of entrepreneurial innovative activity will vary in long cycles, although he did accept the possibility of a bunching of innovations associated with new technologies and of investment activities associated with these bunches of innovations. Such innovations would need to be such, however, that their effects would permeate throughout the economic system and be far-reaching.

Freeman (1978), while basically supporting the Schumpeterian interpretation, has pointed to a number of snags — for example to the very different development in time of the automobile industries in America, Europe and Japan. He also pointed to the need for 'basic science' coupled to 'technical exploitation' followed by 'imaginative leaps' — all preceding the Kondratiev upswing. As Ray (1980) puts it:

> Schumpeter himself emphasised the view that whilst there *is* a relationship between innovation and economic development, it is a very complex one. One innovation is followed by another and the long chain eventually produces new products or processes which are again further developed and/or replaced. If the new product or process is important enough, it generates activity in many allied areas and cascades through the whole fabric of economic and social life.

Work on long-wave formation today falls basically into two camps, the first emphasizing factors of demand, the second emphasizing factors of supply. It is probably true to say that researchers in the United States generally fall into the former category and are looking at indicators of aggregate demand, notably demand for capital goods, while workers in Europe are focusing largely on the supply side, that is, on the role of innovative push.

Perhaps the most rigorous work in the United States is that being done by the Systems Dynamics Group at MIT and Graham and Senge (1980) have summarized the MIT hypothesis of long-wave behaviour as follows:

> Economies move through long waves of approximately 50 years' duration, arising from over- and underexpansion of the capital-producing sector.
>
> The upturn of a long wave, which lasts about 30 years, is characterised by self-reinforcing pressures to acquire more physical capital to meet rising demand for capital, increase capital intensity of production, and to take advantage of high returns on investment.
>
> Productivity per man increases during the upswing of the long wave, due at least in part to increasing physical capital per person.

When the accumulation of physical capital has run its course, adding more capital is no longer more attractive than adding labour. Capital investment peaks out and shows signs of declining, and the economy enters the peak period of the long wave, which can last for a decade or so.

Capital investment eventually falls off dramatically; the economy needs much less new investment to replace depreciation than it did to expand its capital plant. The capital-producing industries collapse and many of the people in them become unemployed.

During the depression, physical capital begins to deteriorate and obsolesce. Eventually, there is a need to replace it, and demand for capital rises. Again the process of capital accumulation is begun in the upswing of the next long wave.

Thus, the MIT researchers focus very clearly on the role of demand for physical capital in the formation of long-waves. The work that emphasizes most strongly the role of technology-push is that of Mensch (1979) in West Germany, who talks about a push of basic innovations opening up new investment opportunities and providing the basis for the growth of whole new industries. According to Mensch there are, over the past 200 years or so, distinct periods in history which uniquely favour basic innovations.* His data are shown in Figure 3.2, which plots the frequency of basic innovations, and the inventions which preceded them, as a times series (Mensch, 1974). It is interesting that Mensch's innovation peaks precede the Kondratiev depressions by about twenty years, which suggests that the seeds of the new upswing were already being sown during the previous downswing. Although Mensch does not address this point, it seems likely that many of the basic innovations will be interrelated: indeed, it would be surprising if they were not.

Graham and Senge have taken up Mensch's data and suggest that their long-wave accumulation of physical capital affects the process of innovation as follows:

Eventually, during an upswing and at the peak of a long wave, the economy's physical, technological and managerial infrastructure is committed to older technologies. There are numerous opportunities for improvement innovations, and large markets for them. Little if any of the current infrastructure is able to support basic innovations, and there are few economic incentives to turn away from the established technologies.

During the downturn of the long wave, very little new investment occurs, and there is little market for technological innovations.

During the late upswing, peak, downturn, and trough, scientific and technical progress continues, even though most of the basic inventions do not yet become commercialised basic innovations.

As a long-wave downturn gives way to a new upswing, old capital plant has depreciated, so substantial amounts of new investment need to be made. This economic climate permits investors to develop the new technologies that may have gone untapped for decades.

The cluster of basic innovations near the trough and in the early upswing of a long wave moulds the technological character of later investments, and the cycle of basic innovations repeats itself.

*It must be mentioned here that concern has been expressed in a number of quarters regarding the validity of Mensch's data, and in particular about the difficulties involved in the precise measurement of dates for the market launch of the basic innovations, as well as about what constitutes a 'basic' innovation. Nevertheless, Mensch's data are extremely interesting and certainly thought-provoking. Mensch (1976) has himself applied a sensitivity analysis to his data, and found a consistently high level of significance.

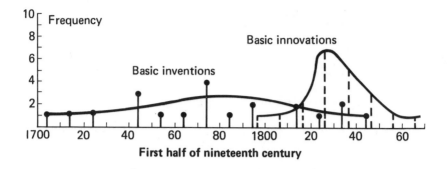

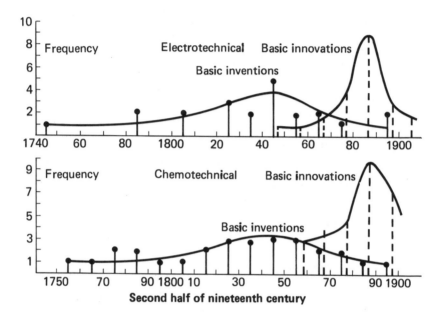

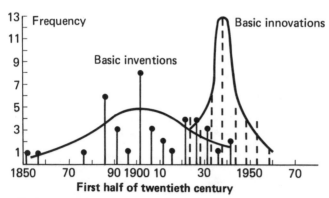

Fig. 3.2 Frequency of basic inventions and basic innovations. Source: Mensch (1974)

Thus, the boom created by the rapid re-equipment by industry in turn creates the right climate for the exploitation and rapid diffusion* of dormant basic innovations which results in the growth of new industries, with subsequent further increases in demand for physical capital, often of a new kind. The fact that Mensch's inventions are rather more spread over time than his 'bunches' of innovations certainly suggests that other factors play a part in forcing their commercialization. A relatively rapid increase in the rate of expenditure on capital goods would certainly contribute towards creating a climate of confidence and optimism in which entrepreneurs could operate, but it is difficult to see how this would have had a sufficiently large impact to, for example, have caused the railway boom in the United Kingdom in the mid-nineteenth century.

Railways were developed in Britain at a time when she enjoyed a very large share of world trade and was opening up new and captive markets in the countries of an expanding Empire. Industrialization was proceeding apace, and much wealth was being generated. There was a pressing and growing need for an efficient and rapid transport system to carry raw materials from various parts of the country and from the seaports to the centres of production, and back to the ports as finished goods. The need for rapid personal mobility of businessmen was also growing. The basic innovations necessary for the development of the railways (the steam engine, Stephenson's first locomotive in 1814) were in being. Cheap and mobile labour was available in Ireland in large quantities. There was thus a 'confluence' of factors — technological, economic, sociological and demographic — which, together, formed the basis of the second Kondratiev built on the rapid growth and international diffusion of the railways and associated industries (iron, coal, construction, mechanical engineering).

Similarly, the economic and political situation in Europe during the 1930s and in particular the Second World War, *forced* the rapid transformation of scientific and technological knowledge and inventions into practical innovations and spawned the modern industries — synthetic materials, petrochemicals, pharmaceuticals, composite materials and electronics — during a relatively short period. This involved massive capital expenditure, mainly on the part of governments, and the concentration of scientific and technical manpower resources. This bunching of new industries formed the basis of the fourth Kondratiev. Again, the influence of a number of factors — including, centrally, new technological capabilities — was necessary before the economic upswing could take place.

Thus, it seems that while technology has played a central role in forcing the world economy out of its major periods of recession, it must be coupled with a great and widely diffused need(s), the availability of large volumes of capital and the presence of entrepreneurs — along with favourable social and political conditions — before commercialization, rapid business development and diffusion occur on a sufficiently large scale.

If this Schumpeterian model of world economic development is indeed valid, and if the world economy is in a Kondratiev recession–depression phase, then this clearly has implications for government innovation policy. These will be discussed later in this book (Chapter 12).

The question to ask now is, what role does technical change play in creating the

---

*We must note here that it is not only the bunching of basic innovations that is important; of greater importance is their rapid diffusion throughout the economy, and the ability of one major innovation to trigger a spate of subsequent innovations.

structural crisis that results first in recession and then in depression? In order to attempt to provide an answer to this question, it is necessary to look at the nature, rather than the rate of technical change in existing industries, as well as at changing patterns of investment and rates of growth in demand. It has been suggested, notably by Utterback and Abernathy (1978), that as industries mature, the underlying nature of innovation changes essentially from a focus on new product development, to one of process optimization and cost reduction (see Figure 3.3). At the same time productivity increases dramatically and, in the final stages of maturity, increased automaticity results in some unemployment. Parallel with these changes in technology, the pattern of investment changes from a net 'expansionary' mode into a net 'rationalization' mode.

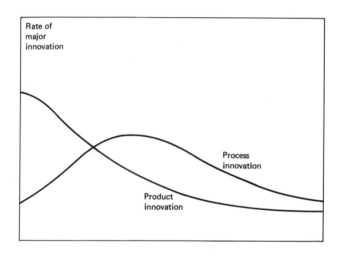

	Fluid pattern	Transitional pattern	Specific pattern
Competitive emphasis on	Functional product performance	Product variation	Cost reduction
Innovation stimulated by	Information on users' needs and users' technical inputs	Opportunities created by expanding internal technical capability	Pressure to reduce cost and improve quality
Predominant type of innovation	Frequent major changes in products	Major process changes required by rising volume	Incremental for product and process, with cumulative improvement in productivity and quality
Product line	Diverse, often including custom designs	Includes at least one product design stable enough to have significant production volume	Mostly undifferentiated standard products
Production processes	Flexible and inefficient; major changes easily accommodated	Becoming more rigid, with changes occurring in major steps	Efficient, capital-intensive and rigid; cost of change is high
Equipment	General-purpose, requiring highly skilled labour	Some subprocesses automated, creating 'islands of automation'	Special-purpose, mostly automatic with labour tasks mainly monitoring and control
Materials	Inputs are limited to generally available materials	Specialized materials may be demanded from some suppliers	Specialized materials will be demanded; if not available, vertical integration will be extensive
Plant	Small-scale, located near user or source of technology	General-purpose with specialized sections	Large-scale, highly specific to particular products
Organizational control is	Informal and entrepreneurial	Through liaison relationships, project and task groups	Through emphasis on structure, goals, and rules

Fig. 3.3 The changing character of innovation, and its changing role in corporate advance. Seeking to understand the variables that determine successful strategies for innovation, the authors focus on three stages in the evolution of a successful enterprise: its period of flexibility, in which the enterprise seeks to capitalize on its advantages where they offer greatest advantages; its intermediate years, in which major products are used more widely; and its full maturity, when prosperity is assured by leadership in several principal products and technologies. Source: Utterback and Abernathy (1978)

Thus, as a new industry grows, initially many new products are created which open up new markets, and business expands rapidly. In order to meet the rapidly growing demand for its products, the industry invests more in physical capital and in increasing production efficiency and productivity. Eventually, markets become saturated, the rate of demand for existing products slackens, and the possibilities for new product development become increasingly fewer. The industry reaches a stage of overproduction, and begins to shed labour. Business confidence wanes. If this happens concurrently in a number of major industry sectors, then a recessionary trend becomes established.

The point is, there is evidence to suggest that a number of major industries have indeed reached a stage of market saturation (synthetic fibres, steel industry, petrochemicals), and that in some areas in which postwar rates of growth have been very high, market expansion is small or nil, and markets are very much ones of replacement (automobiles, consumer electronics, consumer white goods). Stagnation when, as today, coupled to high rates of inflation (stagflation), further reduces effective demand and the recession deepens. Despite rising unemployment, highly organized labour might succeed in obtaining wage increases greatly beyond increases in productivity; this further increases inflation and worsens the crisis of stagflation (already greatly exacerbated by high energy costs).

According to this interpretation, the major industries need to look to the rapid development of new markets (in, for example, the Third World) in order to expand output considerably, or for radical new developments to regenerate demand in existing markets. To some extent the electric light industry achieved a series of such partial reversals from a state of saturation with the introduction of the fluorescent lamp in 1938 and the halogen lamp in 1959 (Haustein, 1980).

A second — Schumpeterian — solution would be the generation of a whole *new* bunch of industries based on technologies currently in their infant stages. Possibilities already being mooted are biotechnology, energy-related technologies (for example, techniques for the reprocessing of coal) and technologies for the exploitation of the ocean bed. These could open up new investment opportunities, generate new and rapidly expanding markets, and create a climate in which entrepreneurial activity — both individual and corporate — could flourish, and drive the world economy into the fifth Kondratiev upswing.

Finally, as regards the regeneration of existing markets, the current situation in the US automobile industry is interesting. Plans are afoot for an expenditure of about $70 billion for the re-equipment of the US automobile industry between 1980 and 1985. This will involve not only process innovations, but also product innovations, that is, the production of a small, energy-efficient car. It will be interesting to see whether this relatively large sum (about twice that expended on the space programme) will create an atmosphere of business confidence leading to the creation of many new small companies — as occurred during the 1950s and early 1960s in the US semiconductor industry — in 'new' areas such as biotechnology and robotics.

Note

If the above 'structural' description of industrial evolution is correct, then this would go a long way towards explaining the change in the relationship between R & D and productivity growth that took place during the 1970s. During the 1950s and 1960s, increasing emphasis was placed on production process improvement. This was particularly true of the 1960s, which was a period of industrial consolidation and rapid productivity increase. Machinery suppliers were rapidly improving the reliability and production rates of their machinery. Semiautomation and automation, based largely on the rapid diffusion of numerical control techniques, became widely diffused. At the same time the process industries themselves were vigorously improving and rationalizing their production processes, gaining both high static and dynamic economies of scale. Thus, the result of a great deal of industrial R & D was reflected in high rates of productivity increase.

By the 1970s, production in most of the 'new' postwar industries (as well as in a number of the older industries, such as textiles) was highly efficient, and undertaken in very large, often vertically integrated, units. In effect, this meant that it became increasingly difficult to 'squeeze' any further productivity increases out of an already efficient system. In other words, the 1970s was a period of diminishing productivity returns to process-improvement investment. The relationship between R & D expenditure and productivity growth therefore became rather weak.

This is not to suggest that high rates of productivity growth will not be obtained in the future; such increases, however, in existing industries, can probably only be brought about by major innovations. This occurred in the textile industry during the 1960s (Sulzer loom, open-ended spinning, carpet tufting machinery, and others) and is currently occurring in the automobile industry through the adoption of robotics.

References

Aukrust, O. (1959), 'Investment and economic growth productivity', *Measurement Review*, **40**, February.

Black, G. (1968), 'Financial variables associated with R & D expenditure by industry', Staff Discussion Paper 300, Program of Policy Studies in Science and Technology, Washington, DC, the George Washington University, January.

Brown, M. and Conrad, A. H. (1967), 'The influence of research and CES production relatives', in *The Theory and Empirical Analysis of Production*, M. Brown (ed.), NBER, Columbia University Press.

Denison, E. F. (1960), *The Sources of Economic Growth in the U.S.*, New York, New York Committee for Economic Development.

Freeman, C. (1978), 'The Kondratiev long waves, technical change and unemployment', in *Proceedings of the OECD Experts Meeting on Structural Determinants of Employment and Unemployment*, March 1977, Paris, OECD.

Graham, A. K. and Senge, P. M. (1980), 'A long-wave hypothesis on innovation', Paper presented to international conference on Innovation Policy and Firm Strategy, IIASA, Schloss Laxenburg, Austria, December, 1979.

Griliches, Z. (1979), 'Issues in assessing the contribution of research and development to productivity growth', *The Bell Journal of Economics*, **10**, 1, Spring.

Griliches, Z. (1980), 'R & D and the productivity showdown', in *Papers and Proceedings of the Ninety Second Annual Meeting of the American Economic Association*, May.

Haustein, H-D. (1980), 'Lighting industry: a classical case of innovation', IIASA, Working Paper WP-80–12, Schloss Laxenburg, Austria.

Jewkes, J., Sawers, D., and Stillerman, R. (1970), *The Sources of Invention*, New York, W. W. Norton and Co. Inc.

Jones, D. T. (1976), 'Output, employment and labour productivity in Europe since 1955', National Institute for Economic and Social Research, London, August.

Kendrick, J. W. (1961), *Productivity Trends in the United States*, NBER, General Series No. 61, Princeton University Press.

Kondratiev, N. D. (1935), 'The long waves in economic life', *Review of Economic Statistics*, November.

Kuznets, S. (1940), 'Review of *Business Cycles* of Schumpeter', *American Economic Review*, **30**, July.

Link, A. M. (1980), *Research and Development Activity in U.S. Manufacturing*, New York, Praeger.

Mansfield, E. (1965), 'Rates of return from industrial R & D', *American Economic Review*, May.

— (1968), *The Economics of Technical Change*, New York, W. W. Norton and Co., Inc.

Massel, B. F. (1960), 'Capital formation and technological change in U.S. manufacturing', *The Review of Economics and Statistics*, May.

Mensch, G. (1974), *Technology Transfer*, Nato Advanced Study Institute Series, No. 6. Nordhoff, Leiden.

— (1976), *IFO-Schnelldienst*, **29**.

— (1979), *Stalemate in Technology*, Cambridge, Mass. Ballinger.

Minasian, J. (1969), 'Research and development, production functions and rates of return', *American Economic Review*, May.

Nason, H. K., Steger, J. A., and Manners, G. E. (1978), *Support of Basic Research by Industry*, Report to the National Science Foundation, Washington, DC.

Ray, G. (1980), 'Innovation in the long cycle', *Lloyds Bank Review*, No. 135, January, 14–28.

Rothwell, R. (1977), 'The role of technical change in international competitiveness: the case of the textile machinery industry', *Management Decision*, **15**, 3.

— (1981), 'Non-price factors in the export competitiveness of agricultural engineering products', OECD Conference on Scientific and Technological Indicators, Paris, September 1980 (to be published in *Research Policy*).

Saunders, C. (1978), *Engineering in Britain, West Germany and France*, Sussex European Research Centre, University of Sussex.

Schumpeter, J. A. (1939), *Business Cycles*, New York and London, McGraw-Hill.

Soete, L. (1979), 'International competition, innovation and employment', Six Countries Programme Workshop on Technology and Employment, Paris, November.

Solow, R. M. (1957), 'Technical change and the aggregate production function', *Review of Economics and Statistics*, **39**, 312–20.

Thomas, E. (1980), 'Recent research on R & D and productivity growth: a changing relationship between input and impact indicators?' Paper presented to OECD Conference on Science and Technology Indicators, Paris, September.

UN Report (1962), *Some Factors in Economic Growth in Europe during 1950s*, United Nations, New York.

Utterback, J. M. and Abernathy, W. J. (1978), 'Patterns of industrial innovation', *Technology Review*, **80**, 7, June/July.

Walker, W. (1980), 'Britain's industrial performance, 1850–1950: a failure to adjust', in K. Pavitt (ed.), *Technical Innovation and British Economic Performance*, London, Macmillan.

4. THE GENERAL PROBLEM OF GOVERNMENT INTERVENTION AND THE MAIN FORMS OF GOVERNMENT INFLUENCE ON TECHNICAL INNOVATION

We shall first consider the issue of the principle of government intervention in relation to innovation, and then the question of form. Many countries have for many years deliberately followed policies designed to encourage inventions and innovations on the assumption that technical change will ultimately help improve the standard of living. It holds true that in contemporary society only a few eccentrics would endorse such policies irrespective of the damaging and social consequences of technical change and it has indeed become rather generally accepted that policies for technical innovation only make sense when placed in a wider social and economic context (SPRU–TNO, 1977).

The supposedly disruptive effects of technical innovation, both on society generally and in the workplace, have frequently led to deep mistrust and often to policies deliberately designed to prevent or hinder innovation. Perceptions of damage and benefit of technical change have varied greatly over time and have deep specific roads in different cultures. It is only relatively recently, and triggered by the question of international competitiveness in a changing world environment, that a more general acceptance of technical innovation has become more widespread. This general acceptance, however, explicitly implies that policies to advance technical innovation must incorporate considerations as to the possible adverse consequences of such innovation.

In the early period of the industrial revolution opposition to the perceived adverse consequences of some technical innovations was sufficiently widespread to involve violent outbreaks. Ever since Adam Smith's *Wealth of Nations* was published in 1776, classical economists have argued very powerfully that the unhindered pursuit of new profit-making opportunities by competing entrepreneurs would lead, as though guided by an 'invisible hand' to the general welfare of society. But it was only gradually during the nineteenth century that these arguments became widely accepted, and *laissez-innover* policies were adopted as part of an overall *laissez-faire* approach to economic policy. The freedom of firms to invest and adopt new methods of manufacture and to develop and produce new products became an essential feature of the competitive process, subject only to minimal constraints in relation to the safety and to the health of users and producers.

More recently, many of the old doubts and fears have been revived and new constraints have been imposed alongside new incentives. Obviously, the extent to which technical change may be perceived as beneficial or damaging will vary with the individuals affected and with the particular type of technical change under consideration.

Those workers who lose their jobs through the substitution of automated processes for older more labour-intensive techniques may very well adopt a 'Luddite' attitude towards process innovations in their own industry. Simultaneously, and by the same group, innovations such as radio, television, longplaying records, cheap air travel and video are being welcomed. The pure logic of classical economic theory is not always immediately apparent to those caught up in the processes of factory closures and redundancies. Similarly, those living close to airports, to chemical plants or power stations may perceive the relative costs and benefits of innovation in a very different way from those more remotely affected.

Contemporary innovation policies may be interpreted as an attempt to achieve simultaneously diverse social goals which cannot always be easily reconciled. On the one hand there is still a very widespread desire to sustain or even improve living standards, the increase of which was such a remarkable feature of the third quarter of the twentieth century. It is generally being recognized that a high rate of technical change was an essential feature of this unprecedented growth. On the other hand, there are increasing pressures to discriminate between various alternative new technologies and to mitigate many of the injurious side-effects of technical change, particularly those relating to employment and to the environment. The daunting but socially indispensable task of those concerned with policies in this area is to achieve a constructive synthesis of these objectives.

One of the main difficulties is that responsibility for policies which affect technical innovation is normally divided between several different government departments. Some have a direct responsibility for stimulating, encouraging and supporting invention and innovation in sectors like agriculture, industry and services. Others have responsibility for safety, employment, consumer protection, education, environmental conditions, international trade, health and so forth.

The government departments involved are often only imperfectly aware of the implications of their departmentalized policies for innovation elsewhere in the economy. Even when they are aware of these indirect connections, they will not usually attach any great weight to them, being preoccupied as they are with their primary mission.

A further complication arises from the perfectly understandable desire of those working in industry and services to participate in the decision-making process which will affect their conditions of employment including, of course, changes in techniques. The printing industry with its employment-affecting new technologies is a major example in this respect.

Thus, the attainment of satisfactory policies for technical innovation is by no means easy. Apparently clumsy methods of coordination have to replace the deceptively simple invisible hand of Adam Smith. Even in the narrower sphere of the effective application of government policies deliberately designed to promote technical change, and when interdepartmental coordination is not a pressing problem, there is great uncertainty about merits and demerits of alternative mechanisms and incentives.

Some would argue that the conflict between these various objectives is so great that the pursuit of one will endanger the others. For example, it is frequently argued that the regulation of food and drug innovation in the United States has become so restrictive as to slow down the process of technical change to an unacceptably low level. Others argue that the environmentalists' opposition to nuclear power in many countries may seriously endanger the future supplies of energy so vital to maintain production in almost all industries. Still others argue that the controls over pollution are now becoming so costly as to endanger the competitive position of some European and American industries in relation to less scrupulous competitors in other continents. Finally, many would argue that taxation and legislation in relation to employment and redundancy are now sometimes so restrictive as to inhibit firms from expanding their labour forces and so are contributing to the very evils they are designed to prevent.

On a more general level some economists, businessmen and politicians are seriously worried by the proliferation of government controls and regulations of all kinds, which take up a great deal of management time and effort. These controls and regulations, as is argued, are diverting management from the pursuit of more urgent and fundamental goals and lead to more defensive actions. *Laissez-faire* theorists have persistently argued that government intervention in industry is usually, if not always, inefficient and that entrepreneurs are the only ones in a position to make rational choices about alternative investments in new equipment and new products. On this view, the springs of productive enterprise are gradually being clogged up by an accumulation of paternalistic legislation and bureaucratic interference.

As against this, others argue that the costs, complexities and risk-taking of technical innovation in many branches of industry are now becoming so great that an even higher degree of government involvement at all levels is quite inevitable. Moreover, it is argued that government-backed international competition is becoming so universal that economic survival dictates state involvement here too. Government participation in new product development, new plant investment, procurement, overseas marketing, and other aspects of innovation would lead logically to a strategy of total state involvement. Explicit socialist centralized policies for industry would be the far end of this spectrum.

But even in several socialist economies the debate on the role of the market continues and so too does the debate on centralization versus regional or enterprise autonomy in major areas of policy-making, perhaps most notably in Yugoslavia. A general problem for all economies therefore is: what types of central government intervention and regulation are most effective in stimulating and sustaining the desired types of technical change? What types of institutional filters or assessment can best discriminate between desirable and undesirable types of technical change?

This is not to deny the central social and political issue of ownership of industry, but only to point out that both capitalist and socialist countries face some similar problems of technical and economic choice in relation to such issues as the future of nuclear power, supersonic aircraft, introduction of new drugs, location of chemical plants, the future of the private car, the pursuit of the information society and so forth. In the light of the realities of maintaining international competitiveness, all countries face the general problem of maintaining increases in productivity growth in the output of their existing product range and problems of stimulating the development of new products and processes.

Critics of socialist centralization point to the bureaucratic incompetence of government controls and the loss of entrepreneurial initiative, which is so vital to innovation. However, only the most rigid dogmatist or pure anarchist would rule out the need for some central government regulation and control. So, the question in the end boils down to one of well-designed policies and instruments of intervention based on a satisfactory theoretical understanding of the nature of innovation and the limitations of central regulation.

Both welfare economists and managers have long accepted that the divergence between private and social costs and benefits necessitates adjustment to the market mechanism in many areas of economic policy, most obviously in relation to environmental pollution, the quality of the workplace, or such areas as the finance of basic research. Ideally, it should be possible to develop the benefits from a continuing flow of useful technical change, while simultaneously foreseeing and averting many, if not all, of the potentially damaging social and environmental consequences.

The aim of such policies should not be growth *per se*, but the introduction of such changes in the economy as would maximize the welfare of the population including health and environmental amenity as well as more directly economic goals. The problem is one of devising policies which increase economic efficiency while also improving the composition and distribution of the national product. What has been generally accepted in economic policy as to do away with the negative aspects of *laissez-faire* economics may now need to have its parallel as to technology policy in the area of technical innovation.

This, at any rate, must be the objective of those who are directly concerned with policy for innovation in government and in industry, both in capitalist and socialist systems, however difficult may be the theoretical and practical problems confronting the attainment of this ideal.

Governments effect technical innovation in innumerable ways. In Chapter 5 we will give an overview of some recent national policy formulations and their appropriateness. In following chapters we will consider some of the most important policy measures: innovation-oriented procurement, regulations, subsidies to individual firms, the role of the scientific and technical infrastructure and policies towards small and medium-sized firms.

Any agency of government may express a demand for new products or systems. This may be a general demand for a group of products or it may be quite specific; it may be an indication of interest or it may be a procurement contract. Whatever form it takes there is no doubt that the government market has an important influence on industrial innovation. It should be mentioned that outside of the military area procurement has not always been explicitly used to advance and direct technical change although experiences and new programmes in a number of countries point at the importance of this policy instrument. For convenience, this form of influence is briefly described here as 'procurement', although of course it is much more than this. Next to weapons development for the military, procurement has been a major factor in relation to the development of synthetic materials in Germany, synthetic rubber in the United States, radar in the United Kingdom, and to many nuclear innovations.

The many problems with which contemporary society is faced within the public sector, and the increased pressure on the efficiency and effectiveness within this sector, will put pressure on innovation oriented procurement policies. Although military procurement has undoubtedly had a major stimulating effect on industrial innovation in some areas, and especially in the United States (semiconductors, for instance), it will not be explicitly included in the discussions in this book.

Secondly, governments may get themselves directly involved in the development of new products, for example through subsidies to R & D activities of individual firms, or through other forms of direct financial support to firms in their attempts at innovation. These subsidies take a great variety of forms, including tax incentives, but again for convenience, they are here summarized briefly as 'subsidy'. This is perhaps currently the most common and most widely applied form of government innovation assistance.

Thirdly, governments may influence innovation to a considerable extent through laws or regulations which affect the provision of a service or the sale of a product. Such laws and regulations may be introduced for a great variety of different reasons like safety, pollution, standards, consumer protection, etc. These laws and regulations are usually exercised by many different agencies, which may be only remotely concerned with innovation as such. All these forms of influence are summarized here as 'regulation'.

Fourthly, governments may influence the course of innovation by their support for background basic research and applied research within the scientific and technological 'infrastructure'. These activities may take place in universities, in government-funded institutions including research associations which, although not themselves producing and selling, may nevertheless contribute a great deal to inventions, to exploratory development, to the demonstration of technical feasibility of new products and processes, to 'debugging' of difficulties experienced by firms, and to the introduction of new technologies in industry.

Of special importance are government policies towards small and medium-sized enterprises. The role of small and medium-sized enterprises towards economic development, to technical innovation and to employment is much underestimated. In addition to more general philosophical aspects relating to the scale of small and medium-sized firms, there is hard evidence of the strategic importance of this group of firms.

Finally, recent studies by Rubenstein *et al.* (1977) and by Allen *et al.* (1981) show clearly that the general economic climate has a major influence on the innovative activities of industrial firms. Many important aspects of this climate are the relative opportunities for profit inside and outside manufacturing industry, the patent system, price and wage controls and general competitive conditions. In this book we will not enter into the discussion of these factors.

A subjective assessment of the importance of the main government instruments towards technical innovation is given in Table 4.1. In this table, we consider some 50 major clusters of technical innovations over the past half-century from the standpoint of government influence. The conclusions which emerge are clear-cut.

The most important way in which governments, according to this table, have influenced technical innovation is through demand, the least important through subsidy. Government regulation has not prevented innovation to any significant extent in the areas shown and may indeed have had a substantial stimulating influence on improving quality and performance. This was true in such fields as mining equipment, transistor technology and aircraft safety.

The infrastructural support provided for by government has also made a major contribution. In the case of electronics and chemicals the universities were especially important in originating major inventions and supplying background technology. In nuclear power, aviation and engines of various types, government-funded laboratories were probably more important, except for the original basic physics. In mechanical equipment and processes for bulk materials, neither government nor university laboratories made significant contributions.

The following major objections may be made to this analysis:

— it is based on a subjective assessment. While it is true that it is founded on a variety of case studies and research projects, nevertheless a highly subjective element is inevitably present in trying to assess the influence of such factors as government demand and public interest in future applications;
— in particular the subjective bias may lead to an understatement of the negative

influence of government regulation and legislation. The rather positive assessment made here stems from the view that stringent safety and environmental standards frequently acted as an important incentive for quality improvements, and that government procurement regulations setting particular standards may have a similar beneficial effect. However, it may reasonably be objected that since the analysis is in retrospect, it fails to take account of the most recent restrictive legislation, for example, in the field of drugs, nuclear energy and agricultural chemicals, which have substantially increased the costs and time needed for radical product innovation;

— the point about the time-period of the analysis also applies to the assessment of 'subsidy'. The use of various forms of subsidy to civilian R & D and other innovation costs became widespread only in the 1970s and any larger scale experience is only being gained at present as to the effect of the several forms in which this instrument is employed.

These objections are all serious ones. We shall therefore go on from this preliminary analysis to a more detailed consideration of other evidence derived from a variety of different sources, including the *Six Countries Programme on Aspects of Government Policy towards Innovation*. However, before considering the role of government in much greater depth, it is worth noting that the key conclusions about the influence of government on innovation are consistent with the main body of economic and social theory and the results of empirical research in the field:

— a strong and clearly expressed government demand has the effect of diminishing risk and uncertainty in the area where it is greatest: the future market. The more radical the innovation, the more important this is;
— the potential inefficiency associated with subsidies has for a long time been a commonplace of economics;
— industrial technology is increasingly related to basic science, so that a strong interaction with universities and government institutes pursuing basic and applied research is to be expected, especially in the more recent technologies. Moreover, pluralistic information inputs are reported beneficial in almost all empirical work on industrial innovation;
— the conclusion on the effects of government regulation is more difficult to relate to a previous body of knowledge, since both negative and positive effects might be anticipated in equal measure, depending upon the nature and the form of the regulations and/or legislation. However, the fact that regulation does have a big effect on industrial innovations, for good or for ill, is supported by one of the most recent surveys carried out for the Six Countries Programme (Rothwell, 1980), although most of the data on this issue are derived from the United States. It should therefore be pointed out that in-depth study of the impact of various types of regulation to distinguish negative and positive elements is an extremely important field of future research. There is no reason in principle why policies designed for consumer and environmental protection and for energy saving would not act as a positive stimulus to innovation, provided that intelligent consideration is given to the innovation impact when legislation is drawn up, or regulations made.

In the following chapters we will go in detail into the potential and the limitations of the several government instruments.

Table 4.1 Government and innovation

		Force of government influence				
		Demand	Subsidy	Regulation	Infrastructure	Universities
Electronic devices and systems	Television	3	1	2	2	4
	Radar	5	2	4	5	3
	Computers	5	3	3	2	5
	Transistors	5	2	4	3	3
	Integrated circuits	5	2	4	2	2
	NC machine tools	5	1	4	3	5
	Electronic instruments	4	2	5	4	5
	Optical fibres	4	1	4	3	3
	Laser applications	4	2	3	3	4
	Satellites	5	3	4	5	3
Synthetic materials and other new chemical products	Polyethylene	4	1	4	4	4
	PVC	4	1	4	2	4
	Polystyrene	3	1	3	2	3
	Synthetic rubber	5	2	4	2	3
	Synthetic fibres	2	1	3	1	3
	Antibiotics	4	2	4	2	4
	Insecticides	3	1	2	2	4
	Fertilizers	5	2	3	2	3
	Herbicides	3	1	2	2	3
	Tranquillizers	3	1	3	4	4
Engines, motors, transport equipment and durables	Turbo-prop engines	3	2	3	4	3
	Large aircraft	4	3	4	4	2
	Jet engines	5	2	4	3	3
	Diesel engines	3	1	4	4	2
	Passenger cars and components	2	1	4	3	2
	Wankel engine	1	1	3	2	1
	Diesel-electric	2	1	4	3	2
	Consumer durables	1	1	5	2	1
Nuclear power	Gas-cooled reactors	5	4	4	5	3
	Turbo-generators	4	1	4	3	2
	Isotopes	4	1	5	5	3

		A	B	C	D	E
	Heavy-water reactors	5	5	4	5	3
	Light-water reactors	4	2	3	5	3
	Fast-breeder reactors	4	5	4	5	2
Mechanical	Shearer-loaders	5	2	4	3	1
engineering	Automatic looms	1	1	1	3	2
equipment	Potato harvesters	1	2	3	2	1
and	Cotton pickers	1	1	3	2	1
instruments	Bulldozers	3	1	3	1	2
	Power tools	1	1	4	2	2
	Tower cranes	3	1	4	2	1
	Biro pens	1	1	1	1	1
	Xerography	1	1	3	2	1
	Optical instruments	3	1	3	3	3
Processes	Direct reduction	3	2	3	3	2
for	Continuous casting	2	2	3	3	1
basic	Oxygen steel	4	3	3	2	2
materials	Float glass process	1	1	3	3	2
	Catalytic cracking	4	1	4	2	3
	Gas reforming	3	1	4	3	3
	Refinery processes	3	1	4	2	4
	Chorleywood bakery	1	4	3	5	2

Notes

Demand, Subsidy, Infrastructure and Universities
 5 Very big contribution or stimulus to success of innovations
 4 Major contribution or stimulus
 3 Significant contribution
 2 Small contribution
 1 Very low or negligible contribution.

Regulation
 5 Big positive effect of government regulation
 4 Some positive effect
 3 Neutral or cancelling out of negative and positive effects
 2 Some negative effect, such as delays, without compensating advantages, such as safety
 1 Major negative effect.

The assessment of effects relates to the whole period of gestation of the 'family' or 'cluster' of related innovations in each group. It starts from the first interest of firms in research and development of products or systems, and it includes subsequent 'improvement' innovations, such as colour television, low pressure polyethylene, and successive generations of computers and aircraft.

References

Allen, T. J. *et al.* (1981), 'Government influence on the process of innovation in Europe and and Japan', *Research Policy*, 7, 124–49.

Rothwell, R. (1980), *Industrial Innovation and Government Regulation*, Six Countries Programme Workshop, TNO, PO Box 215 Delft, Netherlands.

Rubenstein, A. *et al.* (1977), 'Management perceptions of government incentives to technological innovation in England, France, West Germany and Japan', *Research Policy*, 6, 4 October, p. 324.

SPRU–TNO (1977), *The Current International Economic Climate and Policies for Technical Innovation*, report prepared by the Science Policy Research Unit, University of Sussex, in collaboration with Staffgroup Strategic Surveys, TNO, PO Box 215 Delft, Netherlands.

5. INDUSTRIAL INNOVATION POLICY: A COMPARISON OF SOME RECENT GOVERNMENT FORMULATIONS*

Such are the benefits currently believed to be associated with industrial innovation that few governments in developed countries now feel that they can do without an explicit innovation policy. The pressures to construct such a policy have grown as a result of a number of factors, including a worldwide deterioration in the economic climate during the 1970s, major changes in the international economic order (brought about by the development of the newly industrialized countries, and by the sudden acquisition of wealth by various resource-rich nations), and, last but not least, by the general acceptance of the case long argued by certain economists that innovation plays a key role in stimulating economic growth (see Chapter 3). Few would quarrel with the Advisory Council for Applied Research and Development (ACARD (1), 1978, p. 11), who, in their report to the British Government, state simply and boldly, 'innovation must be at the heart of any improvement in the performance of . . . manufacturing industry', a view echoed in a flurry of official and semi-official government reports published over the last two years. Whereas in the past, national innovation policies, in so far as they existed at all, were largely implicit, generally taking the form of government support for big sophisticated R & D projects in a small number of high technologies like defence, aerospace, and nuclear energy (Pavitt (1980), p. 39), now it is increasingly recognized that an explicit, national policy for stimulating industrial innovation is an essential and integral part of any government's overall industrial and economic strategy.

The purpose of this chapter is to analyse and compare a number of reports that have appeared between 1978 and 1980, and which make policy recommendations as to how governments may best induce and nurture industrial innovation. The reports concerned are listed in Table 5.1, and deal with countries in Europe (the Netherlands, Sweden, and the United Kingdom) and North America (Canada and the United States) and with Japan. (We have been unable to cover West Germany or France, since recent and comprehensive policy documents are not available; however, some general comments on government policies towards innovation in these countries are included in the final section.) For each report we shall examine its analysis of those problems which would benefit from a higher level of innovative activity and of the causes ascribed to those problems; the overall strategic goals and the tactical objectives of the innovation policies advocated; the types of measures, and their intended targets, proposed to achieve these aims; the internal consistency of each analysis and set of policy proposals based on it; and, lastly, the similarities and differences, in each of the above respects, between the various reports.

Having outlined some of the themes of this chapter, we must also make clear right at the outset what it does *not* set out to achieve. There is no attempt to examine the extent to which the problems described in each report reflect the real economic situation in the country concerned, nor to assess the degree to which

*This chapter was prepared by Ben Martin of SPRU, in consultation with Roy Rothwell.

Table 5.1   List of reports analysed in this study

Country	Report(s)
Canada	*Forging the Links: A Technology Policy for Canada* Science Council of Canada, Report 29, Ontario, February 1979.
Japan	*The Role of Technology in the Change of Industrial Structure (abstract)* Industrial Research Institute, Japan, April 1978.
The Netherlands	*Summary of the Government White Paper on Innovation* Science Policy Information Department, The Hague, 1979.
Sweden	*Technical Capability and Industrial Competence: A Comparative Study on Sweden's Future Competitiveness* IVA Royal Swedish Academy of Engineering Sciences, Stockholm, June 1979
United Kingdom	(1) *Industrial Innovation* Advisory Council for Applied Research and Development (ACARD), London, 1978. (2) *Technological Change: Threats and Opportunities for the United Kingdom* ACARD, London, December 1979.
United States	(1) *The US Domestic Policy Review on Industrial Innovation* (interim report), May 1979. (2) *Advisory Committee on Industrial Innovation, Final Report* United States Department of Commerce, Washington, September 1979 (3) The President's Industrial Innovation Initiatives (fact sheet), Washington, October 1979.

These reports are referred to in the text by country, rather than by author, for example (Canada, p. 18) or (United Kingdom, 1978, p. 11).

the stated policy objectives represent the government's actual intentions towards innovation. The precise relationship of the problems discussed, and of the policies propounded, to 'reality' is left for others to evaluate.

As one might expect given the different terms of reference imposed on the authors of each report, the different methods they use to assemble relevant information, and the different national economic situations in which the proposed government innovation policy is to operate, the reports examined here, although linked by the common aim of trying to increase the level of innovative activity in industry, are very different in scope and structure. While the American report was compiled by several specially constituted committees established specifically to advise the US president on industrial innovation, the British and Canadian reports each constitute part of a longer term and more permanent effort by ACARD and the Science Council Industrial Policies Committee respectively. In the case of Sweden, the government commissioned the Swedish Academy of Engineering Sciences to carry out the work, and the Japanese report was produced by the Industrial Research Institute. These last two reports represent merely one of the early stages in the process of constructing a government innovation policy, while in contrast the Dutch report takes the form of a government white paper, and the (second) American one is a set of presidential initiatives, and these latter two therefore constitute a far later stage in that process.

In view of this wide diversity between the reports, before we can begin to compare and contrast their contents some consideration must first be given to the process of innovation itself — in particular to the types of benefit it may bring, to the factors needed to ensure successful innovation, to the question of which of those factors a government can hope to influence (the 'targets' for its policies), and to the types of measures (the policy 'tools') that lie at its disposal. Once some sort of classification scheme for all the various options has been established, it should then be possible to identify those on which each report chooses to focus, and those which it prefers to ignore.

POSSIBLE BENEFITS FROM INNOVATION

The benefits assumed to be associated with successful industrial innovation are many and varied. (For a more detailed discussion of the role of innovation in achieving improved productivity, growth, competitiveness, and economic development, see Chapter 3.) As Braun (1980, p. 1) observes, 'It has become an article of faith in all technically developed countries that technological innovation is *the major therapeutic agent* for current economic ills' (emphasis added). Perhaps one of the most important beneficial effects of innovation is that of achieving and maintaining a high level of international competitiveness for a nation's goods. The ACARD report on *Technological Change* has no doubt that the very future of Britain depends on its ability to innovate: 'The rate of technological innovation in United Kingdom industry will need to increase if its products and manufacturing processes are to match those of our major trading competitors. This is a necessary condition for our future survival as a trading nation' (United Kingdom, 1979, p. 7).

However, competitive goods are just one of the possible benefits. There are many others, ranging from the strictly economic benefits (for example, economic growth, or higher productivity) to wider political, social, and environmental benefits, like national security, industrial self-sufficiency, more fulfilling jobs, better public services, and more efficient use of natural resources. Figure 5.1 shows approximately twenty of the major benefits that have been variously attributed to industrial innovation (for example, Pavitt and Walker, 1976, p. 82; OECD (1978), p. 49). We shall see below how countries differ in the importance they attach to each of these potential benefits from innovation.

THE NATURE OF INNOVATION AND GOVERNMENT TOOLS
FOR INFLUENCING IT

As many economists have pointed out, successful innovation depends upon a favourable combination of technology 'supply' and market 'demand' factors (see, for example, Freeman, 1979). On the supply side, the research on, and development of, new products and processes is contingent upon the presence to an adequate extent of three main types of input: (a) scientific and technical knowledge and manpower; (b) information about the likely market for the innovation, and management skills needed to ensure successful research, development, production and sales; and (c) financial resources (Allen *et al.*, 1978, p. 130; Hagedoorn and Prakke, 1979, p. 70). These three inputs are shown on the left-hand-side of Figure 5.2.

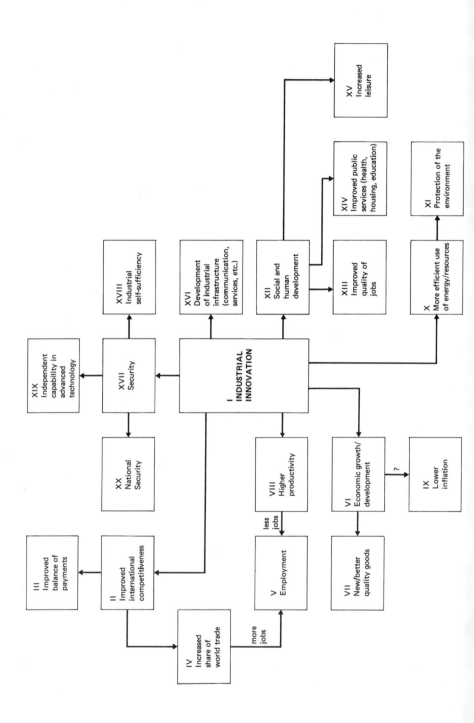

Fig. 5.1 Industrial innovation – possible benefits

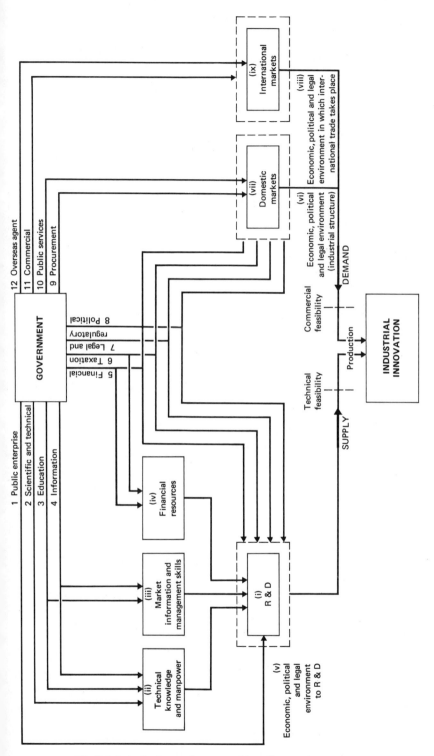

Fig. 5.2 Inducing innovation — possible policy targets and tools

From Figure 5.2, it is clear that a government seeking to influence the supply side of the innovation process can do so either through direct participation in the process itself (target (i)), or through improving the supply of one of the three inputs (targets (ii), (iii), and (iv)), or it can intervene less directly by attempting to modify the wider economic, political and legal environment (target (v)) in which the production of new goods takes place. Alternatively, a government wishing to improve the demand side of the innovation process may do so in domestic markets (either indirectly (target (vi)) or directly (target (vii)), or in international markets, where it could alter the overall environment in which international trade takes place (target (viii)) — by tariffs or trade agreements, for example — or intervene more directly (target (ix)), perhaps to act as an overseas salesman for its nation's goods.

To influence these various targets, governments have a wide range of policy measures available to them, as previous work (such as OECD, 1978) makes clear. A scheme for classifying these measures by the types of tool or mechanism involved has been constructed by Braun (1980, pp. 5–6), and this, with one addition (that of overseas agent, see Table 5.2), forms the basis of the classification employed here.* Table 5.2 lists twelve types of policy tool, together with examples of policy measures coming under each category, while Figure 5.2 shows the possible targets on which the various tools can act.

In addition to distinguishing between different policy targets and tools, there is one further distinguishing characteristic of policy measures towards innovation that needs to be categorized. This concerns the specificity of the measure — some measures may be aimed at *specific* technologies, industrial sectors, or particular types of firms (small firms, for instance), while others are more general in intent, attempting to influence *all* innovative activity, either directly, or indirectly through encouraging improvements in general industrial performance, or, less directly still, through altering the general environment in which industry operates (see Braun (1980), p. 5). Six different levels of specificity, or *target-levels*, are shown in Table 5.3.

THE PROBLEM — ITS NATURE AND ITS CAUSES

Having given some attention to the concepts involved in the process of innovation, and to the various ways in which governments might attempt to influence it, we are now in a position to look in detail at the individual reports on government policies towards industrial innovation. Each report starts from an analysis of the prevailing economic situation — in particular of the problems (both present and future) upon which improved innovation is assumed to be capable of having a beneficial effect, and of the factors believed to be currently limiting the level of innovative activity.

Let us look first at how each report describes the nature of the problem, or problems, which would benefit from more innovation. Although the format of the reports varies considerably, it is possible to establish, relatively unambiguously, what are perceived as being the major problems or areas of concern for each

---

*Other classification schemes can be found in Allen *et al.* (1978), OECD (1978), and Hagedoorn and Prakke (1979), but none make the threefold distinction between policy tools, targets, and target-levels that we have found helpful in analysing government policy measures.

Table 5.2 Classification of government policy tools*

Policy tool	Examples
1. Public enterprise	Innovation by publicly owned industries, setting up of new industries, pioneering use of new techniques by public corporations, participation in private enterprise
2. Scientific and technical	Research laboratories, support for research associations, learned societies, professional associations, research grants
3. Education	General education, universities, technical education, apprenticeship schemes, continuing and further education, retraining
4. Information	Information networks and centres, libraries, advisory and consultancy services, databases, liaison services
5. Financial	Grants, loans, subsidies, financial sharing arrangements, provision of equipment, buildings or services, loan guarantees, export credits, etc.
6. Taxation	Company, personal, indirect and payroll taxation, tax allowances
7. Legal and regulatory	Patents, environmental and health regulations, inspectorates, monopoly regulations
8. Political	Planning, regional policies, honours or awards for innovation, encouragement of mergers or joint consortia, public consultation
9. Procurement	Central or local government purchases and contracts, public corporations, R & D contracts, prototype purchases
10. Public services	Purchases, maintenance, supervision and innovation in health service, public building, construction, transport, telecommunications
11. Commercial	Trade agreements, tariffs, currency regulations
12. Overseas agent	Defence sales organizations

*This table is based on Table 1 in Braun, 1980.

Table 5.3 Classification of policy target-levels

A	Individual specific technologies
B	Industrial sectors
C(i)	Small firms
C(ii)	Large firms
D	Industrial innovation in general, or the technological capability of industry
E	Industrial performance (or the environment to D)
F	General environment (economic, political, etc.) in which industry operates

country. The results are summarized in Table 5.4.* It can be seen that, while all six countries are concerned that there is insufficient innovation, all but Japan are worried by declining international competitiveness, and all except Sweden by growing unemployment. There are nevertheless significant differences between what each country identifies as the major areas of concern — as one would expect given the unique set of economic and political circumstances pertaining to each

*In Table 5.4 (and in later ones), there is inevitably a certain subjective element involved in assessing whether a particular topic has been covered in a report or not — in this case, whether or not each of the possible areas of concern shown in Figure 5.1 is adjudged to be a 'problem'. However, any effects of subjectivity are almost certainly very much smaller than the actual differences in emphasis between the reports, and they should not therefore affect the conclusions drawn here.

Table 5.4 The problem – areas of concern

	Associated benefit in Figure 1	Canada	Japan	The Netherlands	Sweden	United Kingdom	United States
Insufficient innovation	I	✓	✓(a)	✓(b)	✓	✓	✓(c)
Declining international competitiveness	II	✓	–(d) (e)	✓	✓(e)	✓	✓
Balance of payments/import penetration	III	✓	–	–	–	–	✓
Unemployment	V	–	✓	✓	✓	–	–
Declining growth rates	VI	–	✓	✓	–	–	–
Need for better quality goods	VII	✓	✓(f)	–	–	✓	–
Low productivity/industrial inefficiency	VIII	✓	✓	–	–	✓	✓
Inflation	IX	–	–	–	✓	–	–
Need to conserve natural resources	XI	–	–	✓	–	–	–
Non-fulfilling/low-skill jobs	XIII	✓	–	✓	✓	–	–
Need for better public services	XIV	–	–	–	✓	–	–
Foreign ownership	XVIII	✓	–	–	–	–	–
Technological dependence	XIX	✓	–	–	–	–	–

(a) Still a net technology-importer.
(b) In technologically advanced goods.
(c) Loss of world lead.

(d) Problems with high value of yen.
(e) Problems with overseas protection.
(f) In service sector.

country. Canada, for example, is the only country in the group where foreign owner-ship and technological dependence are major issues. The Japanese, British, and American reports focus primarily on strictly economic concerns, in contrast with the Dutch and Swedish reports, which give greater attention to the wider social and environmental benefits (more fulfilling jobs, better public services, conservation of resources) that innovation can bring. As might have been anticipated, Canada and the United States share similar economic concerns (declining competitiveness, balance of payments difficulties, unemployment, and inflation), while, perhaps more surprisingly, there appear to be certain similarities between the economic problems confronting Japan and Britain (unemployment,* the need for better quality goods, and low productivity). However, while Japan is particularly worried by declining growth rates, Britain is less so, perhaps because British economic growth has never been very fast in recent times. Holland and Sweden share this Japanese concern, while Canada and the United States attach less importance to it.

If these are the problems, what causes are attributed to them? Table 5.5 lists some of the national weaknesses pinpointed in the reports as contributing to the problems, along with examples quoted where foreign competitors are felt to have a comparative advantage. It can be seen that Canada is less concerned with the supply side of the innovation process, and more with problems related to the structure of Canadian industry and markets. The reverse is true of the United States, where the technical and financial inputs (targets (ii) and (iv) in Figure 5.2) into the process of innovation are judged to be relatively weak. The United Kingdom appears to be afflicted with all the Canadian and American weaknesses, and a few more besides. For example, there is felt to be a lack of rapport between users and supplying industries, which suggests that marketing information and management skills (target (iii) in Figure 5.2) need to be improved. The Swedish report shares the American worry about inadequate technical and financial inputs, but in addition cites certain 'environmental' factors as contributing to the holding back of innovation, including burgeoning legislation, and 'various safety nets of subsidies, credit guarantees, and "soft" loans', all of which are claimed to have 'reduced the adaptability of industry' (Sweden, p. 7). In addition, Sweden faces one of the structural problems confronting Canada and Britain, namely the threat to its traditional industries from developing countries. The Netherlands, in common with Canada and the United Kingdom, appears to have previously suffered from the lack of a consistent national strategy towards innovation by the government. Moreover, its economy too has certain structural problems because of the con-centration (as in Canada) on primary processing and the production of intermediate goods rather than on advanced (skill-intensive or technology-intensive) goods. The consequence is that Dutch industry is energy and resource-intensive, the one major weakness identified in the Japanese report.

Having looked at the problems that would benefit from a higher level of innova-tive activity and the causes attributed to those problems, there is one further aspect that is worth considering before proceeding to examine the policies recom-mended. This is the extent and the thoroughness of the analysis in each report in dealing with the current economic situation and with the likely future trends prior to establishing where and how the government might best direct and concentrate its efforts to encourage greater innovation.

*In Japan, where in the past there has been a traditional commitment by the firm to its workers, unemployment is now obviously a cause of great concern, although overall un-employment levels are relatively low by international standards.

Table 5.5 Causes of problem — weaknesses of the national economy/industry and strengths of foreign countries

	Associated target in Figure 5.2	Canada	Japan	The Netherlands	Sweden	United Kingdom	United States
Too few engineers/concentration on science rather than engineering	(ii)	—	—	—	✓	✓ (cf. France, West Germany, United States)	✓ (cf. Japan, West Germany, USSR)
Concentration on 'high' technology rather than improved production processes and products	(ii)	—	—	—	—	✓	✓
Lack of rapport between users and supplying industries	(iii)	—	—	—	—	✓	—
Shortage of venture capital for R & D/innovation	(iv)	—	—	✓	✓	✓ (cf. Japan, West Germany, United States)	✓
Low/decreasing profits	(v)	—	—	—	✓	✓	✓
Concentration on short-term returns	(v)	—	—	—	—	✓ (cf. Japan)	✓
'Soft' loans, subsidies, etc.	(v)	—	—	—	✓	—	—

	Associated target in Figure 5.2	Canada	Japan	The Netherlands	Sweden	United Kingdom	United States
Non consistent national industrial strategy by the government	(v)	✓ (cf. Europe, Far East)	—	✓	—	✓ (cf. Japan)	—
Complex, burdensome legislation/ bureaucracy	(v)	—	—	—	✓	✓	✓
Poor coordination between public and private sectors	(v)	—	—	—	—	✓	—
Overmanning	(vi)	—	—	—	—	✓	—
Emphasis on raw material processing and intermediate goods rather than advanced, technology-intensive goods	(vi)	✓ (cf. Denmark, France, Ireland, Japan, Mexico, Norway, Sweden, United States)	—	✓	—	—	—
Industry energy/resource-intensive	(vi)	—	✓	✓	—	—	—
Traditional industries challenged by developing countries with cheaper labour/natural resources	(vi)	✓ (cf. Brazil, Mexico, Singapore, South Korea, Taiwan, Venezuela)	—	—	✓	✓ (cf. Brazil, South Korea, Taiwain)	—
Lack of sufficiently concentrated markets	(vi)	✓	—	—	—	—	—

The extent and the degree of rigour of the analyses varies greatly, with the Japanese and the Swedish ones being particularly detailed — in the Swedish case, this may be partly because a wide-ranging study of the Swedish economy had already been carried out by the Boston Consulting Group (1978) — and the Dutch and American ones apparently far less so, although in both the latter two cases a more extensive analysis did precede the writing of the report but was not included in it. In the United States, the National Science Foundation (NSF) and the Department of Commerce commissioned some ten major reports from the Center for Policy Analysis (MIT), on issues relating to economic performance and technological innovation. In addition, for many years the NSF have been commissioning a variety of such reports. The American reports dealt with here therefore represent only the tip of the iceberg, and are, in fact, based on a wealth of detailed analysis. In the Dutch case, the original white paper contained three major annexes, covering the issues of the extent of the economic problem, the need for innovation, and the role of government. However, these were not published in English, and neither they nor the earlier American reports have been considered here.

In each of the reports listed in Table 5.1, the analysis contains some or all of the various elements listed in Table 5.6. Most begin with a description of the development of the nation's industry and economy over the last few decades, while the Dutch and British also give some attention to the nature and role of technological innovation in economic development. Next, the relative strengths and weaknesses of the economy (the Canadian report is particularly thorough in dealing with the latter because it can draw upon an earlier background study on the causes of the decline of Canadian industry — see Gilmour and Britton (1978)) are assessed as are the rival strengths of industrial competitors (on which the Japanese report goes into some quantitative detail using patent statistics). The Canadian, the Swedish and, to a lesser extent, the Japanese reports have a notably comprehensive treatment of likely trends in international trade and industry, and in the global division of labour, where development in the newly industrialized nations will have a most pronounced effect. This suggests that, in these three countries, there is a clear awareness of the structural nature of the economic crisis confronting us and of the fact that we are entering a new world order, an awareness not obviously apparent in the reports from the three other countries. Besides their recognition of the wider dimensions of the economic problem, the Swedish and Japanese reports, along with the British one, also feature a detailed analysis of trends in technology. Together, these two aspects of the analysis form a powerful basis for the accurate identification of both potential markets and important new areas of technology on which to concentrate the nation's innovative efforts, and hence for constructing an industrial innovation policy.

RECOMMENDED POLICIES — STRATEGIC GOALS, TACTICAL OBJECTIVES AND POLICY MEASURES

In the light of the various problems described in the previous section, what policy recommendations do the reports make? In order to compare and contrast the different policies, it is helpful to distinguish between the overall strategic goals of each report's set of recommendations, the tactical objectives, and the actual policy measures. We shall then examine the degree of correspondence between the

Table 5.6 Extent and thoroughness with which the various aspects of the problem are analysed

	Canada	Japan	The Netherlands	Sweden	United Kingdom	United States
Historical (social, economic, etc.) background	**	***	**	***	**	—
Nature and role of technological innovation	*	—	**	—	***	**
Strengths of national industry/economy	*	***	*	**	**	*
Weaknesses of national industry/economy	****	***	***	**	**	**
Strengths of industrial competitors	*	****	—	*	**	—
Trends in international trade and division of labour	****	***	—	****	*	—
Trends in technological development	**	****	—	****	****	—
Identification of new/potential markets	**	**	*	****	***	—

— Virtually no analysis.
* Only a very brief analysis.
** Moderate analysis.

*** Thorough analysis.
**** Very thorough analysis.

strategic goals and the main problems listed earlier in Table 5.4, and between the tactical objectives and the weaknesses of the domestic economy set forth in Table 5.5.

The overall strategic goals of the policy recommendations are presented in Table 5.7, and to a certain extent these do seem to be linked with the main problems or areas of concern identified in Table 5.4. Thus, Canada, which is particularly worried by the closely associated problems of foreign ownership and technological dependence, sets technological sovereignty as the main goal of its innovation policy. Similarly, four of the countries concerned by a decline in their international competitiveness (the Netherlands, Sweden, the United Kingdom, and the United States) cite this as one of the principal goals; and three of the nations faced by the threat of high or growing unemployment (Japan, the Netherlands, and the United Kingdom) make this one of the policy aims. The Netherlands, which as was noted earlier appears to be more conscious than most countries of the potentialities of innovation for bringing about wider social benefits, lists better public services and better jobs as two of its goals.

However, the match between problems and policy goals is by no means perfect, the American report, for example, making little or no attempt to link its innovation policy with the perceived problems of unemployment, low productivity, and inflation, presumably in the belief that the benefits from improved international competitiveness will eventually filter through to these problems.

Moving to the lower level, tactical objectives of the policies (shown in Table 5.8), we see that, at least for some of the reports, there again appears to be a certain mismatch between these and the weaknesses of the national economy set out in Table 5.5. For example, in the case of Canada, most of the factors inhibiting

Table 5.7 Industrial innovation policies — overall strategic goals

Canada	Japan	The Netherlands	Sweden	United Kingdom	United States
(a) More industrial innovation (I),* to achieve	(a) More industrial innovation (I), to achieve	(a) More industrial innovation (I), to achieve	(a) More industrial innovation (I), to achieve	(a) More industrial innovation (I), to achieve	(a) More industrial innovation (I), to achieve
(b) technological sovereignty (XIX)	(b) security (XVII) in	(b) improved international competitiveness in Dutch industry (II),	(b) improved international competitiveness in Swedish industry (II)	(b) improved international competitiveness in UK industry (II),	(b) improved international competitiveness in US industry (II)
	(c) defence (XX),	(c) more jobs (V),		(c) improved economic performance (VI),	
	(d) energy (XI), and	(d) better quality jobs (XVIII),		(d) more jobs (V), and	
	(e) employment (V)	(e) selective economic growth (VI), and		(e) better jobs (XIII)	
		(f) better public services (XIV)			

*The bracketed Roman numeral identifies one of the benefits of innovation listed in Figure 5.1.

Table 5.8 Industrial innovation policies — tactical objectives

Canada	Japan	The Netherlands	Sweden	United Kingdom	United States
(a) Increased demand for Canadian technology (i, vii and viii)*	(a) Gradual change in industrial structure (vi)	(a) Increased capacity for innovation in industry (iv and v)	(a) Improved performance in traditional sectors (iii)	(a) Strategies for industrial sectors (i, ii, iii, iv and v)	(a) Improved technology transfer (ii)
(b) Expand Canadian industry's potential to develop technology (ii)	(b) Identification of future areas of growth in industry (iii)	(b) More government R & D (ii)	(b) Strengthen the knowledge base (ii)	(b) National policy to coordinate for ample employment (v)	(b) Increased technological knowledge (ii)
(c) Strengthen capacity of firms to absorb technology (ii)	(c) Construction of innovation policies after public consultation	(c) Better consultation and information services (ii and iii)	(c) Identify and exploit new technological prospects (ii)	(c) Increased technological research (ii)	(c) Improved patent system (v)
(d) Import technology under favourable terms (ii)		(d) Increased demand for innovation to satisfy public needs (vi and vii)		(d) Better consultation and information services (ii and iii)	(d) Improve anti-trust policy (v)
				(e) More/better trained manpower (especially engineers) (ii)	(e) Foster development of small innovative firms (iv and v)
					(f) Improved federal procurement (vii)
					(g) Improved regulatory system (vi)
					(h) Facilitate labour/management adjustment to innovation (v)
					(i) Supportive attitude to innovation (v)

*The bracketed Roman numerals refer to the intended target (listed in Figure 5.2) of the various policy measures (see Table 5.9) to achieve this particular objective.

Table 5.9 Industrial innovation policies — main policy measures

Canada	Japan	The Netherlands	Sweden	United Kingdom	United States
**					
a.1 Innovative-conscious procurement (9)*	(Not specified in English abstract version)	a.1 Help large firms meet costs and risks of R & D (5)	a.1 Broaden markets+	a.1 Mature industries import technology (4)	a.1 Information centre on federally supported R & D/technology (4)
a.2 Major government programmes (1)			a.2 Standardization+	(a)	
			a.3 'Niche' strategies+	(b) coordinate public and private sectors (8)	
		a.2 Ensure small firms use advantages (for example, flexibility) (8)	a.4 Search for new markets (for example, in developing countries)+	a.2 'Laggard' industries	a.2 Foreign technology information (4)
b.1 Sponsor companies (5)				(a) R & D batch production+	
b.2 Encourage consortia and joint ventures (8)		b.1 Reorientate Dutch R & D to social and industrial problems (2)	a.5 Exploit national advantages (for example, resources, technical competence)+	(b) monitor technological changes abroad and import (4)	b.1 Generic technology centres (2)
b.3 Aid to small firms (5)		b.2 Research in new areas of technology (2)	b.1 Improve school curricula (3)	a.3 Service industries more R & D (1)	b.2 Regulatory technology research (2)
				(a)	
c.1 Sectorally orientated technical centres (2)		b.3 Better use of existing expertise (2)	b.2 Improve university courses (3)	a.4 New industries coordinated national strategy (8)	b.3 Improved university-industry cooperation (3)
d.1 Secure maximum advantage for Canada from im-		c.1 Coordination of	b.3 More technical and scientific research (2)	(a)	c.1 Uniform govern-

ported technology (2)

d.2 Coordination of importing of technology so as to foster selective development of Canadian technological capability (2)

consultation and information services (4)

d.1 Innovation-conscious procurement (9)

d.2 Innovation-conscious regulation (8)

c.1 Funds for research in new technologies (5)

d.5 Small firms better consulting services (4)

(a) better technology transfer (for example, from large firms) (4)

(b)

(c) aid for R & D (5)

d.1 Better university–industry liaison (3)

ment patent policy (7)

c.2 Improved patent service (7)

e.1 Funds for small firms (5)

e.2 Corporations to sponsor innovation (like NRDC) (5)

e.3 Increased venture capital (5)

f.1 Uniform procurement policies (9)

h.1 Develop a technology forecasting system (8)

i.1 Award for innovation (8)

*The bracketed number refers to the type of policy tool involved (see Figure 5.2 for list of policy tools).

†No policy tool (apart from government exhortation) specified for these policy measures.

**The figures a, b, c, etc., relate to the tactical objectives listed in Table 5.8

innovative activity appear to lie on the demand side, being concerned with the structure of Canadian industry and markets, while three out of the four policy objectives have to do with the *supply* of technology. Similarly, the American report, which is particularly concerned about the levelling off in the number of engineers, the overconcentration of efforts on high technology rather than producing more reliable better quality goods, and the shortage of venture capital, fails to link its policy objectives very closely with these shortcomings, instead preferring to concentrate a great deal of its attention on what are seen as stifling regulations, and flaws in the patent system. By contrast, for the three European countries, the policy objectives are rather better matched to the perceived economic and industrial weaknesses — all three, for example, include measures to remedy the shortage of venture capital among their objectives — and, as far as one can tell from the English abstract version, the same is true for the Japanese report.

To meet the specified tactical objectives, each report recommends a number of policy measures, and these are summarized in Table 5.9.* Because of the diverse nature of the measures, it is difficult to draw many comparisons between the reports on the basis of this table alone. However, one feature that does stand out is that the Swedish report is rather vague about exactly how some of the policies are to be put into effect, a characteristic that it shares with the more recent of the two British reports, for which some of the recommendations take the form:

'Government should examine how . . .';
'The Department of Industry should study how Government can . . .';
'The Department of Industry should examine how . . .';
'Government should pay greater attention to . . .'; and
'It would be prudent for Government to maintain a close watch on . . .'.

This failure to put forward specific policy measures may be because the Swedish and British reports correspond to a much earlier stage in the construction of a national innovation policy than, say, the Dutch white paper, or President Carter's industrial innovation initiatives. However, it is not unreasonable to suppose that a report which resorts to exhortation rather than detailed policy proposals (as the Swedish report tends to do in places: 'Industry must continue to . . .', or 'New efforts in industry are warranted . . .', for example), or whose recommendations consist, to a large part, of calls for further analysis of the problem, are likely to have less immediate impact on policy-makers than one which presents concrete mechanisms for implementing the recommended policies and hence for ensuring that they can be put into effect with a minimum of delay.

ANALYSIS OF THE RECOMMENDED POLICY TOOLS,
TARGETS, AND TARGET-LEVELS

Simply listing the main recommended policy measures is not particularly helpful, as was seen in Table 5.9, because of the great variety of measures involved. In order to draw useful comparisons, it is necessary first to classify the assorted measures into a set of common categories. The typology employed here is that described earlier, which distinguishes the tool or mechanism for implementing

---

*The English abstract of the Japanese report unfortunately does not present detailed policy measures, and this section of the table is therefore left empty.

each policy measure, the target for that tool, and the level of the target — that is, whether the measure is aimed at a specific target (one particular technology, industrial sector, or type of firm) or intended to benefit all likely innovators.

For each of the reports, all the individual policy recommendations have been classified by tool, target, and target-level; vague or imprecise recommendations that failed to specify a policy tool or target have not been included on the grounds that they do not constitute an actual policy measure. The results are shown in Tables 5.10, 5.11 and 5.12. Obviously, some policy measures do not fall simply into one single category. In such cases, a certain amount of (possibly subjective) judgement has to be used in choosing the most appropriate category into which it should be allocated. In a small number of cases (about 5 per cent) this has proved impossible, and the same policy measure has had to be put into two different categories;* this is the reason why some of the totals for individual nations are not identical in the three tables.

Table 5.10 Analysis of policy recommendations by type of tool

Type of tool	Canada	Japan	The Netherlands	Sweden	United Kingdom	United States
1. Public enterprise	0	0	0	1	1	0
2. Scientific and technical	7	7	9	3	4	4
3. Education	3	1	5	11	4	3
4. Information	2	2	8	2	3	8
5. Financial	5	2	6	5	6	4
6. Taxation	1	0	0	1	6	13
7. Legal and regulatory	0	0	6	1	0	46
8. Political	2	4	2	3	4	2
9. Procurement	4	0	2	2	3	11
10. Public services	0	0	1	0	3	0
11. Commercial	2	1	1	0	0	3
12. Overseas agent	0	0	0	1	2	0
Total	26	17	40	30	36	94

Table 5.10 shows the types of policy tool most preferred in different countries, and those that are largely ignored. For Canada, Japan, and the Netherlands, the most favoured tool is the 'scientific and technical' one, for Sweden 'education', for Britain 'financial and taxation', and for the United States 'legal and regulatory' (the results are summarized in the first row of Table 5.13, below). For the United States, this reflects their worry about the economy being overregulated (see Chapter 7), while the British emphasis on financial and taxation measures appears to stem from the preoccupation with obtaining a healthy and stimulating *climate* for industry to operate in, by contrast with the four other countries, which seem to prefer to deal more *directly* with the inputs to the process of innovation.

If we turn next to the targets of these various policy measures, we see from Table 5.11 that, for five of the six countries, the most popular target is that of 'technical knowledge and manpower'. As for the two other major inputs into the innovation process, the Netherlands, Sweden, and the United Kingdom, all provide a variety of measures to improve the 'financial resources', but only the first of

---

*For example, several of the measures using the policy tool of 'information' are aimed at improving both technical knowledge (target (ii)) and market information (target (iii)), and therefore have to be considered as two separate measures.

Table 5.11 Analysis of policy recommendations by target

Target		Canada	Japan	The Netherlands	Sweden	United Kingdom	United States
S U P P L Y	(i) R & D	0	0	0	1	1	0
	(ii) Technical knowledge and manpower	10	8	20	16	11	11
	(iii) Market information and management skills	3	0	6	0	0	2
	(iv) Financial resources	1	1	6	6	7	12
	(v) R & D environment	6	6	5	4	9	34
D E M A N D	(vi) Domestic market environment	1	0	2	0	0	21
	(vii) Domestic markets	4	0	3	2	6	11
	(viii) International market environment	2	1	1	0	0	3
	(ix) International markets	0	0	0	1	2	0
	Total*	27	16	43	30	36	94
	Environmental (per cent) (v), (vi), (viii)	33	44	19	13	25	62
	Supply (per cent) (i) to (v)	74	94	86	90	78	63

*Some of these totals are slightly different from those in Tables 5.10 and 5.12 because a number of policy measures are aimed at more than one target, while a few others involve more than one type of policy tool.

Table 5.12 Analysis of policy recommendation by target-level

Target level		Canada	Japan	The Netherlands	Sweden	United Kingdom	United States
A	Specific technologies	6	6	2	9	1	0
B	Industrial sectors	1	1	5	3	2	1
C(i)	Small firms	5	1	5	2	6	14
C(ii)	Large firms	0	0	1	0	2	0
D	Industrial innovation	7	4	15	5	7	12
E	Industrial performance	6	1	8	4	13	33
F	General environment	1	3	4	7	5	34
Total		26	16	40	30	36	94
Specific (per cent)		46	50	33	47	31	16

Table 5.13 Main* policy tools, targets and target-levels

		Canada	Japan	The Netherlands	Sweden	United Kingdom	United States
Main tools	1	Scientific and technical	Scientific and technical	Scientific and technical	Education	Financial	Legal and regulatory
	2	Financial	Political	Information	Financial	Taxation	
	3						
Main targets	1	Technical knowledge and manpower	Technical knowledge and manpower	Technical knowledge and manpower	Technical knowledge and manpower	Technical knowledge and manpower	R & D environment
	2	R & D environment	R & D environment	Market information and management skills	Financial resources	R & D environment	Domestic market environment
	3			Financial resources		Financial resources	
Main target-levels	1	Industrial innovation	Specific technologies	Industrial innovation	Specific technologies	Industrial performance	General environment
	2	Specific technologies	Industrial innovation	Industrial performance	General environment	Industrial innovation	Industrial performance
	3	Industrial performance				Small firms	
	4	Small firms					

*Included in approximately 15 per cent or more of the policy recommendations these gives much attention to the provision of 'market information and management skills'. Instead, Canada, Japan, the United Kingdom and, in particular, the United States are more concerned that the environment to R & D should be favourable, with the United States also aiming many policy measures at the 'domestic market environment'. (A summary of these results appears in the middle row of Table 5.13.) This difference shows up clearly in the penultimate row of Table 5.11, where the percentage of measures aimed at 'environmental' targets (that is, targets v, vi, or viii) is shown. The Dutch and Swedish reports have relatively few 'environmental' measures, the American and Japanese far more. One further difference can be detected in Table 5.11, and this centres on the relative numbers of policy measures aimed at improving the supply side of the innovation process compared with the demand side. The final row of the table shows that the Japanese in particular, the Dutch, and the Swedish reports direct the great majority of their recommended policy measures at the supply side, while the Canadian, British, and American reports aim about a quarter to a third of their measures at demand-side targets.

Finally, there is the question of the specificity of the various recommended measures, and Table 5.12 analyses these in terms of their intended target-level, with the last row of the table showing the percentage of policy measures that are directed at specific targets (A, B, C(i) and C(ii)). It can be seen that approximately half of the Japanese, Swedish, and Canadian recommendations are specific in nature, compared with only about one-third of the Dutch and British, and just one-fifth of the American ones. The main target-levels for each country are listed in the bottom row of Table 5.13. For Japan and Sweden, the primary target level is 'specific technologies' (such as electronics for mechanical systems, genetic engineering, enzyme and fermentation technology, geological technology, micro-measurement and analysis technology, and so on), while in the case of the Canadian, Dutch and British reports, it is industrial innovation in general, or industrial performance, although all three reports do direct several policy measures specifically at small firms, on the grounds that these possess certain advantages that make them especially fertile breeding grounds for innovation (see Chapter 10). The American policy measures are least specific of all, being aimed mainly at the general environment in which industry operates, or at improving industrial performance.

One further characteristic of the recommendations contained in each report that is worth remarking on is the extent to which the emphasis is placed on aiding existing industry, as opposed to stimulating the development of 'new' technologies and hence launching 'new' industries. The figures in the first row of Table 5.12 on the numbers of measures aimed at specific technologies (target-level A) show that new technology is of particular concern in Canada, Japan, and Sweden, while for the three remaining countries the stress is very much on measures to help existing industry. It is almost certainly significant that Canada, Japan and Sweden are also the three countries in this study whose reports show the greatest awareness of the structural nature of the economic problems confronting the industrialized world (see page 94). For it suggests that an appreciation of the fundamental economic 'facts of life' has led the authors of these reports to the conclusion that any solutions to the problems must be of *a far-reaching, long-term and radical restructuring nature* rather than ameliorative tinkerings at the margins of the existing economic system.

SUMMARY AND CONCLUSIONS

In this final section, we shall summarize briefly the main features of the reports, country by country, highlighting the principal strengths and shortcomings of each. This will be followed by some more general comments pertinent to all the reports.

To take the Canadian report first of all, this, as previously pointed out, has the advantage of being able to draw upon an earlier detailed study by Gilmour and Britton (1978), enabling it to carry out a fairly thorough analysis of those problems that could benefit from greater innovation. Canada, because of its intimate industrial links with the United States, not only shares many of that country's economic problems, but also fears the long-term effects of foreign ownership and technological dependence. Moreover, for various historical reasons, its economy faces several severe structural problems. Where the Canadian report is noticeably weak is in specifying policy measures for innovation that will help alleviate or remedy these structural problems. In addition, it recommends the use of a relatively restricted range of policy measures, ignoring several of the major tools available to governments (such as 'public services' and 'legal and regulatory' – see Table 5.10).

The Japanese report is most concerned with the narrower economic effects of innovation, and shows less interest in the wider political and environmental benefits. It is apparently based on a very systematic analysis involving much quantitative data. However, we have been able to deal only with the English abstract version of the report, and this is lacking in detail on specific policy measures. Hence, it is difficult to draw any broad conclusions about the intended policies apart from remarking on the stress that is accorded (see objective (c) in Table 5.8) by the Japanese to public consultation in order to arrive at a consensus on objectives and policies *before* those policies are implemented.

The Dutch report takes the form of a government white paper. It therefore represents one of the later stages in the process of setting up a government policy towards industrial innovation. Although the accompanying annexes discuss in some detail the nature of the economic problems, the process by which innovation might ease those problems, and the role of government in encouraging that process, the white paper itself concentrates on particular policy measures rather than on analysis. None the less, it does bring out some of the wider implications of innovation as well as the narrower economic benefits. As for the policy measures, a number of the possible policy tools are somewhat neglected (see Table 5.10), as are demand-side targets (Table 5.11). However, the measures do cover most of the target-levels.

Like its Canadian counterpart, the Swedish report can also draw upon the results of an earlier study (Boston Consulting Group, 1978), this perhaps being one of the reasons why the analysis in the report is particularly thorough. Sweden, along with the Netherlands, is apparently more aware of the wider, social and environmental benefits from innovation. However, the report is much weaker on suggesting concrete policy measures, resorting instead in several cases merely to exhortation (although this may be because the construction of a government innovation policy has not yet proceeded very far in Sweden, and this report was not intended to formulate specific measures). About half of the possible policy tools are largely neglected, and little attention is given to demand-side targets.

The British reports by ACARD together give a fairly comprehensive analysis of the prevailing economic situation, and suggest that the United Kingdom is afflicted by more problems than most. In common with the Swedish report, ACARD is rather vague about how some of the policies it discusses could be implemented, although in fairness it should be pointed out that ACARD has produced several reports dealing with more specific areas of technological innovation (for example ACARD, 1978; 1979). As far as the two reports covered here are concerned (United Kingdom, 1978; 1979), the recommended policy measures, while they employ most of the possible policy tools, neglect some of the targets, and perhaps tend to overconcentrate on *general* target-levels, suggesting a preoccupation with getting the overall industrial and economic *climate* right, rather than intervening more directly in the process of innovation.

Finally, there are the American reports. In addition to the somewhat superficial level of analysis contained in these documents and remarked upon earlier, one other major weakness is the apparent failure to coordinate the activities of the various specially appointed subcommittees set up to study issues related to industrial innovation. The Final Report of the Advisory Committee on Industrial Innovation in fact consists of eight separate reports by various subcommittees — each with different but overlapping areas of interest — with no attempt to summarize and link together their proposals into one integrated and coherent strategy. Perhaps because of the low degree of coordination between them, the subcommittees have tended to focus only on the narrower economic problems that would benefit from improved innovation, and on weaknesses in the supply of the technical and financial inputs into innovation. Moreover, given the makeup of the subcommittees, with their heavy representation of industrialists, it is not surprising that the reports exhibit a pronounced preoccupation with the 'over-regulation' of the US economy. The analysis of the economic problems facing the nation, in addition to being weak, is also not particularly well linked to the proposed policy measures. These show a relative neglect of many of the available policy tools and targets, and of *specific* target-levels (apart from the recommendation for generic technology centres), emphasizing instead 'environmental' targets and the tools of regulations and patents.

Before concluding with some more general observations on these proposed government policies towards innovation, it is worth commenting briefly on innovation policy in the two other major West European nations, West Germany and France. In the former, the federal government is continually adding to an existing and comprehensive set of innovation measures. They have long been aware of the crucial importance of technical change for industrial performance, and for many years this has been an integral component of governmental philosophy. Therefore, there already exists in West Germany good government–industry–university relationships. To a great extent, government innovation policy has focused on the development and the successful use of the infrastructure essential for providing the conditions under which innovation can flourish, particularly in small firms. The measures employed by the government are constantly changing and being improved, giving a continuously developing innovation policy. Given the existence of this well-established and relatively successful government innovation policy, it is perhaps not surprising that the German government has not felt it necessary to draw up a report on future policy similar to those produced by western nations.

In France, a white paper on innovation policy in the first half of the 1980s is currently under preparation. It is based on a number of background papers on such areas as microelectronics, biotechnology, and communications (in which the French government has been carrying out some interesting experiments involving the setting up of several 'wired villages'). The overall philosophy behind the measures described in the white paper has been developed from an initial set of broad aims drawn up by the National Planning Commission and further elaborated following discussions by the Economic and Social Council (which is made up of representatives of industry, commerce, workers, and other interested parties). *The French plan is based on 'strategic thinking', concentrating on support for strategic growth sectors like electronic office equipment, energy-saving equipment, consumer electronics, bioindustry, industrial robots, and undersea activities.* For each strategic industry, there will be specific objectives and a set of measures (aids) designed to ensure that industry achieves these objectives. In this respect, there would appear to be certain similarities between France and Sweden, Japan, and Canada, in that all are attempting to identify potentially important new industrial sectors. They seem to have accepted that fundamental structural change in their economies is to be actively pursued, reasoning that *greater advantage is to be gained from exploiting changes in the new world economic order rather than steadfastly resisting those changes through measures seeking to protect ailing industries.*

However, to return to the reports dealt with here, a number of general comments can be made. First, it is clear that systematic international comparisons of the type attempted above are only possible once some all-embracing classification scheme for the various innovation policies has been constructed. Moreover, perhaps the range of conclusions arrived at in this survey points to the usefulness of the particular scheme adopted here, especially in dealing with reports that differ so greatly in nature and scope.

Secondly, many of the reports exhibit little awareness of, or interest in, the wider, non-economic benefits that may flow from a higher level of innovative activity. There is a very real danger that the eventual innovation policies, like much government industrial strategy before it, will suffer from a failure to be fully integrated into the wider political and social programmes of governments.

A third observation is that most of the reports are characterized by a lack of conceptual clarity as to the nature of the innovation process, and consequently fail to consider the full range of targets susceptible to government influence and of policy tools available. Because the problem of industrial innovation is a multi-faceted one, governments need to adopt a pluralistic approach encompassing a wide range of measures which address all the major aspects of the problem.

Another comment concerns the analysis that precedes the drawing up of a set of policy recommendations in each report. In all cases, except perhaps the Japanese, this analysis would be considerably improved by the inclusion of more quantitative data. The authors of several of the reports, in collecting information, seem to have placed undue reliance on the more subjective and qualitative views of 'experts' and interested parties, and resorted relatively little to statistical data. This may partly explain why, for several of the reports, the goals and objectives of the recommended policies have not been sufficiently well linked with the problems seen to be confronting the nation, and with the economic and industrial weaknesses giving rise to those problems.

Finally, there must be doubts as to the degree to which the policy recommendations of all these reports are consistent with current academic views on the relative importance of supply and demand factors in accounting for success and failure in industrial innovation. While the debate over this question still rages (see, for example, Freeman (1979)), many economists have, on the strength of a great deal of empirical research, pinned their flag defiantly to the demand mast. For example, a survey of 50 major clusters of technical innovations leads to the following, unambiguous conclusion: 'The most important way in which governments have influenced technical innovation is through demand' (SPRU–TNO (1977), p. 20). While others may dispute that demand factors are '*the* most important', few would deny that they are, at least, 'important'. Yet in the recommendations of the reports surveyed here, very little attention is given to demand-side targets (they account for less than 20 per cent of all the policy measures). It would appear that, once again, government policies are rooted more in the theories of a previous intellectual generation (one that stressed the importance of supply factors in stimulating technological change and industrial innovation) than in contemporary economic thought.

References

ACARD (1978), *The Application of semiconductor Technology*, Advisory Council for Applied Research and Development, Cabinet Office, London.
—— (1979), *Joining and Assembly*, London.
Allen, T. J. *et al.* (1978), 'Government influence on the process of innovation in Europe and Japan', *Research Policy*, 7, 124–49.
Boston Consulting Group (1978), *A Framework for Swedish Industrial Policy*, report submitted by the Boston Consulting Group, Boston, Mass.
Braun, E. (1980), 'Government policies for the stimulation of technological innovation', mimeo, Technology Policy Unit, University of Aston.
Freeman, C. (1979), 'The determinants of innovation', *Futures*, 11, 206–15.
Gilmour, J. M. and Britton, J. N. (1978), *The Weakest Link: A Technological Perspective on Canadian Underdevelopment*. Background Study 43, Science Council of Canada, Ontario.
Hagedoorn, J. and Prakke, F. (1979). *An Expanded Inventory of Public Measures for Stimulating Innovation in the European Community with Emphasis on Small and Medium Sized Firms*, report prepared by the Staffgroup Strategic Surveys TNO, Apeldoorn.
OECD (1978), *Policies for the Stimulation of Industrial Innovation, Vol. 1 — Analytical Report*, Paris.
Pavitt, K. (1980), 'Technical innovation and industrial development', *Futures*, 12, 35–44.
—— and Walker, W. (1976), 'Government policies towards industrial innovation: a review', *Research Policy*, 5, 11–97.
SPRU–TNO (1977), *The Current Economic Climate and Policies for Technical Innovation*, report prepared by the Science Policy Research Unit, University of Sussex, in collaboration with Staffgroup Strategic Surveys, TNO, Delft.

6. GOVERNMENT SUBSIDIES TO PRIVATE FIRMS

Before the 1940s government policy for invention and innovation rested mainly on three pillars: the patent system, technical education, and the promotion of basic science. Presently a whole new array of government measures and instruments has been introduced to try and accelerate technical progress (Pavitt and Walker, 1976). Unfortunately, many of these measures were deployed hastily with very little regard for any theoretical understanding of the system which was being influenced. Often these measures were based on simplistic but false analogies with the military system, on a desire to maintain employment in design and development departments no longer required for military purposes, or on the primitive tendency to equate accelerated technical change with a simple increase in R & D expenditure.

None the less, some theoretical arguments have been advanced to justify subsidies for research and development to private firms. Galbraith (1969) has argued that the growing scale imperatives of modern technology are such that governments increasingly have to intervene financially to underwrite technical and market risks; any justification, civil or military, commercial or political, will be found for government financing the R & D for industry's technological development.

Although based on observations of experience in the United States, Galbraith's justification for government intervention has already been put forward by practitioners in Western Europe, in order to justify increasing government expenditures in, for instance, the aircraft and computer industries. The importance of these 'key' sectors (together with nuclear energy and space) for Europe's future was stressed at the time by people as different as Harold Wilson, Jean-Jacques Servan-Schreiber, Charles de Gaulle, and members of the French communist party (Servan-Schreiber 1968; 1973). All argued that without vigorous government intervention and strong R & D programmes, Europe's industrial independence and economic wellbeing would be in jeopardy in the 1980s.

A number of economists, however, have questioned the usefulness and the need for subsidy, especially at the stage of full-scale commercial development. Eads and Nelson (1971) have argued that, while governments should continue to finance the development of basic skills and knowledge (including engineering skills and knowledge), industrial firms still do have the capacity to finance even very large-scale development projects, provided that both the technology and the market conditions are right. Government-financed projects of full-scale commercial development will be one result of pressures from government and industrial lobbies committed to a particular technology, without sufficiently cool appreciation of its commercial prospects. In other words, governments are running the risk of commercially financing second-best projects, which, given governmental financial and political involvement, will also be more difficult to stop than regular commercial projects. Jewkes (1972) and Clarke (1973) have argued that this will ultimately lead to an intervention-breeding system, as industrialists seek profits increasingly through political lobbying and government subsidies, instead of through producing and selling.

At least in analytical terms, the latter group of economists critical of large-scale government involvement have had the best of the debate. Pavitt and Worboys (1977) have questioned the validity of Galbraith's scale imperatives of modern technology, arguing that there is no unequivocal evidence of increasing government involvement in financing industrial R & D. Some technologically sophisticated countries (like Switzerland and the Netherlands) have relatively little government-financed R & D in industry, while others (like the United States) have a considerable amount. Most government-financed R & D is concentrated in the aerospace, nuclear and electronics industries; there is very little in the materials transformation and processing industries (for example, the chemical, iron and steel, and non-ferrous metals industries), where the scale requirements of modern technological innovation are often very big. Finally, there is no uniform tendency for governments to intervene increasingly over time; in some countries, such intervention is on the increase, and in others it is decreasing.

There is also evidence that governments have been left to finance 'second best' projects. In the United Kingdom, Gardner (1976a and b) has shown that government-provided 'launching aid' for civil aircraft development has been highly unprofitable; he has also argued (along with Jewkes) that justification on the basis of 'external benefits' is not valid, given that commercially financed industrial R & D creates many of these same benefits without large-scale government funding. In the nuclear energy sector in the Federal Republic of Germany, Keck (1977) has found that commercial industry has been willing and able to finance the development of light water reactors. On the other hand, it has not been willing to finance the development of the sodium-cooled fast-breeder reactor, not so much because of lack of financial ability to do so, but through lack of commercial prospects for the foreseeable future. Based on Gardner's data, Walker (1976) has shown (like Keck) an inverse relationship between scale, technical sophistication and government involvement, on the one hand, and commercial success on the other. Zysman's (1975) analysis of the French government's programme of support of the computer industry points in a similar direction. He argues that government intervention hindered rather than helped the necessary adjustment of the French industry towards profitable products, markets and management methods.

Finally, economists in many countries argue that the high technologies have pre-empted too big a share of government and industrial R & D resources, that the opportunity cost of such programmes has been considerable, and that technological autarchy is undesirable and unnecessary, since technological knowledge can often be readily transferred on the world market (Freeman, 1976 and Williams, 1967).

Most of the above discussion relates to 'big' science or technology or sectors of 'high' technology, in other words, the nuclear, aerospace and electronics industries. What can be said about experience outside these sectors?

In most countries, direct government funding of industrial innovation outside the high technologies is negligible compared to what industry finances itself. Sufficient information on the distribution of government funds by industrial sector is lacking. Data for France and Canada suggest they reflect pretty closely the total distribution of industrial R & D. A large proportion of the funds are concentrated in the electronics, chemical and aerospace sectors.

Sufficient information on the distribution of the funds according to size of company is also lacking. For France it is known that the programmes of *aide au developpement* and of *actions concertées* are distributed across size of company in almost exactly the same proportion as all industry's R & D expenditures. It is also known that most funds from the German Ministry of Research and Technology go to large firms. In the Netherlands, on the other hand, the big five companies responsible for some 70 per cent of all industrial R & D receive hardly any development credits. In general, however, it seems that big firms are more able to profit from government programmes, so that special efforts need to be made to reach small firms.

Although studies show the dangers and difficulties of large-scale government intervention in commercial development activities without sufficient regard to cost and market realities, it would be illusory to conclude that trust can always be put in the market, or that government need finance only basic research and the development of skills. Such an approach neglects three important and interrelated problems: market imperfections, dynamic comparative advantage, and the problems of adjustment.

Market imperfections do exist, especially in the high technology sectors, where there is considerable monopoly power and barriers to entry, and where lead times for the development of new technologies are long. For example, in the 1960s, falling real energy prices led to the neglect in the market sector of R & D on coal-related and new and unconventional energy technologies and of energy conservation technology. Governments did not compensate for these deficiencies, but instead concentrated most of their energy R & D resources on nuclear energy development and, within nuclear energy, on fast-breeder reactors: in other words, a 'narrow front' approach. This experience clearly shows the difficulties of dealing with market imperfections and long lead times and suggests the advantage of broad-front incrementalism. Given the possibility of discontinuous changes in energy supply in future, government intervention is quite justifiable. Such an approach could go as far as full-scale demonstration of, say, coal gasification and liquefaction plants, large numbers of offices and housing equipped with solar energy devices, heat pumps and conservation devices and systems, etc.

Secondly, there remains the problem of dynamic comparative advantage, or how to sustain infant industries in an internationally free trade world. Europe has been at a comparative disadvantage in some high technology sectors, given the US government's stimulus through their military and space programmes (Walker, 1976). The French *Plan Calcul* may have failed to produce a viable French computer industry, but perhaps the UK government expenditures, coupled with management and marketing changes, may ultimately lead to a viable self-sustaining industry.

Finally, there is the problem of adjustment. In an open world, with rapid technical, competitive and political change, how can firms and the labour force adjust? In this context, the aircraft industry is not really different from shipbuilding. Government responsibility to tackle the social costs of transition cannot be escaped, but manpower training policy may be more helpful than subsidies to redundant R & D groups.

Taking into account the existence of these three problems, the notion of government responsibility cannot simply be banished. In such a context the institutional setup can be very important. The Dutch aircraft industry has, with government support, been relatively successful in concentrating on market niches not demanding major resources or technological skills; and since profits from sales are ploughed back into a revolving fund from which the industry can finance future generations of aircraft, it has a major incentive to perform well commercially. On the other hand, the UK industry has a long history of major technological achievement and close industry–government relations, mainly in military aircraft.

Attitudes and habits, born of this and other relationships, have carried over into civilian areas where they do not work (Concorde, for example). In addition, as it is being argued, the system of obtaining and repaying launching aid is perverse; there is little or no financial penalty for failure, and the terms of repayment become harder, the greater the commercial success. These examples indicate the great importance of selecting the right means of intervention and of devising the appropriate institutional structures where there is a good enough case for government involvement.

Given that the reason for government involvement is clearly specified at the outset, it is still difficult to assess its effect on a firm's actions or whether the assistance was indeed necessary. Where the project is large (for example, an aircraft) and likely to cost as much as or even more than the capital of the company is worth, it may reasonably be assumed that the project would not have gone ahead without government assistance.

The situation is different where the project may cost only a small fraction of the value of the firm's capital and there is no obvious reason why the firm should not have financed it if it had a reasonable hope of commercial success. The financial results of direct assistance tell us if the projects which received assistance were commercial successes or not. Such information is relevant to evaluating the effectiveness of the assistance where it was given for projects intended to be commercially successful. It is, however, not the complete test — substantial external benefits may have accrued, even in apparently unprofitable projects.

Assessment of the effects of direct financial assistance on a firm's actions is essentially a question of judging what was the marginal activity for the company. Was the injection of assistance necessary for the project in question; did it enable the firm to sustain some other development project or piece of investment; did it increase the dynamic efficiency of the firm so that it became better adjusted to providing products and services in a changed environment; or did it merely increase the dividend paid to shareholders by improving the general liquidity of the firm? Appraising the effects of government assistance, even for a relatively small development project, would require a view of the whole of the firm's operations during the development of the project.

Governments in the western industrialized world do not have primary responsibility for industrial performance, but they have concern as representing the community as a whole who depend on the present and future performance of industry. Governments must therefore be involved, though the extent to which they can influence industrial performance by direct methods is rather limited except where industries have been nationalized. The sum total of direct financial assistance is a small proportion of the amount spent by industry independently. Up to 80 per cent of the government financial assistance provided in the United Kingdom, France and Germany has gone to high technology sectors like aerospace, electric (including nuclear) and electronics, and computer industries. Of the remainder, most assistance has gone to relatively large firms for relatively small projects — in other words, those which on the face of it are most likely to be undertaken without government assistance so long as they are expected to be profitable. The justification for such support could have been the external benefits which might have accrued to the rest of the economy or a reduction in the cost of imports, though there is little evidence to this effect.

The machinery of government for the selection and monitoring of special assistance programmes is invariably cumbersome and seldom equipped to assess the market prospects of a development project though market acceptance is a critical factor in innovation. They rely heavily on industrial firms not only for their market assessments, but also for their assessments of technical feasibility, costs and development times without in some instances having the capability to assess any of these variables realistically and independently. They have difficulty in designing contractual systems which reward success and punish avoidable failure and have had difficulty in developing adequate incremental review procedures to ensure that projects are terminated when more precise technical and commercial knowledge had shown them to be unviable. To a degree, therefore, governments are susceptible to the pressure of the large or technologically advanced firms in their decisions, while their procedures can discourage smaller firms from applying for assistance because of the effort involved and the time taken to reach a decision. The comparative lack of commercial success achieved by large projects in the past suggests that the firms involved have not themselves been particularly strong in market research and assessment.

With a few notable exceptions, government instruments for providing assistance have been general — available on application to industry at large — rather than specific to sectors of industry identified by government as priority areas for government assistance in terms of employment, exports, regional development, acquisition of new markets or maintenance of existing markets, and problem areas like energy, the environment, etc. They have also tended to concentrate more on supporting research and development rather than the marketing of the results of these efforts, and on the general improvement of the management and the organization of technological change in industry.

Against this background, it is significant that the procedures, scope and mechanisms of government direct assistance are currently, or have been recently, subject to review in a number of countries.

INSTRUMENTS AND THEIR SCOPE

In France, by contrast with most other countries, the instruments are identified not only with a stage of the progress from research through development to exploitation but also with the types of organization which may receive the financial aid. Thus, technical research contracts are available to collective research centres, CNRS laboratories, engineering schools; predevelopment aid to collective research centres on condition that industry is also involved; *actions concertées* for collaborative ventures involving any combination of public, semi-public and private sector laboratories; and *aide au developpement* for industrial firms.

The emphasis is on development of new products or processes and has contributed to the tendency for assistance to have gone predominantly to large firms or technologically advanced industries with strong research and development capabilities who were best equipped to submit projects. These industries already had well-established links with the departments concerned through their defence or other high technology contracts or through their representation on advisory committees, etc.

In most countries governments have become increasingly aware of the need to reorientate their instruments so as to concentrate more effort on priority sectors of industry determined by national industrial, economic, regional and employment policies; to ensure a more equitable distribution of assistance to all sizes of firms in industry, particularly the small and medium-sized firms; to establish better interfaces between government laboratories or semi-public laboratories and industry; to extend assistance beyond research and development to the more commercial (and often more expensive) phases of innovation and to the more generally acceptable field of consultancy services for the improvement of technology, management and marketing. The transfer of technology into marketable and profitable new products and processes is now being recognized as no less important than the generation of new knowledge.

It is of course easier to change policy than to effect rapid and substantial changes in the distribution and allocation of existing resources without a major input of new finance. There are, however, strong indications that the period of transition has begun.

In the United Kingdom, a series of industry schemes have been set up whereby selective assistance for product development is a feature of a package of assistance aimed at encouraging a selection of industries to improve their technological competence and become competitive; preproduction orders and support for collaborative development programmes involving users as well as manufacturers of equipment are aiming to overcome market resistance.

In Germany, the programmes for the encouragement of primary innovation and for the use of *Fraunhofer* facilities have put new facilities and financial assistance at the disposal of small firms. Tailored schemes have also been undertaken to modernize, for example, the watch industry and to develop practical uses of solar energy.

In a limited sense, NRDC (the National Research and Development Council) in the United Kingdom, ANVAR in France, Canadian Patents and Developments Ltd. assist in the development phase. More generally there have been established, in the Netherlands, the National Investment Bank and Risk Capital BV.; in Germany, the Venture Financing Bank; in France, SOFINOVA; in Ireland, *Foir Teoranta*.

Surveys carried out in France and the Netherlands in 1976 assessing the reaction of industry to the direct financial assistance schemes available from government indicated that there was a pressing need for them to be made known more widely in industry so that more firms could make use of the assistance available. In France, general complaints were the length of delay between application and approval or rejection; and lack of knowledge about official contact and selection criteria.

Where firms had received assistance, the general consensus was that the assistance had been necessary and beneficial: not all projects had proved commercially viable and about half had produced income from the sale of products indirectly linked to the assisted project. Firms in traditional industries (textile, glass, construction) felt that the assistance was not sufficiently adapted to their particular needs.

In the Netherlands, emphasis was on the need to shorten the review process in the development credits scheme. The results of a sample study in the Netherlands of sixteen development credit projects suggested that the assistance was effective in accelerating developments which would otherwise have taken longer, rather than in causing new developments which would otherwise not have been attempted.

The general trend in all countries is towards more commercial terms of assistance for development work, even where government laboratories do work for industry. This approach has been carried furthest in the United Kingdom. Until recently, Germany was an exeption to this rule in its large programme on new technologies but policy was changed there in 1975. There is no agreement on what constitutes a reasonable balance between commercial terms for assistance and providing a positive incentive for industry to take up the funds available; nor on the extent to which commercial criteria encourage stronger market-oriented projects or inhibit longer-term objectives and projects with strong external benefits. There is some evidence in the UK industry schemes for the machine tool and wool textile industries that the original criteria were set too high to secure full industrial response; they have now been lowered.

NRDC has had more cash at its disposal than it has been able to invest. It is probably true in this context as in others that there must be flexibility in any industrial assistance scheme to tailor the whole package of instruments and the terms on which they are offered to match the technical and commercial needs of each particular sector of industry selected for such assistance. Given such flexibility, it is imperative that adequate arrangements are made for monitoring progress, amending the scale or terms of assistance to suit each successive stage of development as it is reached, and terminating the project as soon as it ceases to be a viable proposition.

DISCUSSION

Direct financial assistance for development projects in industry receives support from economic theory on three bases, namely: market imperfections, dynamic comparative advantage, and coping with adjustment problems. Despite the lack of success which has attended the past heavy government investment in large high technology, prestigious and 'lobby' projects, there is a need to continue direct assistance to technological change in industry. Lessons should be learnt from both categories as to why some succeeded and others failed.

- There should be much more emphasis on assistance to manufacturing industry, at all levels, and more concentration on helping industry to get the products and processes it develops on to the market.
- governments should identify priority sectors of industry on which assistance should be concentrated. This presupposes better forecasting of the future shape and technological requirements of industry — high 'knowhow' or high technology;
- industry should be involved in planning assistance schemes but should not be allowed to use the assistance for other than the prescribed purpose. Assistance should not be confined to research and development activities only but should embrace the other management and marketing skills essential to efficient transfer into saleable goods and services;
- there should be more management consultancies (technoeconomic as well as financial) particularly for the smaller firms; and better advisory services including those on product/market strategy. More attention should be directed to designing packages of assistance, including technical assistance, tailored to match the needs of industries in difficulty and raise their performance and competitive status;

- the interface between government and semi-public laboratories and industry should be improved so that full use is made of either facilities and technical skills by contract or collaborative work.
- governments must, in establishing direct assistance measures, be clear at the outset on their objectives; they must make adequate provision for monitoring progress, periodically adjusting the scale of assistance to match the needs of the next stage, and if necessary terminating the project; they must set up machinery to assess the value of the assistance given and the continued relevance of their instruments;
- the terms and conditions on which assistance is offered should be flexible enough to be made attractive to the various sectors of industry involved while continuing to satisfy broad policy requirements, for example, as to eventual recovery of exchequer costs if this is relevant;
- government procedures for providing assistance should be simplified in the interests of speeding up the decision process. The attraction of decentralizing or subcontracting responsibility to an agency (NIVR, NRDC, ANVAR) should be reviewed, as also should the arguments in favour of operating on a revolving fund rather than an openended grant basis.
- finally, because of the enormous volumes of cash required to regenerate existing industries, and to seed the growth of new technology-based industries, we feel that the banks should become much more involved in the financing of industry in general, and innovative activities in particular. This issue will be discussed in more detail in Chapter 12.

References

Clarke, R. (1973), 'Mintech in retrospect', *Omega,* 1, 1 and 2.
Eads, G. and Nelson, R. (1971), 'Government support of advanced civilian technology', *Public Policy,* 19, 405.
Freeman, C. (1976), 'Disussant's Comment', in A. Whiting (ed.), *The Economics of Industrial Subsidies,* HMSO.
Galbraith, J. K. (1969), *The New Industrial State,* Harmondsworth, Penguin.
Gardner, N. (1976a), 'Economics of launching aid' in A. Whiting (ed.), *The Economics of Industrial Subsidies,* London, HMSO.
—— (1976b), letter on state-aided technology in *Financial Times,* 24 February.
Jewkes, J. (1972), *Government and High Technology,* Occasional Paper No. 37, London, Institute of Economic Affairs.
Keck, O. (1977), *Fast Breeder Reactor Development in W. Germany: an Analysis of Government Policy,* doctoral dissertation, University of Sussex.
Pavitt, K. and Walker, W. (1976), 'Government policies towards industrial innovation: a review', *Research Policy,* 5, 1.
—— and Worboys, M. (1977), *Science, Technology and the Modern Industrial State,* London, Butterworth.
Servan–Schreiber, J-J. (1968). *The American Challenge,* London, Hamilton.
—— (1973), *L'Humanité,* 29 May.
Walker, W. (1976), *Direct Government Aid for Industrial Innovation in the UK.* Report to TNO, Delft, Netherlands, February.
Williams, B. (1967), *Technology, Investment and Growth,* London, Chapman.
Zysman, J. (1975), 'Between the market and the state: dilemmas of French policy for the electronics industry', *Research Policy,* 3, 312.

7. INNOVATION-ORIENTED PROCUREMENT POLICIES

INTRODUCTION

Innovation policy must not only concern itself with influencing the manner in which firms react to changes in their environment, however great these may have been in the past; government must also realize that it is itself a major element in that environment. It is heavily involved in setting the rules of the marketplace in general and is for many particular market segments a major customer. Government influences demand through *regulation* and *procurement*. In fact, a variety of studies that stress the importance of 'demand pull' as the critical input in the process of innovation support this standpoint. If innovation policy is to become more than the traditional science and technology policy, governments cannot neglect the manner in which they influence demand. This contention was borne out in a joint SPRU–TNO report (1977) which gave a number of cases of procurement leading to innovation: the empirical evidence presented supported the conclusion that 'the most important way that governments have influenced technical innovation is through demand' (p. 20).

There is also a different ground on which the need to study government demand can be argued, namely the present stage of technological development and the economic stagnation in the industrialized world. It has been argued in Chapter 3 that the present economic crisis has underlying causes related to the *type of technological change* that has characterized the latter part of the third quarter of the twentieth century. The spectacular increase in personal income in this period and the development of a number of technologies based on major innovations of the 1930s, has led to a situation in which many individual needs are now much better fulfilled by industry than ever before. In fact a certain saturation of the market for many consumer goods can be pointed to, as well as a lack of recent major innovations in this area. On the other hand, many public or collective needs go unfulfilled and the impact of innovation in this area seems to be much less. The modern industrial corporation, one might conclude, has found it much easier to respond innovatively to private than to public sector demand. One can also use the concept of 'natural trajectories' of technological change, 'technological regimes' or 'technological imperatives' (Nelson and Winter, 1977) to signal that perhaps industry is locked into a certain kind of behaviour and a given set of priorities in its present attitude toward innovation. New 'trajectories' must be developed and one area that seems a natural candidate for providing the opportunity for technical change is the public sector.

With the exception of military hardware, the public sector has lagged behind technologically. Public transportation technology has developed much slower than the automobile. The telephone system lags behind development of computer terminals and other non-collective communication equipment. Block heating has lost out to the one-household central heating unit. Developments in preventive medicine and productivity in the health system look pale when compared to innovation in the pharmaceutical industry.

Having argued the need and potential benefits of studying an innovation-oriented procurement policy leaves us with the problem of how to best go about it. Only in very few countries is such a policy seriously being implemented or even being considered. Of course there is a great deal of procurement activity going on and there is no lack of war stories about effects. However, there is considerable diversity in goals pursued, policy, and organizational structures that serve as an all-important background. Often elements of procurement policy are not brought out into the open or are purposely concealed, as the stakes can be quite high.

To arrive at some delimitation and mapping of the large field of government procurement we will discuss the different stages of the process of innovation at which procurement policy may be aimed. We will also discuss market structures on the supply and demand sides as their importance to the possibility of initiating procurement aimed at innovation is great. We will describe three types of objectives, namely: influence on innovation for the public sector; influence on innovation in the private sector; and objectives stemming from industrial policy. Finally, we will deal with the limits on the use of procurement as an instrument for innovation, and with some tentative conclusions and recommendations to help focus the discussion.

The subject of innovation-oriented procurement has also been studied in the framework of the Six Countries Programme and led to a report by Overmeer and Prakke (1978). This chapter is to a large extent based on the latter report.

CONDITIONS FOR SUCCESSFUL PROCUREMENT POLICY

Government procurement concerns technology in different stages of development and takes place under different market conditions. We can use these two aspects to map the many different types of conditions under which government procurement activities take place and play a role in the innovation process.

Stages of Technological Development

In the process of innovation a number of stages can be identified. We choose here to differentiate between *applied research, feasibility studies, prototype development, diffusion* and *maturity.*

Every area has its unique characteristics, so it is unjust to make any attempt at generalization, but we hope that the chosen five stages will make an intelligent discussion of technological change possible in a large number of different fields.

The above scheme serves a number of objectives. First of all, the order is chronological. Most case histories of particular innovations can be presented along these lines. Secondly, the stages correspond to recognizably different types of activities of people involved in the management of technology, be it in industry or in government. For example, applied research corresponds to the management problem of research project selection in large industrial firms and to the contracting-out of research by a government department.

Diffusion corresponds to a firm's possible second-in-the-market strategy or to government's efforts to promote technology transfer. The stage of maturity corresponds to the buying of goods off-the-shelf by procurement officers. From the standpoint of costs, projects at the early stages of development carry a much lower price-tag than those at later stages. The important consequence of this differentiation is that in the early stages the possibility of risk-taking, parallel projects and competition among suppliers are much more obvious.

Thirdly, the ordering reflects a dimension of decreasing uncertainty for decision-makers involved in the funding of a procurement process and concurrently an increasing degree of possible demand specification. For our purposes it is of importance to recognize the fact that the nature of the management of the innovation process changes as the degree of demand specification changes and with it the degree of environmental uncertainty. This fact is realized in the management of R & D in large industrial corporations. Decisions concerning different degrees of demand specification (uncertainty) are taken at different levels and places in the organization. It is generally considered good practice not to let R & D projects with different levels of uncertainty compete with each other for funding. Decisions involving a great deal of uncertainty for the organization because they involve non-standard technology or unfamiliar markets, are often placed outside the existing hierarchy, for example, by creating new venture units, where specialized knowledge of technology and of markets may be concentrated and where the inevitable result of uncertainty, namely a large chance of failures, will not effect the regular operations.

With respect to the management of technological change, when government uses procurement for stimulating innovation, the degree of demand specification similarly has great influence on the type of activities that can successfully be pursued. Relatively little in-house competence is required for procurement activities when buying goods off-the-shelf. No attempt is made to encourage the supplier to be innovative in any other way than producing at the lowest possible cost.

Most present government procurement activities fall within this category. Specialized central buying agencies have usually been set up to maximize the potential for driving down prices by ordering in large numbers. To prevent favouritism and to encourage price competition, the lowest-bid principle is in some cases even prescribed by law.

It is only under the pressure of special circumstances that the buyer will accept a more than minimal uncertainty. Likewise, the producer will only respond if extra compensation is offered. The difficulties become greater and the chances of failure increase as the degree of demand specification is lower. It is for this reason that the general process of government procurement concerns itself mostly with buying off-the-shelf and less frequently with the diffusion or transfer of technology.

Using procurement to influence the prior stages of the innovation process requires the willingness to run larger risks, spend larger amounts of money, and there is, therefore, a compelling sense of national purpose usually based on national security, prestige or grave social problems. The example *par excellence* of such a use of procurement to support a technological development from the stage of applied research all the way to complete specification is the American military microelectronics programme. Not only were certain manufacturers stimulated to achieve specific advances, but a whole climate was created (Kleiman, 1977) in which a branch of industry and a technological community was given a set of well-defined goals, to create (without regard to costs) electronic devices of minimal size and absolute dependability. Although it is undeniable that all stages of development were affected, it is interesting to note that commentators such as Golding (1978) emphasize that the real advantages of procurement were not in influencing invention and innovation but 'in accelerating the diffusion process'. In this case the effect on the learning curve was of particular importance.

Market Structure

The influence of government on a certain market, and therefore on the possibility to promote innovation in that market by means of an innovation-oriented procurement policy, depends on the market position of that government. Such market positions are likely to determine the success or failure of future extensions of the use of procurement policy for the purpose of innovation.

Purchases of central government are sizable. Procurement by local government and government-linked organizations (such as the Post and Telecommunications (PTT) in most countries) are generally a multiple of these. In Canada, for example, the figures for 1977, were 3 and 11 billion Canadian dollars, for central and local government respectively. However large these sums may be, they are spread out over many markets.

One can make the theoretical distinction between monopsony, oligopsony and polyopsony to describe the market structure on the demand (procurement) side.

In the case of monopsony the government is the sole buyer in (a segment of) a market. This is generally the case with military goods, the building of dams and dykes, and — in most countries — telecommunication technology. It is clear that the potential for an innovation-oriented procurement policy is greatest in the case of monopsony. It should be emphasized that government specifications should not interfere with demands set by experts. In the case of oligopsony a number of other large buyers besides the government are in the market, either in the public or the private sector. In Holland such a situation exists in low-cost housing, where government as well as large cooperative housing associations operate on the demand side. In the United States there is an oligopsony in the market of capital goods for electric utilities.

The public Tennesse Valley Authority (TVA) is a large purchaser next to a number of privately owned utilities. Because the number of buyers on the market is limited, the possibility exists of coming to agreements concerning the technology to be procured. The relationship between local governments or semi-government purchasers can also be termed oligopsonistic, for example, hospitals, port authorities, and regional electrical utilities. Although the latter take pride in their independence and reject any interference by the central government, they often cooperate with respect to the procurement of power stations. It is interesting to note that, analogous to the behaviour of the 'price leader' in the theory of oligopoly, one of the oligopsonists can play the role of 'quality leader'. Such a role was clearly written by the 'new dealers' into the charter of the TVA, according to which this public utility was to be 'a goad and example' to the other utilities when it came to technical innovation.

It is also clear that within the framework of an oligopsonistic market situation it is quite possible to come to cooperative relationships between purchasers and suppliers — one method is an agreement between purchaser and suppliers to buy in the future only goods according to certain standards.

An important factor contributing to an NRDC supported development of a mobile toilet for the elderly and disabled was the 'call-off contract' placed by the British Department of Health and Social Security (DHSS). This is a contract that closely defines the product (in this case including patented features like seat shape), thereby guaranteeing quality, and also publishes the seller's product price. It is therefore an official indication that the product is a good buy. Although it does not guarantee sales, it estimates them and lists the possible demanding authorities; in that sense it can be called off. Also when it is written on patents, it strengthens the position of the licensee in relation to competition from other non-licensed firms.

Another method for concentrating demand with respect to innovation in an oligopsonistic market, and similarly one in the public sector, is the practice of cooperative *trend analysis*, carried out by oligopsonists together with producers and experts. A study of this nature was carried out by the STU in Sweden in 1975 (STU, 1976) with respect to the increasing needs, quantitatively and qualitatively, of the elderly. The study indicates future demand and opportunities for innovation in an area of the economy that, as we noted in the introduction, seems to lag technologically behind such well-developed sectors as durable consumer goods and private transportation. The reference STU report also concludes that stimulation of innovation for the demand of the elderly should lead to an advanced capability and export potential for Swedish industry in the future. A trend analysis with respect to future needs in telecommunications has been carried out in West Germany by a panel consisting of people from industry, the *Bundespost*, government, as well as journalists and communication experts.

Having discussed monopsony and oligopsony, we should now turn to polyopsony, the usual position of government with respect to the market. Government is only one of many buyers and its share of the market is relatively small. Under conditions of polyopsony government can still attempt to pursue an active procurement policy aimed at innovation. But the effect will in principle be limited to that small share of the market, and the influence on the innovative efforts of the producers will be commensurate.

Government should not overestimate its influence nor suggest to the producer the existence of a larger market for new products to be developed than is actually there. This point was illustrated by the experiences of the American Department of Housing and Urban Development (HUD), which, based on the success of such practices in the military sector, made public its intention in the future to buy a number of innovative new products according to certain specifications. However, lacking the military's unity of command and the complex nature of building practices, HUD was not able to follow up on its declared intentions and a number of innovative firms were left 'holding the bag', destroying the climate for 'innovative' procurement practices in this area for some time to come.

The market structure on the supply side also puts constraints on the possibilities of a government procurement policy. A number of problems can be listed. First of all there is the situation of monopoly. If there is only one supplier in a certain market there is considerable danger of an incestuous relationship between it and the government, leading to a lack of competitive pressure on this firm and, quite likely, lack of technological performance.

Oligopoly also poses its special problems. Some countries have used such a market structure creatively by forcing parallel and competitive developments of different technological approaches to a certain problem.

A situation in which the market power of the suppliers is not sufficient to allow adequate profitability for financing R & D and other innovative activities can also be a serious obstacle to promoting innovation with procurement. It should be noted finally that, as is recognized in economic theory, market structure is not the only determining factor for competitive performance. Market behaviour, on the side of government as well as on the side of producers, is often a factor of considerable importance. It is the purpose of this chapter to show some of the potential for attuning market behaviour of the government to the potential for stimulating and directing technological innovation in industry.

Objectives

In general more than one objective is served by a particular policy; and since the 1978 Nobel prize for economics was awarded to Herbert Simon, it is certainly no longer revolutionary to observe that policy is not the end-product of a rational decision-making process. By the very nature of policy-making and the coalition building it entails, the existence of a complex of objectives behind a certain government policy or programme is always to be expected. Support will always be coming from diverse quarters in and around governments, each serving their own ends. For that reason alone it will be difficult to find an act of procurement which serves one objective only. Nevertheless it seems useful to formulate a number of separate objectives which figure prominently in government procurement programmes studied.

We see three broad categories of objectives of innovation-oriented procurement policy.

— improving the quality of goods used in the *public sector*;
— improving the quality of goods used in the *private sector* according to certain social goals;
— improving the *international competitiveness* of the industry.

Improving the quality of public sector goods, or achieving an optimal relationship between costs and benefits is the primary and generally accepted objective of almost all procurement. It is important to make the distinction between the short-term and longer-term relation between costs and benefits. Short-term efficiency confines itself to the comparison of goods off-the-shelf. It is the area of competence of central procurement offices. A number of the programmes in this field set themselves the goal of making such competence more widely available, especially to local government authorities. Important in this respect is the dissemination of lifecycle costing techniques (LCC), that include factors in the decision-making such as energy and maintenance costs.

Longer-term efficiency becomes the objective when government takes on the added responsibility of encouraging industry to produce technologically improved goods. The government tries explicitly to influence prior stages of the process of innovation thereby raising the technical capability of industry. Procedures typically used are the setting of performance specifications and value incentive clauses.

In a number of traditional areas of public responsibility, particularly in defence (in almost all countries), but also in waterway and dyke construction (especially in Holland), in rapid public transit systems in densely populated areas (Japan), and in space technology, government has followed this way. By definition these are areas in which government has a monopsonistic market position. Since Archimedes, most examples can be found in the military sector. The decreased importance of price differences when it comes to national security or safety is vital. Certainly much of the favourable experience with procurement policy for the promotion of innovation stems from this area. We should realize, however, that it is not an easy thing to transplant such experiences to other areas of public concern where conditions may be quite different. The goals of society in such areas as energy conservation, public transportation and health care are much more complex than the proverbial 'bigger bang for a buck' of the military. Nevertheless it does seem useful to learn from the military in attempts to stimulate long-term improvement in the production of non-military public goods.

While we have distinguished between short-term efficiency of procurement as buying the best that industry has to offer, and long-term efficiency as improving the offering that industry has to make, it is clear that the former can (of itself) lead to the latter. Highly informed public procurement will naturally lead to rewarding and will therefore stimulate technologically competent producers. This process can be speeded up by explicitly taking the long-term capability of suppliers into account.

The second objective of innovation-oriented procurement policy that can be listed is improving the quality of goods *in the private sector*. This is no easy proposition as it is generally assumed that individual consumers can decide best for themselves and through their decisions they can influence the manufacturers of goods. In addition, the market position of government is by definition weak in the private sector, where its relative market share is small. It can, moreover, be argued that the technological performance of industry is relatively strong in areas of private demand. However, a number of exceptions can be mentioned here. For example, there is the situation of market imperfection because of lack of information on the part of the consumer. This would result in the wrong message being transmitted by the market mechanism to the producer. It is not illogical for the government to assume that the public would pay more for energy-saving products if these were offered and clearly advertised as such. This means that government can support a campaign of public information (for example, the required labelling of the energy consumption of washing machines) and by buying such machines for its own use. Similarly, a policy of regulation (such as new safety or pollution rules) can be supported in the political discussion as well as in the courts by procurement of products according to such regulation.

The third category of objectives of procurement policy lies in the area of promoting international competitiveness of industry. This objective stems from traditional industrial policy. We can distinguish between short-term and long-term aspects of this objective. In the short term it is clear that most governments, under pressure of firms, labour unions and parliamentarians use government procurement to save jobs. This is generally called protectionism. A more interesting and probably also more defensible objective for national policy is to use procurement for the longer-term competitiveness of industry. This corresponds to what economists call the 'infant industry' argument. Protecting such infant industry by procurement policy is an important objective for countries that do not wish to become technologically dependent upon their trading partners. Technological competitiveness — and therefore industrial competitiveness in general — does not currently depend as much on the static comparative advantages in factor prices but rather on the dynamic advantage of a firm's position on the learning curve. The theory of the learning curve tells us that the speed of technological development in an industry depends on the number of units produced. The firm that can sell more units advances faster, which in turn allows it to sell more. In addition, it has been shown that innovations have a strong tendency to be created in the market that offers the greatest initial demand. In the eyes of many the result is that, as long as the European Economic Community does not form a real homogeneous market, new technology will still be introduced initially in the United States and that American firms will continuously improve their position on the learning curve, and gain by exporting to countries lagging behind. Countries will want to protect their infant industry or 'infant technology', by the use of procurement.

GOVERNMENT ORGANIZATION AND PROCEDURES FOR EFFECTIVE PROCUREMENT

Government organization and procedures are important, because to stimulate innovation, government must reduce the degree of uncertainty for the potentially innovative firm. This requires an articulation of a demand that is clear, stable over time and based on sufficient knowledge of the technology to arrive at good specifications. A number of organizational and procedural aspects are of particular importance.

Organizational Aspects

Centralization of government is often mentioned as a way to articulate demand more forcefully; a monopsonist has more market power than an oligopsonist. Centralization may either refer to the degree in which the central government has power over local government decisions or over such semi-government functions as the post and telecommunications, the utilities, or the railway system. In America it is often said that it is much easier for the French government to improve the quality of, for example, swimming pools or school buildings than for federally governed states such as Canada or the United States. In fact, market aggregation has been a main theme of the discussion on procurement policy. The United States government has typically selected hospitals of the Veterans Administration for its efforts of promoting innovation in the health sector, because they are under the control of central government. Decisions on the procurement of certain drugs and on the introduction of the X-ray thermography scanner seem to have been more effectively taken in the strongly centralized British health system, than in the disaggregate system of the United States. Japan has made effective use of centralized decision-making in such areas as telecommunications and nuclear energy. Nevertheless, it is too early to draw the conclusion that from the standpoint of innovation governments should always try to centralize procurement as much as possible. It has been observed in the German study on local procurement that centralization can also be a strong conservative factor. Building codes and rules for subsidies in the public sector were often found to be a hindrance to the introduction of innovations. While centralization increases the possibility of innovative procurement by creating a monopsony, this does not mean that innovative behaviour will always be the result. In many cases a degree of competition between oligopsonists may be preferred, even if it is the competition between municipalities for prestige, based on civic pride.

A second important organizational aspect is the management of the R & D interface. This relates to the necessity for the effective exchange of information between users and suppliers of innovations. Because the decision-making on innovation is characterized by uncertainty of the environment, effective linkages or integrating devices are of the greatest importance for successful innovation (Prakke, 1974). In large industrial organizations such linkages are typically applications research departments, marketing — R & D coordinating groups, R & D planning, integrators, new venture managers, etc. In government procurement such linkages are provided by joint industry–military committees or exchange of executives between government and industry. Their role is more important when the degree of uncertainty is relatively high, that is, when procurement attempts to affect prior stages of the process of innovation. Again, most of the examples here are from the military sector.

The French tradition of dual industry–government careers is important in this respect. Japan systematically sets up special coordinating councils to guide technical development of various industries. The council of the ministry of communication decided, after reviewing Japan's future needs in the field of communication, that the development of space technology (that is, rockets and satellites) was indispensable. Similar decisions were taken by the council of the ministry of transportation (maritime and weather information) and the ministry of construction (geographical information). While Japan offers an example of an extremely formalized system of organizational linkages, such informal measures as the semi-annual briefings about expected procurement given by the Canadian Department of Supply and Services to the electronics industry may also be quite effective. All these examples are given to emphasize the point that extraordinary organizational measures may be needed to use procurement for innovation.

Using procurement to stimulate innovation generally goes against traditional practices in government. Resistance is to be expected from existing structures. From the point of view of organizational change it may therefore be useful to create new departments or groups, or change agents, with the explicit responsibility to promote innovation-oriented procurement. The ETIP* in the United States is an example of such a change agent and also a lesson of how not to complicate the functioning of such a group by giving it too many roles to play.

Procedures

One of the main successes of ETIP is reported to have been the introduction into general usage in the government of performance specifications. The tradition had been to issue design specifications, followed by price competition. Specifications phrased in terms of performance allow industry to search for better solutions to given problems. The classic example is the noise level specifications issued by the California Department of Education for a school building. While traditionally a certain thickness of isolation material had been specified, the winning design based on the noise level specification made use of internal carpeting, rather than thick isolation. Of importance has also been the wider use of lifecycle costing in government. A related procedure is the use of value-incentive clauses. This rewards the producer for a more effective design by sharing the financial benefits.

Another procedural lesson seems to be that some form of competition between suppliers needs to be introduced in the procurement process. If this is not done, there is considerable risk of excessively high costs and, perhaps worse, technological complacency on the part of the favoured firm.

Competition is especially effective in the less costly, early stages of the innovation process and for technological developments on a scale that is not too large relative to the size of the country. An illustrative example is the development of a

*Experimental Technology Incentives Programme, US Department of Commerce (see Wolek, 1978).

communications satellite in Japan, for which a competition in the development of prototypes was organized among a number of firms for the design of the satellite itself, but for which the development of the rocket was awarded to a single company.

Finally, there are such rather mundane but not less important activities of government to improve the efficiency of procurement as the training of procurement officials and the support of independent testing facilities. They are important elements of the British LAMSAC and the Swedish STU programmes.

LIMITATIONS ON THE USE OF PROCUREMENT AS AN INSTRUMENT FOR INNOVATION

We have already indicated the conditions under which procurement may stimulate innovation. Before going into the presentation of experiences with such a policy, we should discuss a number of limitations. Procurement should not be seen as the panacea of innovation policy, however important it may be in specific cases. The following limitations can be listed:

- first of all, there may be a lack of consensus in the government, resulting in frequent changes in policy. This increases the uncertainty to firms and makes successful innovation unlikely. A similar case is when government is decentralized and the different elements do not have the political will to pool their resources. Such a situation can severely hinder the coordination of procurement;
- a second limitation is the absence of market power on the side of the government. In case of a polyopsony, government should not pretend that it can effectively influence innovation without supporting measures such as regulation;
- a third factor that can dull the procurement instrument is the absence of competition by producers. This affects especially the smaller countries;
- a fourth limitation of procurement policy is that government is not always capable of rational and evenhanded decision-making. Reasons for this are that in-house competence is usually lacking, especially in areas of high technology, and that government may let itself be used by such interested parties as the scientific community, large agencies, and industry.

EXPERIENCES WITH THE USE OF PROCUREMENT AS AN INSTRUMENT FOR INNOVATION

Introduction

A number of programmes from different countries will be described here and evaluated. All these programmes aim at the use of government procurement as an instrument for technological innovation in the private sector. Our intention is to show how different countries choose different approaches. The reason for these differences can be type of technology, market structure, organization of government, attitude of civil servants, ideas on the role of government, differences in local circumstances, etc. It will appear that the procurement instrument has a potential power but that careful assessment of the circumstances in advance is a prerequisite for its use. Wrong estimations of the influence of the instrument may mean that instead of incentives for innovation, disincentives are generated and introduced.

It is not our intention to suggest that the selected cases are characteristic. Nor is it our intention to give overall evaluations. We will limit ourselves to the procurement aspects, and intend to show the variety of possibilities and problems that can arise.

The United States: The Experimental Technology Incentives Programme (ETIP)

One of the early programmes, concerning experiments with government procurement policies to enhance technological innovation in the civilian sector, was the Experimental Technology Incentives Programme (ETIP). The programme was conducted by the National Bureau of Standards (NBS) of the US Department of Commerce, and coordinated with the companion Experimental R & D Incentives Programme of the National Science Foundation (NSF). Both programmes were initiated after the presidential speech 'Message on Science and Technology', delivered in 1972. Funds became available during the fiscal year 1973.

Among the reasons ETIP was brought into being were:

- a declining positive result in the balance of trade concerning technology-based products;
- a growing awareness in the nation of its new needs (energy sources and conservation, pollution control, urban transportation, health services);
- the unused potential in commercial application of technology, already provided through the mostly military R & D procurement;
- a need for better understanding of the market environment for research and innovation.

ETIP's task was to explore stimulation mechanisms and acquire the results of experimental approaches for the purpose of developing new policies and practices to be implemented by the federal government. In ETIP, federal procurement procedures and practices were examined, approaches recommended, and experiments as well as fields of experimentation selected.

Within the confines of existing legislation ETIP recommended among others: introduction of performance specifications and lifecycle costing; technology utilization as a pre-award qualification factor; a government-wide policy; competitive negotiated procurement with guaranteed follow-on; potential use of multiple procurement approaches and subsidization of purchases made by other bodies, in other words directing the lines of innovation, for example in building industry and urban transportation. ETIP anticipated that sometimes multiple incentive approaches would be necessary, such as a combination of direct research subsidy, regulation and procurement.

Two types of experiments were distinguished:

- 'piggy-backing', meaning the modification of an ongoing or planned programme of a federal agency. It required close cooperation with the agency, as well as agreement with the agency to share the additional costs. Moreover, ETIP should be involved in the very early phase of the procurement process. This method was preferred;

— 'demonstration-experiment', showing the feasibility of a new technology, establishing a scale production, convincing people with a conservative attitude towards technological innovation.

Important conditions were: the contribution of a programme to solve the national problems; existing market structures have proven unable to stimulate new solutions; industry, lacking sufficient incentives, should be willing to support; government agencies should have a purchasing power, based on a market position.

Some ETIP Proposed Experiments

Health Care

The major problem in this field was that introduction of new technology had been discouraged by resistance to change and by the disaggregation in the market. The federal government had only very limited influence in this field through its market position. Less than 10 per cent of 2000 major hospitals were under direct government control, mostly via the Veterans Health Administration of the Department of Defense. The others were independent and had established their own practices and standards. A miniature fast blood-analyser was selected in order to reduce medical costs.

Four demonstration approaches were possible:

— the government could buy a limited number of one prototype and insert them into government-controlled hospitals;
— the government could purchase a large enough number of one prototype to introduce 'economy of scale' and place them in government controlled clinical settings;
— the government could purchase several prototype models (up to three) after proof of commercialization, and guaranteed sole-source follow-on;
— the government could purchase a large enough number of one prototype to introduce 'economy of scale' and sell them to physicians with the promise to buy them back after two years if desired.

Energy Conservation

That energy generation and conservation were a national problem goes without saying. Three deficiencies in the past were stated: a lack of understanding about the complex interrelationships in this field; a naïve conception that the ability to meet the growing demand for energy is limitless; a lack of centralized planning and control of energy policy.

Some of the proposed experiments were:

— in order to stimulate the commercialization of Syncrude (synthetic fuel), government could purchase fuel for its own use at a price above current market value for equivalent sources, provided that fuel was produced using an innovative and previously uncommercialized process;
— on solar energy: since the required technology is not new, what appeared to be needed is broader-scale demonstration of such systems 'to convince the construction community and the population of their feasibility', and 'The main barrier to commercialization appears to be uncertainty about the economics of producing power from such systems on a large scale'. ETIP proposed a full-scale

plant to meet the electric power requirements on a military base. In August 1978, Congress approved a defence bill authorizing $4 billion in military construction, with the addition that all new military family housing units and 25 per cent of other military constructions should be equipped with solar heating and cooling systems. This means that the Department of Defense will spend about $100 million a year, while industry annual sales previously accounted for only $150 million;

energy consumption of airconditioners. Although manufacturers of aircraft airconditioners had already achieved greater efficiency, the technology had not been applied into household airconditioners because industry leaders feared that consumers would not buy a higher priced unit. ETIP suggested that the Department of Defense would use performance specifications.

Transportation Systems

Special attention was given to urban transit buses. It appeared that this type of bus was last redesigned in 1956, due to the decreasing revenues in the transit industry. Virtually no new technology, such as supported by federal government subsidies and procurement in the aerospace industry, had been applied in buses. ETIP proposed 'piggy-backing' on an ongoing programme, which initiated the development of prototype vehicles.

Evaluation of ETIP

Three considerations in the initial phase of ETIP were influential (Berke, 1977). First of all the US economy was lagging and it was believed that this was largely due to government's regulation, bureaucracy, etc. ETIP was regarded as an important vehicle to solve these problems. Secondly, there was faith in US technology. The United States had just successfully beaten the Russians in the race to the moon, and the importance of technological innovation for economic performance was emphasized. Altogether this caused considerable political pressure on ETIP and asked for fast results. Moreover, since the agency goals often required immediate payoff, ETIP was seeking fast and riskless success. Only those products were selected which were based on a technology well in hand, but also where the government version lagged behind the commercial version. Thus the aim of ETIP was simply to upgrade the performance of those versions being purchased by public agencies, and in the process to upgrade governmental procurement procedures. ETIP's initial experiments were product-oriented and contractor-designed and were selected to establish ETIP's credibility with agency partners.

Focusing on the procurement aspect of ETIP the following lessons can be derived from the experiments:

— ETIP failed to recognize the full strength of the public contracting traditions and the specific roles of specification analysts and the purchasing agencies;
— one of ETIP's criteria for selecting an experiment was whether a product would contribute to the solving of a national problem or not. It appeared that a national problem is not necessarily a problem for either an agency or a local government;
— technical and financial miscalculations were made;
— early involvement of industry has been lacking;
— as there was lack of a major objective ETIP became involved in too many products;
— various organization problems were underestimated during the course of events.

To these lessons can be added that ETIP assumed that agencies were already interested in technological innovation. Furthermore, ETIP was performing conflicting roles, of which those of advocate, promoter, supporter and evaluator can be distinguished.

Although ETIP hardly influenced private industry, it did have an impact on government, and was most successful in the field of procurement practices. It introduced concepts such as lifecycle costing, performance specifications and the value-incentive clause in many federal and state agencies. The Federal Supply and Services as well as the Veterans Health Administration created their own Experimental Technology Division. It initiated various courses concerning more innovative procurement gradually being taken over by the agencies themselves.

Most important, although ETIP experiments started without a thorough conceptual framework of government's impact on innovation, they have been an extremely valuable source of information afterwards — a unique learning process.

BRD: The BMFT Research Project

One of the West European programmes influenced by ETIP is the 'Public Procurement and Technological Innovation' project from the Federal Ministry for Research and Technology (*Bundesministerium für Forschung und Technologie* — BMFT). BMFT initiated the project at the end of 1977 and contracted IAGB (*Industrie anlagen-Betriebsgesellschaft mgH Ottobrunn*) to conduct the actual research. The procurement research project started in June 1978.

The Objective of the Study

BMFT expects IABG to define 'both pragmatic and effective methodologies and an outline of measures and instruments, that the government can use in stimulating the technological transfer and innovation by public procurement'. Unlike ETIP, which started without a thorough conceptual framework in mind on governmental intervention in the technological innovation process, and attempting to gain knowledge through experiments, BMFT has chosen for a thorough analysis of already existing data of successful cases in the past. ETIP was considered to be an interesting and encouraging example, but answers were not yet firm enough to be used as a base in the German context. The research conducted by IABG is aimed at the following questions: (1) Are there any special fields in which public procurement has been or could be applied successfully for stimulating technological transfer and innovation? (2) What are the possible hindrances of regulations and procedures? (3) What are the eventual risks for public purchasers? (4) Which conditions should be taken into account when a government wishes to use the procurement instrument in this context?

Field of Investigation

The following selection criteria were used to determine the fields of investigation:

— there should be a technological potential for innovation;
— the government should hold a significant part of the market in order to be able to exercise a certain influence through its purchasing power;
— there should be the 'probability of provoking response from the private demand sector', in other words, the government is clearly seeking to influence private demand;

— it should be a centralized versus decentralized public demand-type problem;
— the selected productlines should have social relevance;
— the selected products should be representative of broader productlines;
— the applied technologies should exist already, at least as prototypes. In other words, a 'technology well in hand'.

The following fields of investigation were selected:

— *solar energy and heatpump technology*, characterized by: a great social importance; a large-scale government interest; an obviously increasing private demand; a great technological change compared with conventional equipment;
— *motor vehicles*, characterized by: an increasing social consciousness concerning the more negative impacts of motor vehicles; large efforts in the private and public sectors; a dominating private demand; a relatively slow but steady rate of technological progress;
— *medical technology, in particular equipment demanded by general practitioners*, characterized by: a high priority based on national consensus; large government subsidies and considerable private R & D; fragmented private demand; a high rate of technological innovation;
— *geriatric and disabled people's equipment*, characterized by: small financial support for R & D, a modest social interest, a small increase in private demand, minor technological improvements which may produce significant benefits;
— *fire-protection equipment*, characterized by: financial support for R & D concentrated on selected and narrow product lines; a sufficiently large private demand; a low rate of technological progress.

Some Tentative Conclusions

(The investigations in various productlines are in different stages)
Heat pumps. One of the preliminary questions of the research team was: 'Why has such an important technology not yet been realized by procurement agencies without a substantial financial subsidy?' Successful cases were investigated and it appeared that, for instance, in one case the technology was introduced because the *Bürgermeister* of a city wanted to demonstrate his progressive image. In another case it was introduced through the efforts of a private company, already heating a swimming pool and looking for a profitable use of its surplus capacity. It also became clear that centralization of authority and subsidies by the federal government can lead to inflexible regulation and increasing bureaucracy, both tending to make procurement policies more conservative. Furthermore, small municipalities are, in terms of technical competence dependent on engineering consultants who, in practice, are conservative concerning the application of new technologies.
Motor vehicles. One of the preliminary questions was whether 'a procurement agency uses the opportunity which may be given by a large-scale purchase to stimulate technological innovation?' The *Bundespost* buys approximately 8000 motor vehicles of a certain type. By using this quantity as a leverage the *Bundespost* is now trying to have new types of safety-belts developed as well as new devices to decrease the costs of crank-case and gearbox oil replacement.
Medical technology, that is, analysing equipment for general practitioners.
Geriatric and disabled people's equipment. In this case a cooperative procuring agency does exist; however a continuous effort by the management of the institutions to minimize costs seems to be a major hindrance for technological innovation.

Solar energy. Again one of the preliminary questions was why the diffusion of this technology proceeds at such a slow rate. Among others it appeared that the government-procurement regulations were a hindrance. Furthermore, the fact that solar energy devices did not yet fit into the DIN-system seemed to be a major barrier.

Fire protection equipment. Public demand is 80 per cent of the total demand, although largely fragmented. The *Bundeswehr* is the quality leader. One would expect to find advanced equipment among the·municipalities, but this is contradicted by the findings. Reasons given are: (1) severe testing and DIN-regulations as a prerequisite for federal government subsidies have been a major barrier for innovation; (2) as well as a strict replacement scheme, allowing replacement only on a predetermined replacement schedule, and not in response to equipment innovation. An accounting scheme, not the emergence of an advanced product on the market, determines when a certain piece of equipment will be replaced. Purchased products have in general a very high quality.

Sweden: The STU Programme

The National Swedish Board of Technological Development (*Styreisen for Teknisk Utveckling, STU*) is one of the public-service agencies in the Swedish administration, associated with the Ministry of Industry. STU's primary task is to act as the central governmental agency for non-military technical research and development activities carried out with governmental support. One of the important ways through which STU carries out this task is via the setting-up of collective research programmes, efforts within certain branches of industry, with the objective of conducting research on a specific problem common to most enterprises in that branch. Out of the 30 programmes going on, three deal with technical problems of local government. These programmes have procurement aspects. Some six new programmes, focusing on procurement problems at local and county level are expected to be initiated. The approaches towards procurement policies are based on the results of a feasibility study, which will be discussed below.

The Feasibility Study on Procurement

A feasibility study on the subject 'an innovative procurement policy' (Swedish: *Teknikupphandling*) was initiated on 29 June 1973.

The Commission on Public Procurement and Technical Development (*Teknikupphandlings Kommitten, TUK*) was installed, consisting of, among others, civil servants of the Ministry of Industry, STU, local government, and officials from the electric utilities, the telephone company and the Association of County Councils. The study was completed in December 1976.

The report refers to two main motives for investigating public procurement in relation to technological innovation. By a proper definition and long-term planning of their needs, public agencies can initiate innovations, and improve their own efficiency. Moreover, in Sweden public purchases are an important market. The government therefore has an instrument to affect the direction of technological innovation, and through this to improve the competitiveness of Swedish products on the international market. The need for long-term planning, improvement of in-house competence, and the establishment of cooperation both within industry and the public sector are recognized.

Proposals Made in the Feasibility Study

(1) Agencies should investigate their present and future needs and set up long-term planning.
(2) Agencies should establish which in-house competence is needed in terms of knowledge concerning technology and procurement policies, and which knowledge should be acquired from outside.
(3) Cooperation between procuring agencies should be initiated in an early phase of development.
(4) Introduction of courses for procurement officers should be considered.

Field of Interest

While ETIP started at the federal level in the United States, STU has started at the local level. The reasons for doing so are: (1) local government purchases account for 50 per cent of the total purchases of the public sector; (2) there is a lack of in-house competence in local governments; (3) through the fragmentation of the market of 'urban technologies', the rate of technological innovation has been very slow. Through aggregation of demand via the Association of Local Authorities, it is believed this rate can be increased significantly; (4) there are many 'not-articulated needs' especially on the local level; (5) the Swedish military procurement model, a case of a monopsonistic market, is considered to be successful. As 'urban technologies' have similar characteristics, it is expected that the military model can be transplanted. Through this, experiences can be gained for the more oligopsonistic and polyopsonistic markets.

Based on the outcome of the subject feasibility study, STU has started preparation of the following frame programmes with local and county authorities:

— collection and treatment of household garbage;
— development of a data processing system for technical information for management of municipal public works, for example, concerning the location of electric cables and waste-water pipes in road constructions;
— development of regional public transportation systems;
— information processing system for the maintenance of municipal housing;
— crime prevention measures in hospitals;
— fire prevention and firefighting techniques.

The utilization of external competence by local and county governments is considered to be an important part of the programme. For example STU will set up procurement courses in which local procurement officers will be taught by procurement officers of the Swedish telephone company and the Department of Defence. Other activities of STU include: investigation of approaches concerning innovation-oriented procurement policies abroad; development of STU's own competence on procurement matters; and the initiation of a procurement advisory committee within STU to assist local and county authorities.

Canada: The Department of Supply and Services and its Science Centre

In Canada there exists a special ministry, called the Department of Supply and Services (DSS), which has initiated experiments with procurement policies, after the ETIP experiments of the United States. For example, the effectiveness of 'value incentive clauses' is tested; in other words, the financial benefits of cost reductions due to innovations in goods for the public sector will be shared between the supplier, who originated the idea of the innovation, and the public sector.

Department of Supply and Services

In Canada the DSS purchases *all* goods for federal purposes. Its organization is based on the former Department of Defence Production, which originally purchased goods for the military sector. The DSS does not purchase for the Crown corporations, except the Post Office; its task is not merely to purchase according to the 'off-the-shelf' and 'for the lowest bid' principle like the central procurement offices in European countries. Recently, it has also taken into account 'socioeconomic objectives'; for example, Canadian companies should benefit as much as possible from Canadian government purchases, unless the price difference between a Canadian and a foreign supplier is more than 10 per cent.

If the criterion of 'the lowest bid' is not employed any longer as the decision criterion, it becomes necessary to formulate other criteria. At first the DSS, like ETIP, did not have serious problems. However, when the DSS, and especially its socioeconomic objectives, became more and more well known the number of claims of various interest groups increased rapidly.

The DSS has an operating budget of $5 million per year. Every month a profit and loss account is made. The DSS charges for its intermediary services; 50 per cent of the total turnover per year of the DSS concerns military equipment, but the percentage of military goods declines year by year. Per year the DSS purchases for $3 billion; total Canadian government procurement stands at $11 billion.

The DSS is attempting to make the departments aware of its 'procurement power' and their impact on markets. The DSS is also trying to aggregate local and provincial demands; drugs are already centrally purchased, for example. Once a year the DSS holds a briefing for the electronics industry concerning future public sector demand especially for military and space sectors. Regarding the in-house competence of DSS, it employs 60 contracting officers, most of whom have a technical background.

The Science Centre within the DSS

The promotion of technological innovation is one of the objectives of Canadian industrial policy. Government procurement policies are considered to be a means to achieve it, and within the DSS the promotion of innovation is delegated to its Science Centre. The following activities of this centre are of importance with respect to procurement policies:

— all research, development and feasibility study assignments of all federal governmental bodies are put out to contract by the Science Centre. The departments remain ultimately responsible. After the recommendations of the Lamontagne report (1972), a great number of assignments is given to industrial enterprises. It is stressed that the lowest bid is not the only criterion, and that it is also possible that assignments are given to more than one company;

— the Science Centre publishes a monthly bulletin listing all assignments for research, development and feasibility studies that have been contracted out during the previous month, as well as possible future assignments. The intention of these bulletins is to achieve a better 'tuning' of the capacities of suppliers to the demands of the public sector;

— the Science Centre also functions as a national suggestions box. Any company in Canada which has an idea that it is able to develop or can carry out research beneficial for one of the departments, may apply for a contract. In such cases, the Centre acts as a broker between the company and the department. These unsolicited proposals have to be approved by a department at the assistant deputy minister level and the subject department has to be willing to pay a third to two-thirds of the total cost. The Centre has a budget of $12 million in order to finance its contributions to the unsolicited proposals.

The Contracting-out Policy

A second aspect of the Canadian innovation policy deserves attention — the contracting-out policy. It is formally described as: 'Contract-out signifies a situation where a science and technology requirement is purchased by the federal government from Canadian industry or from other performers in the private sector'.

Because government institutes and universities took a large part of the research activities, a lot of knowledge was 'inactively stored'. The private sector had difficulties in getting access to this passive knowledge and the relationship between research and market was far from ideal. The lack of 'demand pull' was seen as the major barrier for this deficiency, in other words, a lack of communication between potential and needs. Since the Lamontagne report (1972) it is the government's policy to have as many research, development and feasibility studies as possible carried out in the private sector; basic research will remain part of the task of the universities. Part of the contracting-out policy is that government is not allowed to start new R & D activities unless the private sector is not willing and/or able to carry them out.

The United Kingdom: Activities at the Local Level

Several activities at the local level concerning procurement policy take place.

First of all there is the Local Authority Management Service and Computer Committee (LAMSAC). It has two functions:

(1) LAMSAC's Advisory Service aids local authorities in a variety of ways to suit individual needs and circumstances. It gives general advice, including courses for purchasing officers and technical specialists, collects and disseminates information, gives training courses, and investigates, appraises and develops new systems for local government, both in management and computing
(2) LAMSAC also provides a consultancy service to local authorities of a more detailed nature and over a longer time-span than can be given through the advisory services. It carries out comparative studies in order to enable the transfer of best practices between authorities.

These services are aimed at increasing the efficiency of local government in the procurement of goods and services and in providing up-to-date knowledge on technical specifications for those goods. LAMSAC facilitates the dissemination of technological innovation in local government; it can also be an instrument to increase technological innovation through procurement of goods adapted to requirements existing at local level.

JACLAP

Another activity is the Joint Advisory Committee on Local Authority Purchasing (JACLAP). The White Paper on *Public Purchasing and Industrial Efficiency* (Cmnd. 3291), published by HMSO in May 1967, drew attention to the role that the public sector should play by the use of its purchasing power both to promote industrial efficiency and to help exports. With this objective in view, the government invited the local authority associations to join with central government departments in setting up a Joint Reveiw Body on Local Authority Purchasing to review the ways in which the government's objectives set out in the 1967 White Paper could best be attained in the field of local authority purchasing. The joint review body recommended, in 1968, the creation of national machinery to coordinate the purchasing activities of local authorities and to encourage and promote more efficient purchasing by local authorities. It also recommended that the government should introduce legislation which would allow all local authorities to supply goods one to another and to contract, purchase and store for that purpose. The second of these recommendations was implemented by the enactment of the Local Authorities (Goods and Services) Act 1970. Orders were made under this act in 1972 and 1975, specifying public bodies to which local authorities are enabled to supply goods and services.

Merger of JACLAP with LAMSAC

With a view to strengthening and rationalizing the work of the central advisory bodies for local government in relation to purchasing, the local authority associations decided to merge the activities of JACLAP with those of LAMSAC. The latter's new responsibilities for local authority purchasing will be handled at the policy level by the main LAMSAC committee and a purchasing subcommittee involving elected members appointed by the associations, aided by a panel comprising purchasing officers and chief officers of the other main disciplines in local government, together with central government assessors.

Terms of Reference of LAMSAC

Within the broad guidelines and estimates agreed through LAMSAC and with the guidance and assistance of (specialist purchasing advisers and) the purchasing panel, the purchasing subcommittee will seek to improve purchasing performance in local government by:

(1) advising local authorities on the organization of central and coordinated purchasing;
(2) providing guidance as to the application of good purchasing techniques and practices and the adoption of specifications suited to local authority needs;
(3) representing local authority interests in work at national level on legislation and administrative measures having implications for local authority purchasing and participating in central activities in relation to specification and public sector cooperation in purchasing;
(4) the direction of future research into the development of coordinated purchasing.

The particular activities of the new purchasing section of LAMSAC in carrying out these objectives are likely to include:

(1) the establishment of a database about the way purchasing is organized in local authorities;
(2) coordinating the necessary purchasing information from specialists in order to advise and assist local authorities;

(3) the publication of a periodical bulletin and other advisory memoranda about developments in purchasing for circulation to individual authorities and purchasing officers;

(4) the promotion, in conjunction with Local Government Training Boards and other appropriate agencies, of training at various levels of supplies staff, and the organization of conferences, seminars, etc., for local authority elected members and chief officers on particular aspects of materials management;

(5) the organization of the effective representation of local authority purchasing interests in relevant work carried out by or on behalf of central government, the British Standardization Team etc., and also by LAMSAC itself and the other central local government bodies.

The United States: The Impact of Military Procurement Policies on the Innovation Process in the Electronics Industry

The United States government procurement policies for electronics components and finished products, especially computer application, are often described as examples of government procurement policies which successfully influenced the innovation process in the electronics industry.

To understand the impact of US government procurement, the following remarks are important:

— it is necessary to make a distinction between three stages in the technological innovation process: the invention, the innovation and the diffusion;

— the US government, in fact, the Airforce, the Army, the National Aeronautics and Space Agency (NASA) and to some extent the National Bureau of Standards, Department of Commerce (NBS), do not only use the procurement instrument to influence the innovation process in the civilian electronics industry. Simultaneously, they gave direct financial support for research and development, used procurement policies for R & D contracts, generated an innovation-oriented climate, etc.;

— we shall confine ourselves to the innovation process itself, and refrain from discussing whether the same innovation could have been achieved in another way;

— we should like to stress that due to the type of technology, the manufacturing of the products, the type of market (monopsonistic in an early phase), and the budgets of the Department of Defense (DOD), experiences and theories cannot easily be transplanted to other technologies, products, markets or governments;

— we shall distinguish between three products that were purchased by the US government: components such as transistors, integrated circuits (IC), and finished products, such as computer applications.

The Innovation Process

There are differences in the invention stage between the various products. According to Golding (1978) commenting on the invention of the transistor: 'In general, there is no obvious reason why procurement policies should have any impact on invention and the case of the transistor suggests that the motivation came entirely from within the Bell System.' A similar statement is made by Utterback and Murray (1977):

Substantially none of the major innovations on semiconductors have been a direct result of defence sponsored projects. Major advances in semiconductor technology have, with a few exceptions, been developed and patented by firms or individuals with government research fundings. Far fewer patents have resulted from defence supported R & D than from commercially funded R & D, and a far smaller proportion of those which resulted from defence support have had any commercial use.

Concerning the invention of the IC, Kleiman (1977) notes: 'The two basic patents and key technological contributions that underly the IC innovation were made by private companies on their own with no government support'. In the case of the IC, however, after the experiences with transistor procurement, it was known in advance to companies that the Department of Defense was willing to buy these types of components. According to Golding (1978), 'The Armed Services, by stressing their willingness to buy small quantities of high technology items, were successful in creating a climate of opinion conducive to invention'. Kleiman (1977) adds: 'The government influence helped to create the landscape which these companies and their key managers viewed, but the government support in no way dictated the nature of the technological route to be taken'.

Concerning the invention of the computer, Schnee (1978) states: 'the first US computer, the Automatic Sequence Controlled Calculator, was developed by a Harvard–IBM team between 1937 and 1944'. In the case of the innovation of the transistor, it was again an initiative of private industry, although a conductive environment had some influence. According to Golding: 'government procurement had a fairly limited direct effect on the emergence of the transistor as a commercially acceptable device'.

In the case of the innovation of IC government initiated some programmes. According to Kleiman: 'None of these programmes was successful, although as argued later, they did contribute in more tangential ways to the IC innovation process. For the successful IC innovation the government backed initiatives already taken by private industry.'

Concerning innovations in the field of computer applications, Schnee (1978) notes:

> The major advances during this period [the 1940s and 1950s] were made in the large computers demanded by the military and other government agencies. The advances were subsequently incorporated in the medium and small computers, which were designed for smaller scale, less complex applications. In the 1950s government contract R & D accounted for about 60 per cent of total R & D expenditures at IBM; by the early 1960s, government sponsored R & D was a small part of the company's $125 million R & D budget. The very large IBM computers, were built on contract for government agencies, but the highly successful transistorized 1401 series and the 360 and 370 series have been privately funded projects.

According to the literature, US government procurement of high technology had its real impacts on the diffusion process. Golding (1978):

> Immediately after a (Military) Diffusion Symposium in 1956, the Department of Defense became convinced that a broad usage awaited transistors and other semi-conductor devices in defence equipment. Accordingly, the focus of government support shifted towards production refinement projects (Industrial

Preparedness Studies) designed to provide a large-scale industrial capacity for particular types . . . The influence of government procurement on invention and innovation in this industry were probably greater than the impact of the government R & D support, but the real advantages of procurement were to be found in an acceleration of the diffusion process.

Schnee (1978) makes the distinctions: 'Whereas military demand accelerated the advance of transistorized component technology, the US space programme was dominant in accelerating the development of integrated circuit technology'. Concerning computer applications:

> The MIT Instrumentation Laboratories served as NASA's prime contract for this project (Apollo Guidance Computer). Twenty-two different component manufacturers participated in the procurement process for the Apollo Guidance Computer. Several of these firms worked with MIT's Instrumentation Laboratories for seven or eight years although their components were never purchased by NASA. The firms remained potential suppliers for such a long period because of the learning experience generated by NASA's demanding technical specifications.

Aspects of the US Procurement Policies

In order to stimulate innovation in the electronics industry, the US government used various instruments, such as financial support for R & D and procurement incentives, and it created a general climate favourable to innovation. The mix of these three instruments was the most important reason for the success of the project. Direct R & D subsidies were given, and companies were sure to find a willing purchaser. Companies even funded several times as much R & D support as from the Department of Defense, due to the fact that the government considerably reduced uncertainty at the demand side. This is stressed by all authors on this subject.

The US government clearly articulated their interest in electronics improvement, without specially detailing that the IC was the means to accomplish the desired ends. This articulation was persistent, public, and punctuated by support of various candidate programmes which, in hindsight, never succeeded but contributed to the groundswell that ultimately materialized in the IC innovation. The Department of Defense and NASA purchased large quantities of components, directly or indirectly via the procurement of systems. In some years, half the industrial output of certain components was bought by the government. Altogether, the US government created a conducive environment for product innovations at the beginning of the product lifecycle, although it had no direct contribution to inventions. Because of the quantity it purchased, it enabled industry to take advantage of the 'learning economics' or the 'dynamic economics of scale' in the manufacturing phase, a phenomenon occurring particularly in the early phases of the product's lifecycle.

It should be noted that a major part of the Department of Defense's success in influencing the civilian market was due to the following facts: (1) components for the civilian market were similar and could be produced in a similar way; (2) the nature of the manufacturing process enabled companies to achieve the dynamic economies of scale; (3) the hesitating and even conservative industrial market was convinced by the fact that the Department of Defense and NASA were using components and systems in their spectacular projects which received great publicity.

Production and Design in the Metal Industry (ICAM and ICAD)

Some years ago, the US government went a step further. According to the US Airforce, it was considered a vital aspect of national security that the most advanced production techniques were diffused in the US metal industry. The US Airforce included in its procurement contracts the so-called 'technology utilization clause', in other words, supplier companies would have to use certain ways of manufacturing. This has been applied especially to numerical control of manufacturing processes, and it speeded up diffusion considerably. Based on the same philosophy, the US Airforce is now spending $75 million on demonstration projects concerning computer-aided manufacturing — a programme called Integrated Computer Aided Manufacturing (ICAM). Another programme has also been initiated quite recently — Integrated Computer Aided Design (ICAD). Two explicitly mentioned objectives are pursued: (1) to obtain better military equipment; and (2) to improve the efficiency of US industry in the long run. Against the background of the US anti-trust tradition especially it is interesting to note that, in order to accomplish the diffusion of a new technology, the following aspects are usually part of the contracts: (a) more than one supplier has to be involved; (b) traditional industries have to be involved; (c) one or more universities should participate in the project. Accountants and management consultants, sent by the Airforce, evaluate potential suppliers concerning their financial situation and management capacities. Two man-weeks for an initial small contract are normal. In this expensive way a whole range of potential suppliers are screened in a short time, and companies with an innovative attitude are preferred. These practices are not only found in ICAM and ICAD programmes, they are nowadays used in a great number of other military contracts.

France: 'La Péri-informatique'

During the 1950s and 1960s the French central government intervened in a number of high technology sectors at the level of private industry, as part of national plans. The plans generally included large direct subsidies for research, reorganization of a particular industrial sector, protection of the home market, various kinds of favourable financial arrangements and guaranteed public sector procurement. The rationale for these interventions was technological autonomy in relation to national prestige. One of the sectors in which the French government intervened is the electronics industry, in particular the computer industry. It is beyond the scope of this book to describe all these interventions in detail, so we shall only deal with a quite recent intervention in the computer industry concerning the *péri-informatique*, that is, all computer equipment except the central processing unit. We feel this intervention is rather characteristic for the present French situation.

The objectives of the French government are more or less similar to those mentioned in previous cases. First of all, a country like France, trying to establish a knowledge-intensive industry cannot allow itself to have an increasing deficit on the trade balance for these knowledge-intensive products. According to the overall industrial strategy France should be a net exporter (PIF, 1976). Secondly, due to defence and space contracts, American enterprises are on the frontier of technological development, which gives them an advantage. These factors make it almost impossible for French industry to either enter the market or to survive under this severe competition (PIF, 1976).

Thirdly, it is said that foreign enterprises, due to their monopolistic position, can impose supply of equipment which does not exactly fit the French government and other French consumers (PIF, 1976). Fourthly, the public sector market accounts for about 40 per cent of the total sales in France, and it is expected to increase. The market is dominated by foreign firms. Fifthly, the technological development in the *péri-informatique* in France, was based largely on research contracts and purchases of the French public sector. Again it was the foreign firms which took advantage of these contracts. Finally, even though it is not explicitly mentioned in PIF, the national prestige of France and efforts to establish a technological autonomy (also a military argument) are important objectives, and were used to justify previous programmes like the *Plan Calcul*. Zysman (1975) adds to this: 'Foreign firms may be less responsive to French government policy and less bound by the rules of the business game in France. For example, they may be less willing to assure stable employment and exports, two central elements of French economic policy.'

Procurement Policy

An important instrument to achieve successful governmental intervention in the market is the use of procurement policy. According to a team of the ministry for industry and research it is even vital. As justifications for public procurement policy are given (PIF, 1976): — as described before, the procurement instrument appears to be an effective means to stimulate innovations;

 - by a technological development suited to the needs of the public sector, government organizations will be able to decrease their costs, and even be able to restructure their total need for information;
 - the prevailing tendency of public sector purchasing officers is to turn to foreign companies with extensive productlines. This is a severe disadvantage for French firms. There should be a systematic consultation of all producers. Even a price which is higher than the lowest one, but which takes into account small and medium-sized enterprises, should be considered;
 - public procurement will be a demonstration of quality and thus facilitate exports, as the foreign market frequently consists of government organizations. Moreover public procurement will make it possible, by the cashflow it provides to French firms, for them to finance their exports.

In summary: the objectives of a procurement policy are: defence against imports, increase of industrial ability to produce goods for the public sector, infant industry stimulation and creation of export potential.

Suggested procedures (PIF, 1976) are:

 - both the public and private sector should be aware and take into account possibilities on the world market and settle agreements to enhance exports;
 - a systematic consultation between the public sector and French producers should be initiated. In this way producers will know and can anticipate what the government requires and the government will have a technological development in private industry better suited to its own requirements;
 - cooperative trend analyses by the public and private sector should be set up;
 - procurement policy should focus on the middle long-term planning. Through this, 'normal' depreciation is possible. In other words technical and economic obsolescence should coincide.

One way French industry and public sector are cooperating is as follows: Within the French central government every department has a *commission informatique*. The members consist of civil servants of the particular ministry and a representative of the *mission de l'informatique*. This mission is in charge of the purchase of computer equipment in French industry and is part of the general directorate for industry. It means, that industry, through the *mission de l'informatique* with its representatives in the *commission d'informatique* in every department, can have extensive knowledge of future demands of the public sector.

References

Berke, J. G. (1977), *New Direction in Public Government Policy or Procurement Policy Revisited*, Experimental Technology Incentive Programme, National Bureau of Standards.

Golding, A. M. (1978), 'The influence of government procurement on the development of the semi conductor industry in the US and Britain', paper presented to the Six Countries Programme Workshop on Government Procurement Policies and Industrial Innovation, Dublin, Eire.

Kleiman, H. S. (1977), *The US Government Role in the Integrated Circuit Innovation*, Paris, OECD.

Lamontagne, M. (1972), *A Science Policy for Canada*, report of the Senate Special Committee on Science Policy, Ottawa.

Nelson, R. R. and Winter, S. G. (1977), 'In search of a useful theory of innovation', *Research Policy*, 6.

Overmeer, W. and Prakke, F. (1978), *Government Procurement Policies and Industrial Innovation*, TNO, PO Box 215, Delft, Netherlands, December.

PIF (1976), 'La péri-informatique Française', in *Études de politique industrielle*, 14.

Prakke, F. (1974), 'The Management of the R & D Interface', doctoral thesis, MIT.

Schnee, J. E. (1978), 'Government programs and the growth of high-technology industries', *Research Policy*, 7, 2-24.

STU (1976), *Tecknikkupphandling*, statens offentliga utredningar, Stockholm.

SPRU–TNO (1977), 'The current international economic climate and policies for technical innovation', Report to the Six Countries Programme on Innovation, TNO, PO Box 215, Delft, Netherlands.

Utterback, J. M. and Murray, A. E. (1977), *The Influence of Defence Procurement and Sponsorship of Research and Development on the Development of the Civilian Electronic Industry*, Cambridge, Mass., MIT, Center for Policy Alternatives.

Wolek, F. W. (1978), 'ETIP, an experiment in experimentation', paper presented to the Six Countries Programme Workshop on Government Procurement Policies and Industrial Innovation, Dublin, Eire.

Zysman, J. (1975), 'Between the market and the state: dilemmas of French policy for the electronics industry', *Research Policy*, 3, 312.

8. GOVERNMENT REGULATIONS AND INNOVATION

INTRODUCTION

While many forms of governmental intervention in industry are essentially a recognition of a failure of the market mechanism, which gives rise to various externalities of industrial production, this is most explicitly the case with government regulations. Here, the stated objective is to minimize externalities by controlling environmental impact, improving worker health and safety, minimizing the danger sometimes inherent in the use of new products, etc. While the satisfaction of regulatory requirements might itself require some product or process innovations, regulations are rarely, if at all, formulated with the stimulation of business innovation as a primary objective.

The process of regulation and its interaction with innovation can be illustrated by reference to Figure 8.1.

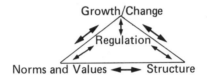

Fig. 8.1

Society's norms and values determine the rate and direction of regulation. At the same time the need for growth and/or change might well demand technological innovations. The direction of innovation (and to some extent its rate) is in turn at least partially determined by government regulations, but also by the structure of industry, society and the marketplace.

During the 1950s and the 1960s the advanced western nations enjoyed unparalleled rates of economic growth and greatly increased prosperity for most of their peoples. Social benefits increased and the quality and availability of health care improved enormously. Education, especially higher education, expanded rapidly. There was full employment with exceptionally good prospects for the highly educated. At the same time there was an abundant — and seemingly endless — supply of cheap energy (oil) and abundant and cheap raw materials for industrial production. There was widespread appreciation of the benefits derived from a thriving industry with little thought to the potential disbenefits in the form of various externalities.

From the mid-1960s to the early 1970s, however, while economic growth and general standards of living continued to increase and remained high, there was a growing awareness of the impact of rapidly intensifying industrialization on both the physical environment and the quality of life. This led to questions concerning both the 'benefits' of unrestrained economic growth and demands for more regulation of the operations of industry. Early fears about the potential dangers of new drugs following the thalidomide tragedy had already led to severe regulations being imposed on the US drug industry in 1962. From the late 1960s onwards the rate of promulgation of new regulations increased rapidly, especially in the United States. This is demonstrated for the US chemical industry in Table 8.1.

Table 8.1 Legislative milestones in chemical pollutant and product control

1906	Pure Food and Drug Act
1910	Insecticide Act
1938	Federal Food, Drug, and Cosmetic Act (FFDCA)
1947	Federal Insecticide, Fungicide and Rodenticide Act (FIFRA)
1956	Water Pollution Control Act
1962	Hazardous Substances Labelling Act
1967	Federal Hazardous Substances Act (FHSA)
The 1970s	
1970	Consumer Product Safety Act (CPSA)
1970	Occupational Safety and Health Act (OSHA)
1970	Clean Air Act (CAA)
1972	Federal Water Pollution Control Act (FWPCA)
1974	Safe Drinking Water Act (SDWA)
1976	Resource Conservation and Recovery Act (RSCA)
1976	Toxic Substances Control Act (TSCA)

Thus, from the 1950s to the mid-1960s, society's norms and values changed, resulting in an increase in the rate of promulgation of regulations – notably in the United States – often of increasing severity. During the past six or seven years, following the so-called energy crisis of 1973–4, there has been a marked reduction in the rate of growth in the world economy. This general recessionary trend has led to a decline in the quality of social and health care services in a number of advanced western countries, as well as, in some cases, a move towards decreasing the length and/or availability of higher education. Further, there now exist high levels of structural employment with lowered expectations for graduates.

Because of these factors, governments in all the advanced market economies are seeking means to increase rates of economic growth and there is a growing belief among these governments that one means of at least partially breaking out of the current recessionary cycle is via the stimulation of high rates of industrial innovation. At the same time, at least in the United States, there is a widespread acceptance both in industry and on the part of government (as evidenced in President Carter's 1979 domestic policy statement on innovation), that the current stringent regulatory climate is inimical to high rates of technological innovation. As a result, there is a growing movement in the United States in favour of de-regulation, or at least towards modifying some regulations and their method of implementation. Certainly, during the past three years of Carter's presidency, very little has happened in the United States on the regulation front. Thus we appear to see, that as the world's most advanced economy feels its world technological and economic leadership challenged and high standards of living threatened, society's norms and standards have once again changed towards a 1950s mode: the perceived benefits from industry are growing while perceived disbenefits have begun to fade a little. This will in turn affect the possibilities for, and acceptance of, technological innovations.

Within EEC Europe, the situation is rather different and, generally speaking, neither the rate of promulgation of regulations nor their severity have, in the past, been as great as within the United States. There is, however, evidence to suggest that the member countries of the EEC are undergoing a 'catching-up' process, and a number of rather severe regulations relating to the chemical industry and to product liability are currently in the legislative pipeline.

The question is, of course, just what impact does regulation have on determining the rate and direction of innovation? How important is regulation in relation to a myriad other factors affecting the technological innovation process? If regulation is important, what can governments do to mitigate possible adverse impacts and to encourage potentially positive ones? The remainder of this chapter discusses evidence — taken, mainly, from the United States — that throws some light on these points. The data are taken from a recent report to the Six Countries Programme and to the National Science Foundation (Rothwell, 1979).

INFLUENCE OF REGULATION ON INDIVIDUAL INNOVATION PROJECTS

During the past two decades there have been a number of detailed studies of the innovation process covering a variety of industry sectors and countries (Rothwell, 1977). Most of these studies, however, have concentrated more or less exclusively on factors endogenous to the firm in attempting to explain innovative success or failure; that is they have considered the innovation process more or less exclusively from the point of view of what managers have — or have not — done and have by and large neglected external factors such as the role of government.

There have been some exceptions to this pattern, notably in the United States, where several studies have looked in some detail at, among other things, the impact of regulation on the industrial innovation process. In this section these studies will be reviewed in order to assess the role that regulation has played in stimulating — or retarding — *individual innovation projects*, which can have important implications for government policy.

Gerstenfeld (1977) studied the efforts of performance regulation on the direction of innovation in eleven industry sectors in the United States. The study included a total of 107 projects, 68 successful and 39 unsuccessful. Gerstenfeld found that performance regulation was cited as an influencing factor in 44 per cent of successful innovations and in 25 per cent of unsuccessful innovations. However, in only ten cases (seven successful, three unsuccessful) was government regulation a *primary* factor in the innovation (in other words, the innovation was a *direct* response to a government action). In a further 29 cases (23 successful, six unsuccessful), government regulation was a *secondary* factor in the innovation (in other words, it shaped the development of the innovation and management decisions).

The type of regulation which appeared most frequently was safety (this factor was an important stimulant for innovation for eleven of the 39 innovations in which government regulation was a factor), and this affected innovations mainly in textiles, shoes, and wood and wood products. Pollution was cited as the next most important regulation affecting innovation (in eleven of the 39 affected innovations), and this appeared in industries such as pulp and paper, chemicals and food processing (that is, three-process industries).

Thus, Gerstenfeld found that government regulation was most often a secondary, as opposed to a primary, factor affecting innovation; that while government regulation was often in the background, it clearly affected the shape and direction of innovation. Further 'one can no doubt conclude that regulation can be a doube-edged sword. As new products and processes are evaluated, management must now carefully consider regulatory requirements along with their previous criteria of cost and performance. Some innovations are encouraged (in fact necessitated), while others are thwarted'.

Finally, Gerstenfeld did not find any different effects when considering the size of the innovating firm. Thus 'One cannot conclude that government performance regulations affect larger or smaller firms in differing amounts'.

Allen *et al.* (1978) studied the influence of government policy on the conduct and outcome of 164 innovations (66 successes, 51 failures, 47 on-going) in five industry sectors in Europe and Japan. Their results showed, perhaps surprisingly, that while none of the policies directly aimed at stimulating innovation had any relation to performance, regulatory constraints, not directly aimed at stimulating innovation (mostly environmental and safety), were related to performance (a factor of 15.2 per cent of successful projects and in only 2.0 per cent of unsuccessful projects). It appears that government regulation afforded a very high priority to the project, since Governmental requirements for entering or remaining in a market affect a large proportion of sales; often one hundred per cent. Thus, in effect, government regulation *demands* innovation, and can lead to the speedy allocation of relatively large resources to solve an often highly specified problem, which enhances the likelihood of a successful outcome.

According to the authors, the technology for accomplishing innovation to meet product safety, pollution, etc., was often readily available. The only reason these improvements had not been introduced prior to the new regulation was because the dimension of safety or reduced pollution was not seen by the engineer as a critical dimension in his problem. Government regulatory action, however, re-ordered priorities among dimensions, and once long-neglected dimensions were given some importance, a reservoir of technology could be tapped, which allowed fairly rapid improvement.

The influence of regulation on innovation was by no means evenly spread across the five sectors studied. It was a factor in 18.2 per cent of the 44 industrial chemicals projects, and in 35.7 per cent of the 28 automobile projects. It figured in none of the computer ($N = 30$), consumer electronics ($N = 32$) or textiles ($N = 30$) projects.

In a study of innovation among 32 suppliers to automobile manufacturers in the United States, Rubenstein and Ettlie (1979) looked both at factors which acted as barriers to innovation, and at those which facilitated innovation. Their results are summarized in Tables 8.2 and 8.3. It can be seen that the most important barrier to innovation was a federal law or regulation:

> This barrier acted in a variety of ways. Changes in regulation or procedure required adjustment on the part of the suppliers. The uncertainty of the regulatory climate or vacillation of the government's position caused many problems for suppliers in focussing development efforts and setting priorities for projects. In five of the cases in this category firms had difficulty in meeting federal standards. Many firms developed products in one area (e.g. energy) also recognized the need to meet other federal standards (e.g. noise).

Similarly, the most important single facilitator to innovation was a federal law or regulation: 'A federal law or regulation concerning safety, the environment (usually

Table 8.2 Categorization of barriers to innovation

Barrier	Number of innovations in which barrier acted	Percentage (n = 32)
1. Federal law or regulation	15	46.9
2. Cost	14	43.8
3. Technical reliability	14	43.8
4. Market considerations	8	25.0
5. Maintain integrity of vehicle	8	25.0
6. Lack of adequate testing procedure	7	21.9
7. Lack of top management support	4	12.5
8. Change in manufacturing process required	3	9.4
9. Lack of federal interest or competence	3	9.4

Table 8.3 Categorization of facilitators to innovation

Facilitator	Number of innovations in which facilitator acted	Percentage (n = 32)
1. Federal law or regulation	14	43.8
2. Challenge and incentive of solving a pressing problem	13	40.6
3. Recognition of market potential	10	31.1
4. Direct government R & D or grant	6	18.8
5. Technological capability of supplier	5	15.6
6. Federal procurement policy	4*	12.5
7. Availability of federal information	4**	12.5
8. Government financial incentives	3**	9.4

Source: Rubenstein and Ettlie (1979)
* Only two firms reported this facilitator
** Only one firm reported this facilitator

an emission standard) or energy (usually fuel economy) stimulated development or adoption of a particular innovation.'

Rubenstein and Ettlie (1979) also discussed the impact of the content of the regulation:

> The specificity of these mandates varied greatly. Some just set performance standards, others set standards and specified the means or methods by which these standards are to be met. There appears to be a trade-off between the type of facilitation that results from these two types of mandate. On the one hand, very specific regulation or law focuses development efforts on a particular component or process but on the other hand it may retard development of an alternative and, perhaps, better solutions to the problem addressed by the mandate . . . In addition one regulation was changed in response to an application of a new technology.

Finally, a study by Gellman Research Associates (Feinman and Fuentevilla, 1976) which looked at 500 major innovations in a variety of industries in five countries during the period 1953-73 considered, among other things, the key elements in the process of innovation. Their results indicated that 'government regulation' was only a minor factor in the innovation process. However, since 78 per cent of these innovations were introduced onto the market prior to 1968, and since it is really during the 1970s that the pace of legislation began to accelerate, and its impact began to be felt on a large scale (outside pharmaceuticals), it is not surprising that government regulation figures minimally as a key factor in innovation.

A number of studies have also looked explicitly at regulation as a barrier to innovation. One such, an NSF-sponsored study carried out by Arthur D. Little Inc. (1973), looked at barriers to innovation as perceived by 24 firms in a variety of industries in the United States. The results of their study showed that three of the eight groups of 'barrier factors' to business innovation related to aspects of government regulatory action; patents, anti-trust and other regulations. If the sample of firms chosen is at all representative of US industry generally, then these results indicate a very high level of *perception* within the US of government regulatory action posing a significant barrier to industrial innovation.

A second major NSF-sponsored study, this time undertaken by the Denver Research Institute (Boucher *et al.*, 1976), focused on the impact of EPA regulatory action on innovation in industry. The study, based on detailed interviews in 41 organizations representing both the industry and non-industry points of view, identified fourteen barrier categories relating to EPA regulations. In order of importance, these categories were:

(1) Regulatory time pressures leading to non-optimal innovations;
(2) Prohibitively high costs of complying with regulations;
(3) Unclear scope or implications of regulations;
(4) Delays by the agency in promulgating guidelines required by the law;
(5) Inability or unwillingness of agency to modify regulations in view of altered circumstances;
(6) Disagreement within the agency about the application and meaning of regulations;
(7) Inconsistency over time in the agencies application of regulations;
(8) Inability of firm to develop or allocate the resources necessary to comply with regulations;
(9) Conflicts and inconsistencies between regulations;
(10) Inability of firm to meet prescribed deadlines in regulation;
(11) Lack of mechanism within the agency for explaining regulations;
(12) Lack of effective appeal procedure;
(13) Differential treatment by the agency of the entities affected by the regulations;
(14) Unwillingness of the agency to explain regulations.

An important positive aspect to emerge from this study was a belief that innovation in process technologies made to comply with EPA regulations has led to greater productivity for some firms. 'Difficulties' created by the EPA often function as incentives for industry to innovate; regulations *force* companies, albeit not necessarily the target companies, to innovate in pollution control and in production processes, resulting in more efficient production processes.

It was also concluded that: 'There was a general agreement that EPA regulations impose considerable *indirect* barriers to innovation. These arise primarily from the need to divert management, engineering, capital and energy resources in order to comply with the regulations.'

Finally, Gerstenfeld (1978), found that one of the major causes of the apparent technical backwardness of the US construction industry was the US (state) regulatory process:

> A cumbersome regulatory process exists which relies upon local standards in the materials, design, performance and safety characteristics of residential structures. Local regulations may mean that potentially profitable regulations in one area are illegal in another location. This obviously reduces the scale at which an innovation can be marketed. . . . This obviously inhibits research and development by suppliers of building materials and capital equipment. . . .

Thus, Gerstenfeld found that regulation was a significant barrier to construction-related innovations. Furthermore, since the severity and nature of regulation varied from one local authority to the next, the magnitude of the 'innovation barrier' (or more correctly in this area the innovation diffusion barrier) varied also. This is illustrated in the differential acceptance rates Gerstenfeld found for the following four innovations in different localities.

(1) The first innovation is the provision for using 2 X 3 inch (50 to 75 mm) instead of 2 X 4 inch (50 to 100 mm) studs in non-load-bearing interior partitions.
(2) The second is the provision for placing studs 24 inches (600 mm) apart instead of 16 inches (400 mm) apart in such partitions. The wider placement of the studs reduces the wood required in such partitions by 33 per cent and concomitantly reduces the labour required for such partitions.
(3) The third innovation is the use of preassembled drain, waste, and ventilating systems instead of the onsite assembly of these components. This innovation reduces the demand for skilled labour.
(4) The fourth innovation is the use of non-metallic (chiefly plastic) sheathed cable for electrical wiring systems instead of metal conduit. This system is cheaper, easier to install, and reduces the skill requirement for electricians and thus labour inputs.

Over a wide range of authorities Gerstenfeld found that, because of regulations, 29 per cent did not allow innovation (1), 47 per cent did not allow innovation (2), 47 per cent did not allow innovation (3), and 31 per cent did not allow innovation (4). It is clear from the evidence presented above that regulation is only one of many factors influencing the innovation process. Nor is it by any means always the most significant factor, although its relative importance varies from sector to sector (that is, high in chemicals, automobiles and textiles; low in computers and consumer electronics). Certainly, in some areas there is strong evidence to suggest that the impact of regulation on 'business' innovation is *indirect* rather than direct. It is, however, significant, according to the findings of Allen *et al.* (1978), that in Europe and Japan at least, regulation had a greater impact on innovation other than government measures which were formulated specifically to facilitate innovation in industry.

A second point to emerge is that regulation *forces* innovation, although not necessarily 'business' innovation designed to offer the firm a comparative advantage in the marketplace. It seems that this element of necessity affords the project high priority, with consequently a relatively high resource allocation. This, coupled with the high specificity of the mandate, enhances the project's probability of success. It is important to note, however, that Allen *et al.* (1978) found regulation to be associated with successful innovation even after the cases in which innovation was required to comply were subtracted (that is, when the regulation-forced cases were removed) from the universe of cases. That is, the *indirect* effects of regulation on innovation were in some instances found to be positive. On the other hand, a number of instances have been quoted which show that regulation can also act as a significant *barrier* to industrial innovation.

There appear to be two main areas of impact through regulation on the firm. The first is that the very existence of a regulation adds to the firm's costs and causes an often unwelcome diversion of technical and management resources away from business innovation.* The second is administrative, and relates to problems of uncertainty, of too little time available to find optimum solutions and lack of information, etc. These issues will be dealt with in more detail below.

REGULATION AND THE RATE AND DIRECTION OF TECHNICAL CHANGE

While the main purpose of regulation is not the stimulation of technological innovations, nevertheless many regulations are formulated that are designed to bias technological development along preferred paths. Also, while regulations can make impossible innovations which were planned disregarding them, alternative technical routes can open up just because of these regulations. Thus, it is possible that regulation can affect the direction and also the pace of technical change, and this section offers evidence for these·effects in the pharmaceutical, chemical and automobile industries.

The regulation–technical change relationship is by no means always a simple or a direct one, and the measurement of regulatory impacts is fraught with difficulty. Before describing evidence of this relationship in the above three areas, a number of *caveats* need to be borne in mind. First, as shown above (page 122) regulation is only one — and not always the most important — factor affecting the industrial innovation process. Outside those areas where regulation has forced *specific* changes in technology, it is difficult to identify areas where the broad trend of technical change has been determined *largely* by regulation; it is extremely difficult to separate regulation effects from other factors determining the rate and direction of innovation.

Second, it is extremely difficult to separate innovations which would have occurred in the absence of regulation from those in which regulation played a part. For example, while regulation has clearly played an important role in the trend in the United States to smaller automobiles with lower rates of fuel consumption, it is reasonable to suppose that rising energy costs, energy shortages and competitive pressures would have eventually forced these changes in the absence of regulation. In this case perhaps it would be true to say that governmental regulation caused these changes to occur sooner than would otherwise have been the case, that is, affected the *rate* of innovation along these particular paths. (In the case

---

*This is not to say that compliance R & D and business R & D are *necessarily* mutually exclusive. Indeed, some firms have found that regulatory compliance can be made one criterion for successful R & D along with other goals such as maximizing profits, minimizing the use of energy, etc. Certainly firms can take advantage of regulation to offer them a comparative advance in the marketplace. Here, response to regulation becomes an important component of company strategy.

of the US automobile industry it is probably true to say that regulation has induced innovation in other areas which are socially desirable, but which simply add to the costs of the producer and have only a marginal impact on his competitiveness — passive restraints and emission standards, for example.)

A third area of uncertainty lies in the actual measurement of the rate of innovation. Clearly, if the innovative output of a particular industry cannot be measured accurately, then the impact of regulation on innovative output cannot be properly assessed.

Perhaps more has been written about the effects of regulation on the rate of innovation in pharmaceuticals than in any other single sector of industry, and much that has been written has focused on the impact of the 1962 Kefauver–Harris Amendments to the US Food, Drug and Cosmetics Act.* As Ashford, Butler and Zolt (1977) have pointed out, however:

> While the 1962 Amendments represent the major stimulus to changes brought about by regulatory action, the Amendments have been implemented in an evolving fashion since 1962 and policy and agency practice are changing all along. Thus, the 'signals' seen by the pharmaceutical industry are constantly changing. It is, therefore, simplistic to regard the analysis of regulation-response as a single cause and effect task.

While it is necessary to bear in mind this *caveat*, it is nevertheless true to say that most analyses of the effects of regulation on innovation in the US drug industry have treated the 1962 Amendments as a watershed, true or not. According to Peltzman (1973), for example, the 1962 Amendments significantly reduced the flow of New Chemical Entities (NCEs), and furthermore all the observed differences between the pre- and post-1963 NCE flows could be attributed to the 1962 Amendments.

Figure 8.2 shows the number of new pharmaceutical products and new chemicals introduced in the United States between 1948 and 1975. It demonstrates a marked decrease in both quantities during the 1960s, but indicates that this decrease began *before* the introduction of the Kefauver–Harris Amendments in 1962 (Steward, 1977). Figure 8.3 presents comparable data for the United Kingdom which also indicate a decline in total pharmaceutical products and in new single chemicals beginning about 1960. Steward has also presented data which show that the decline in new pharmaceutical chemical introduction is a *global* phenomenon, and that this decline, in fact, began around 1960 (Figure 8.4).

Thus, it would appear from this evidence that the Kefauver–Harris Amendments were not the only factor in causing a decline in pharmaceutical innovations in the United States, but that the decline was part of a broader, underlying phenomenon which was operating worldwide. Comparison between Figures 8.3 and 8.4 does show, however, that the *rate* of decline was very much sharper in the United

---

*Following the thalidomide tragedy the US Congress passed the Kefauver–Harris Amendments to the Food Drug and Cosmetics Act in 1962. This extended the mandate and regulatory control of the FDA in several ways:

— it required firms to provide documented scientific evidence on a new drug's efficiency in addition to the proof-of-safety required by the original law.
— it gave the FDA, for the first time, discretionary power over the clinical research process. Thus, prior to any tests on human beings, firms are now required to submit a new drug investigational plan (IND) giving the results of animal tests and research protocols for human tests.

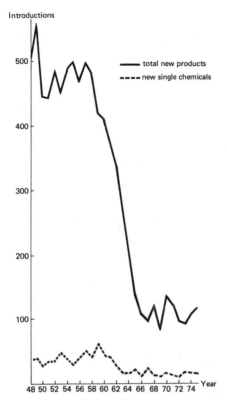

Fig. 8.2 United States – pharmaceutical products introduced 1948–75. Source: De Haen, *New Products Index* taken from Steward (1977).

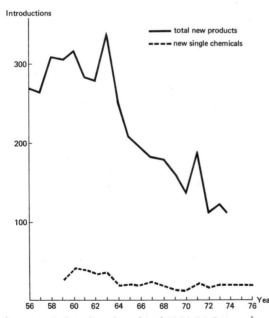

Fig. 8.3 U.K. pharmaceutical products introduced 1956–76. Source: Steward (1977).

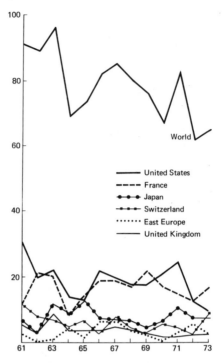

Fig. 8.4   Introduction of new drugs 1961-73 by nationality of innovating firm. Source: Steward (1977)

States than in the United Kingdom, which might be taken to indicate the added impact in the United States of the 1962 Amendments.

It is not only the *quantity* of new drugs which is important, but also their *quality*, that is, their therapeutic significance. Thus, Steward (1977) states:

> Although, in commercial terms, a high rate of innovation may be desirable, and a decline is to be deplored, in terms of broader health consideration what is more important is the therapeutic significance and character of innovation rather than simply the rate.

Figure 8.5 shows the annual approval of new drugs by degree of therapeutic gain in the United States between the years 1950 and 1973. It shows that while there was a general downward trend for drugs with modest gain and little or no gain, the 1962 Amendments had little impact on the rate of introduction of drugs offering an important gain. From the point of view of the innovating firm, of course, it might be that the latter category of drugs are the more difficult to produce in terms of R & D expenditure, while the others represented the 'cream' on the sales cake. If this is true, it could mean that in the long-term less cash will be available for fundamental research into future high-therapeutic gain drugs.

What is interesting about Figure 8.5 is that it shows a marked decrease in new introductions for all three classes of drug between 1966 and 1969. This might represent the true impact of the 1962 Amendments taking into account the lead times inherent in new drug development.

Ashford, Butler and Zolt (1977) have offered two alternative explanations to

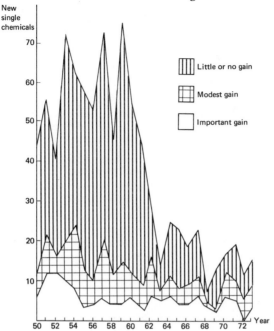

New single chemicals

Little or no gain

Modest gain

Important gain

Fig. 8.5   United States — annual approvals of new drugs by degree of therapeutic gain 1950–73.
Source: Steward (1977)

that emphasizing the impact of the 1962 Amendments concerning the decline in pharmaceutical innovation in the United States during the 1960s:

(1) The increasing scientific difficulties inherent in finding new drugs for the diseases which are receiving attention.
(2) Market distortions traceable to government involvement of a non-regulatory nature in the pharmaceutical area, for example, government research and the utilization of technical manpower.

Concerning point (1), Peltzman (1977) questions whether the major drug discoveries of the 1940s and 1950s exhausted the promise of drug research; whether there may be no undiscovered potential drugs for the remaining unconquered diseases. He also points out that the areas of disease currently receiving attention such as arthritis and arteriosclerosis are intrinsically more difficult.

Bearing the above arguments in mind it is likely, as Steward (1977) states, that:

The lengthening of the R & D process and the decline in introduction reflects a combination of more stringent requirements on safety and efficacy, increasing difficulty in drug discovery and a rise in the costs of research. It is difficult to separate these influences.

Nevertheless, stringent regulations in the United States have clearly affected both the rate and direction of pharmaceutical innovation there.

In a novel approach to determining the impact of regulation on the *nature* — as opposed to the rate — of innovation, Ashford and Heaton (1979) looked at the changes induced by regulation in both products and processes produced by 'rigid' and 'fluid' production segments in the US chemical industry.* Thus, they allow for technological response variations which differ according to the nature of the underlying production technology in use by different segments of the regulated industry. A number of their more interesting findings are:

— there was a strong relationship between the type of regulation and the nature of the technological response, which leads to the conclusion that the characteristics of the existing technology largely determine the nature of the compliance technology. This conclusion was strengthened by the fact that technological responses for firms within a given productive segment were highly uniform;
— a number of important innovative responses arose from new entrants to the industry, whose entry was a direct result of the opportunities created by the new regulations;
— most responses were developed over a relatively short period of time; they were relatively non-novel and in a late stage of development, thus requiring only moderate development to achieve compliance;
— only a very few examples could be found of regulation-induced radical technologies, and these arose in areas outside the regulated segment. In most cases they were unsuccessful;
— since compliance responses in rigid segments were often as novel as those in fluid segments, it appears that regulation can alter the overall character of innovation in rigid industries, particularly when the regulatory impact on the rigid segment is potentially very great.

These results are interesting in that they show that, in the US chemical industry at least, regulation rarely leads to the development of radical new technologies and that most technological responses to regulation are not novel, but relate closely to the technology currently in use or in development. Nevertheless, regulation, while not resulting in novel, new technologies, did have the effect of guiding existing technologies along certain preferred paths.

As regards the automobile industry, the US Office of Technology Assessment (1978) offered the following list of major technological developments in the US automobile industry expected by 1985, which will be brought about mainly in response to regulation:

— downsizing programmes will reduce the average size and weight of the vehicle fleet. Waste space from styling and image requirements will be greatly reduced;
— material substitution — greater use of lightweight materials such as aluminium, plastics and high-strength low-alloy steels — will further reduce vehicle weight;
— changes in vehicle layout, such as front-wheel drive, will allow further size and weight reduction;
— additional improvements in fuel economy will be achieved by improvements in transmission and drive-chain efficiency and by reduced power requirements for accessories. The application of electronic controls for fuel metering and ignition will help the engine maintain efficient performance and reduce the need for tune-ups;

*Ashford and Heaton utilize the concept of *technological rigidity*, which is a continuum that has at one extreme evolving (fluid) product lines and uncoordinated production technologies, and at the other extreme mature, commodity-like products and highly integrated cost-effective production technologies (rigid). A group of firms, or units within firms that employ a particular technology (for example, all the firms that polymerize vinyl chloride), are termed a productive segment.

— several new or refined engines may be widely offered: diesels (several now offered); stratified charge (now offered by Honda); single-chamber stratified charge (under development by Ford, GM and Texaco); valve selector (expected on the market by 1980) and turbocharging (now offered by GM and Ford); These engines will afford greater fuel economy and/or reduced emissions;

— vehicle safety will be improved by the addition of passive restraint. However, the decrease in vehicle size may offset these gains unless additional crashworthiness is designed into small cars. Advanced propulsion technologies (such as Stirling and turbo-engines) and electric vehicles will not significantly penetrate the market by 1985;

— most of the actual or proposed regulation-induced changes discussed above have been brought about by environmental and worker health and safety (EWHS) type regulations.

Thus, regulations are clearly both stimulating innovations in the US automobile industry, and to a large extent shaping the direction these innovations will take; since most regulations impose a time-limit for compliance, they are affecting the rate of innovation as well. Further, since the United States is now a large market for foreign-built automobiles, US regulations are influencing car design in Europe and Japan as well as in the United States itself.

Finally, regulation is likely to have a number of subtle effects on technological change in that it helps to create the general climate in which researchers and designers operate. Thus, for example, product liability regulation will generally bias designers towards safer products and, in the longer term, this will become an accepted part of 'design culture' rather than be seen as a direct response to regulation.

THE REGULATION FORMULATION AND IMPLEMENTATION PROCESS

There appear to be a whole range of problems associated with the process of regulation formulation and implementation, which can cause a great deal of uncertainty in industry, particularly with regard to the development of new and improved products and processes. Two problems which, in particular, cause a great deal of concern to managers relate first to the competence of regulatory bodies to set realistic and meaningful standards and to ·operate them efficiently and, second, to the competence of these bodies to properly assess the impact of their activities on industry.

According to Schweitzer (1977), the US regulatory agencies are generally ill-equipped to analyse a broad spectrum of possible impacts, especially secondary and delayed impacts. They do not possess the technical expertise to enable them properly to assess regulatory impacts on technological progress. What assessments they do undertake relating to technology are generally of short-term perspective, and based largely on the testimonies of interested parties.

Lack of technical expertise within regulatory agencies can also result in inflexibility towards changed circumstances. This is because those responsible for regulations often have difficulty in recognizing what the changed circumstances are — in other words, they do not always fully understand the implications for, for example, environmental regulations of major changes in technology and technique. Thus, they tend to play safe and adhere to unnecessarily severe, or inappropriate, regulations.

Williams (1977) points to similar problems in the operations of the Occupational Safety and Health Administration (OSHA) in the USA:

> Employer criticisms of OSHA have included demands for more precise standards. Further, by 1976, the (OSHA) implement programme involving the states was said to be 'in a shambles', only 23 states having, even after 5 years, had their plans approved. The original consensus standards were not widely recognised as needing revision . . . and OSHA's head acknowledged a 'pressing need' for more and better compliance officers . . . In the case of the National Institute for Occupational Safety and Health, two quotations well illustrate the general tone of the criticisms directed at the organisation:
>
> — There are no deliberate attempts to formulate any kind of research policy based on real problems in the workplace. They don't bring input from labour into the design of their research projects.
> — They have a lot of deadwood and meaningless programmes . . . Their hazard evaluation programme is a total failure. The evaluations they do are meaningless . . . All they do is measure how close companies come to TLVs. And when they get important information they sit on it without alerting anyone.

Thus, there are clearly very real problems associated with the expertise of regulatory agencies in both administering regulations, and in assessing their impact on industry. Another serious problem for industry is the lack of clarity in certain regulations or in the means mandated by the regulatory agency by which they should be met. A further problem, particularly with environmental regulations, is that they are sometimes seen by industry to be too broad in scope in that they are made to apply to an entire industry and make no allowances for differences in the local environments in which different plants operate. For example, a plant located on a polluted river and serving an urban area has different problems from a plant located on a clean lake in a rural area.

If standards are too stringent, then this can also create severe problems for industry. Certainly there seems to be evidence to suggest that in the area of pharmaceuticals a number of new chemical entities, which promised benefits to mankind, have been abandoned by firms because of the high cost of meeting seemingly over-stringent regulations.

Having said this, it is true to say that industry, especially in the United States, has repeatedly claimed that particular regulatory requirements were unrealistic or unattainable, but has nevertheless subsequently met them. An example of this is the US automobile industry's opposition to the passive restraint (airbags) rule which was based initially on the technical difficulties involved in compliance. The argument that meeting the standard was 'not reasonable or practicable' was rejected in an early court case on the matter, which decision was vindicated when General Motors began to market airbag-equipped cars in 1974. As most of the technical difficulties were solved, the industry's arguments shifted to economic problems and emphasized the cost of airbags relative to seatbelts and the effects of consequent price increases on sales and on employment. (It is interesting to note that while General Motors have offered airbags, the public has shown a marked reluctance to buy them.)

A number of experts have suggested that one means of overcoming many of the problems associated with lack of technical expertise on the part of the regulator is to employ lay experts in the regulation formulation process. Gabrowski and

Vernon (1976) have discussed this issue when comparing the US system of drug regulatory control with that followed in the United Kingdom. They offered the following quotation by Sir Derrick Dunlop, who was for many years the head of the British drug licensing system:

> The main difference between the two systems is that ultimate power to license medicines in the UK rests with the Licensing Authority (the Minister responsible to Parliament) acting on the professional advice of the Safety Committee. The decisions of these Committees are taken by professional men whose careers in no way depend on their membership of the committees on which they serve part-time in a virtually honorary capacity as an altruistic chore. They are assisted, of course, by a small staff of expert professional civil servants who do most of the preparatory work, but the decisions are taken by the committees. It is probable that the experience gained from the eight years' informal Safety of Drugs Committee will tincture their subsequently official actions.
>
> In the United States, on the other hand, ultimate power rests with the full-time professional civil servants of the FDA whose careers depend on the correctness of their decisions, and who are subject to formidable grillings by Congressional Committees. The FDA has to work under fairly rigid rules by Congress which seem to rely more on animal experiments than is usual in the UK.

Gabrowski and Vernon suggest that the greater use of external professional advice in the United Kingdom has produced a regulatory incentive structure less prone to bias in the direction of caution and delay, a regulatory system with shorter review times and lower development costs than has recently been the case in the United States. Whether in the long term the British systems acts to the greater benefit of society is a matter for both debate and further analysis.

There does, however, seem little doubt that regulation can, and often does, add a substantial element of uncertainty to the operations of would-be innovators. This uncertainty can derive from a variety of sources: unclear regulations; rapidly changing regulation; inconsistencies between local and national regulations; the creation of a general climate of uncertainty. Manners and Nason (1979) have addressed this issue in some detail:

> No one can really estimate the extent of pejoration in technological innovation induced by the uncertainty of today's regulatory climate. Nevertheless, it is the fourth most frequently articulated outcome of regulation. The outcome is observed simply as a reduced tendency to take risks. The tendency is *factual* both in an overall business sense and in the innovative sense. It is observable in reduced R & D, in the shifts within R & D, in the patent records, in the new incorporation records, in mergers and takeovers of established firms and in the current assets on corporate balance sheets. Is regulatory uncertainty the primary culprit? The authors feel that regulation per se, is the primary culprit in the above trends but that the uncertainty component is the catalyst in the actual *willingness* to take risks.
>
> The nature of regulatory uncertainty is manifested by both intra-agency ambiguity and inter-agency ambiguity, the latter being the most significant. As to intra-agency ambiguity, one only has to read the wording of the Delaney Amendment and observe the constant shifts in interpretation to understand the effect on risk-taking. Whole plants now stand empty, and significant new products have been taken off the market simply because an agency changed its

position. The effect of EPAs shifts in enforcement (i.e. 'old' pollution versus 'new' pollution) or of Congress shifting extent of enforcement, are not designed to aid prediction of the future. The possibility of loss of proprietory information through regulatory compliance can have a significant impact on risk-taking. Would one want to plan where to perform R & D with Treasury Regulation 1.861–8 hanging around unsettled?

Probably the greatest contemporary example of intra-agency uncertainty in the US is the problem presented by the Toxic Substances Control Act of 1976 (TSCA). TSCA 'can' regulate the input (raw materials) to a production process and 'can' regulate output including intermediates, products, by-products and co-products (i.e. potentially everything). The initial inventory of chemical substances being compiled will run from 50 000 to 70 000. EPA will require a premanufacturing notification 90 days before planned manufacture and the Act further requires data to demonstrate 'no unreasonable risk' to health or environment. Given this ambiguity it is not too surprising that an Arthur D. Little study estimated that TSCA will cut chemical introductions by 50%.

It is, however, the problems presented by inter-agency ambiguity that really impact on US innovative tendencies. Although a definite count is seemingly impossible, it is safe to say that there are over 80 federal agencies that regulate private enterprise from a tremendous number of directions (5000 regulations issued by 27 agencies in the steel industry alone). There are more than 20 federal laws that cover the regulation of chemicals. Four separate agencies operate from four separate policies relative to cancer. (The reader must remember that delay was our primary impact category when interpreting these numbers. Our intention at this point is to underscore the effects on uncertainty.) The musical chairs played by the personnel occupying policy positions in these agencies only magnifies the ambiguity. In addition, to the extent innovation still occurs. . . which it does . . . the threat of patent protection is next. (The chances are 6 out of 10 that a court will rule a patent invalid.) *Really* successful innovation will then bring the company into possible antitrust regulation or litigation, as evidenced by Dupont's titanium dioxide. Finally, one must keep an eye on product liability and third party suits.

Although it has been stated above that regulation increases the risk and uncertainty which accompany innovation decision-making, Lederman and Morrison (1979) have argued that a stable regulatory climate can reduce risk and uncertainty:

The establishment of fixed (EWHS) regulatory standards (accompanied by some assurance that they will not shortly be modified) assures a market for the product and process innovations necessary to comply with them. The assurance of continuing regulation may, in fact, provide a stimulus to product/process technological innovations not otherwise justified in the short term by market conditions, and these innovations may ultimately yield cost and resource savings which offset some or all of the initial investment cost needed to comply with the regulations. This appears to have taken place in the US pulp and paper industry. In addition, investments made initially to comply with EWHS regulations may spin off marketable goods and services.

It might be, of course, that compliance innovations are made outside of the regulated sector. Thus, the regulated sector bears the costs of compliance while the supplier sector reaps the benefits of a new market for innovative products or processes.

Finally, Lederman and Morrison (1979) conclude that:

> Unfortunately, the assurance of stable regulatory requirements is infrequently given or sustained, with the result that technological innovation to meet EWHS is often aimed at a moving target. On balance it is probable that EWHS regulations tend to increase, rather than reduce, risk and uncertainty.

This contention is most certainly borne out in the considerable literature in this field.

One of the problems touched upon earlier in this chapter was that of the speed of response of regulatory agencies to changes in circumstances (technical, economic) within regulated industries which themselves require changes in previously promulgated regulation. This so-called 'regulatory lag' can have a marked impact on firms affected by rate-of-return regulations (for a detailed discussion on this point see Capron 1971). Since the regulatory agency's response to changes in the circumstances of regulated firms is often very slow, a technological innovation which substantially reduces costs, thereby increasing its net income, allows the firm to enjoy greater profits until the agency gets around to readjusting the rate structure. On the other hand, if the net income of the regulated firm is reduced because of increased costs, it must press for a rate increase.

The point is, an often quite lengthy period can elapse between a firm requesting a rate adjustment due to higher costs, and the granting of that adjustment. Reduced cash-flow during this period might result in a fall off in R & D expenditure with a subsequent impact on the firm's innovative output. On the other hand it might stimulate firms to look for cost-reducing innovations. According to Gillette (1979) this has occurred in the US telecommunications industry:

> It is not unknown that a commission may take a year or two to decide whether a request for a rate increase is justified, and during that same one or two years, economic inflation may have continued to the point that the rate increase granted may simply return the telecommunications company to the earning position it had at the start of the proceedings. In the United States this phenomenon is called 'regulation lag' and it can force innovation. Economist Elizabeth E. Bailey has stated the proposition neatly: 'The regulated firm finds that, in a period of rising costs, its profits decline. Since the decline occurs with increases in any of the cost parameters, the firm not only has an incentive to avoid payment of inflated costs but will also seek out cost-reducing innovation.' It has certainly been my experience at Bell Telephone Laboratories that the economic pressures to meet service demands in periods of inflation has been a strong forcing function in designing equipments for lower cost services and for creating operational methods to reduce annual expenses.

Finally, innovation can be retarded when a 'lag' exists between development in industrial technology and the response of regulatory agencies to these charges. Greenberg, Hill and Newburger (1977) have discussed this when commenting on the influence of regulation on ammonia production in the United States.

COST TO INDUSTRY, INCREASING LEAD-TIMES AND
CONFIDENTIALITY

Innovation often requires quite substantial cash and manpower resources if it is
to be carried through successfully, and regulations, if they impose a severe burden
on the resources of the firm, will inevitably reduce its ability to undertake innovation endeavours. A great deal has been written concerning the costs to US industry
of Federal Regulations, and Weidenbaum (1978) has calculated that the aggregate
cost to the private sector of regulatory compliance in 1976 was $62.9 billion,
and that the estimated cost in 1979 would be $97.9 billion.

Figure 8.6 shows pollution abatement expenditure as a percentage of new plant
and equipment expenditures in US industry in 1975; the all-industry average is
6 per cent. Not surprisingly, expenditure on pollution control varies greatly between sectors, and is particularly high in the basic metals processing industry. For
example, the US copper industry in 1965 spent $1.17 million on pollution control
(1.5 per cent of total capital expenditure). In 1975 the industry spent $162 million
on pollution control (36.8 per cent of total capital expenditure). In 1965, the US
zinc industry spent $0.3 million on pollution control (2.5 per cent of total capital
expenditure): by 1975 this figure had risen to $21 million (36.3 per cent of total
capital expenditure) (Weiss, 1978).

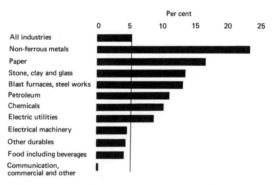

Fig. 8.6   Pollution abatement expenditures as a percentage of new plant and equipment expenditures (1975). Source: US Department of Commerce (1976)

According to Lederman and Morrison (1979), another measure of the burden
of compliance costs is the conversion of EWHS regulation-imposed dollar costs to
effects on productivity, and a recent US study has concluded that, due to regulation, the growth rate of output per unit of input in the non-residential business
sector of the economy was 0.35 per cent lower in the 1974–75 period than it
would have been under 1967 (pre-regulation) conditions.

Commenting on the problems associated with the measurement of compliance
costs, Lederman and Morrison (1979) go on to state:

Gross estimates or assertions of costs expended for compliance with EWHS
regulations may be misleading for a variety of reasons. They generally fail to
distinguish between expenditures incurred to comply with regulations and
expenditures incurred as R & D and operating expenditures for development
and production of marketable goods and services for pollution control, health
and safety monitoring, and related administrative costs. They frequently allocate

entirely to compliance cost expenditures which would have been incurred even in the absence of regulation. (As an illustration, CEQ indicates that of the $40.6 billion estimated to have been spent for pollution control in 1977, only $18.1 billion is attributable to compliance with Federal legislation. CEQ states that the remaining $22.5 billion would have been spent even in the absence of US government regulation of the environment.) Finally, these estimates of compliance costs are not reduced by savings or productivity improvement realized from changes resulting from regulation.

As an indication of the difficulties involved in estimating the likely costs to industry of new regulation, the Bureau of Medical Services (1978) received the following four estimates of the probable annual net cost to industry of good manufacturing practice regulation for the manufacture, packing, storage and installation of medical devices: $58.46 million; $31.68 million; − $19.03 million; − $3.61 million, that is, two estimates of net cost and two of net benefit to the industry.

Finally, an element of regulation-induced cost, which is perhaps less direct than those described above, is that associated with product liability, and this is of increasing importance in some areas of US industry particularly. (In the United States, in 1976, the number of product liability cases was about 70 000, which was 2.8 per cent of the entire civil case load.) Product liability insurance has increased rapidly in the United States, for example from between 100 per cent to 500 per cent in the first eleven months of 1976 depending on industry sector: in some instances claimant awards have been very high, all of which places an increasing burden on firms, especially small firms, with potentially less cash available for R & D.

Though the costs to industry of government regulation are, in some cases, clearly very considerable, there probably exists an understandable tendency on the part of industry to overestimate these costs, and to underestimate any regulation-induced benefits. (This would appear to be an area that would reward careful and independent study.) What is highly significant, however, is that all estimates of regulation-induced costs expressed as a time series, even though some may be overstated, show a marked upward trend.

One of the most widely quoted effects of regulation on innovation which can also increase costs considerably, is its impact in delaying the market launch of new products and processes through lengthening development times and, in the case of pharmaceuticals, imposing considerable additional delays in waiting for regulatory approval. According to Manners and Nason (1979):

Certainly, the most often articulated outcome of regulatory activity on the process of technological innovation can be categorized as simply delay. The data supporting this outcome are overwhelming, although the most visible and quantifiable results appear in the drug industry — which was the first sector to bear the brunt of the new regulatory *Zeitgeist* in 1962 . . . The factor of delay has been presented just as definitively in the power generation sector, the transportation sector and the chemical sector. The impact of TSCA with its 'premanufacturing notification' requirements on the delay factor in chemicals has not yet been experienced, but our opinion is that it will be at least as pernicious as any experiences in the drug industry.

Not only has pharmaceutical regulation delayed the market launch of new drugs, but the delay has become increasingly great. Garrett (1974) has offered the following figures for increasing lead times of new drugs in the USA: 1958–62; 2.5 years; 1963–67: 7 years 1968–72: $7\frac{1}{2}$–10 years. Figure 8.7 offers parallel data for lead times in the UK pharmaceutical industry. These data show that while average lead times have increased significantly between 1960 and 1975–76, there is a great deal of variation among different products. While regulation has undoubtedly had a major impact in increasing lead times for drug development in both the United States and the United Kingdom, a second significant factor might also be the increasing technical difficulty experienced in discovering new drugs suggested earlier. Separating these factors is clearly an area for careful research.

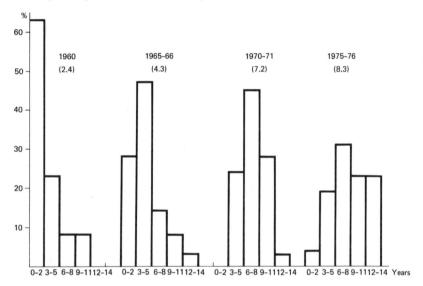

Fig. 8.7   Time from first patent or publication to UK marketing. Source: Steward (1977)

Finally in regard to drug regulation, there is evidence to suggest that, because of the greater severity of regulation in the United States important new drugs are sometimes marketed there, many years after their acceptance in other countries. Thus, Gerstenfeld (1978) states:

> Both academicians and FDA officials have acknowledged that other countries often market drugs before we do. Our source of delay has been the FDA's demand that two controlled trials be conducted in the US regardless of the number of foreign tests already completed. This seems to be little more than chauvinism (recently acknowledged by the FDA).
>
> I cite the case of volporic acid to illustrate the above point. Volporic acid is an anticonvulsant drug that has been used in Europe for decades but was only recently approved by the FDA for marketing in the US. The benefits of the drug are profound . . . Although volporic acid was already available in ten countries, the FDA required additional human subject tests, claiming that only one of the 200-odd foreign studies of volporic acid published since 1967 was fully acceptable.

In the US chemical industry much concern is currently focused on the potential of the recent Toxic Substances Control Act to significantly delay the introduction of new chemicals. This was mainly based, as Manners and Nason (1979) have suggested, on the requirement in the Act, for premanufacturing notification. It is felt that this will result in a massive backlog of new chemicals awaiting clearance and consequently long delays between development and marketing. Whether or not this fear is justified remains to be seen.

Other countries have followed suit. The EEC 'Sixth Amendment', due to be approved by the Council of Ministers will, like the US TSCA, require companies to assess the effect of new chemicals on human health and the environment before they are marketed. This has generated fears among chemical firms in Europe, as in the United States, about the likelihood of increased delays in the market introduction of important new chemicals.

A number of examples exist of the effect of regulations in delaying the market use of innovations in the area of public utilities. Gellman (1971), for example, has described how action by the ICC in the United States retarded the use of an innovative new railway grain car for four years, and Gillette (1977) has shown how lack of clear legislation has delayed the introduction of highly innovative communication systems into public use in the United States.

Of all the utilities it is, perhaps, in the area of nuclear power plant that lead times have increased most. Lester (1978) has suggested that in many cases lead times are approaching utility planning horizons, and sometimes exceeding them. He estimated current total planning lead times for nuclear power plant projects in the United States, Japan, West Germany and Canada as 12–15 years, 9–12 years, 9.7 years and 7.3 years respectively. The very long lead times in the United States reflect the very stringent regulatory requirements there. Further, not only are lead times increasing, but they are also becoming more unpredictable. Lester (1978) listed the main reasons for longer and more unpredictable lead times as:

— technical problems encountered when increasing the size of power plants;
— lack of design standardization;
— the variable economic climate of the past decade;
— the increasing number and stringency of nuclear safety and environmental regulations and the continuing fluidity of the general regulatory environment;
— more generally, an inadequate level of political consensus over what constitutes an appropriate role for nuclear energy.

Lester further states that perhaps the most important cause of increased lead times is that associated with the regulatory process. One of the more important aspects of regulatory-induced lead times — apart from greatly increased costs — is that as the period from patenting to marketing increases, so the period of effective patent protection decreases. In areas where development costs are high, this can pose a serious disincentive to invest in innovation. It is increasingly being mooted, both in the United States and in Europe, that because of the serious consequences for company profits, and for future rates of innovation, of the regulation-induced reduction in effective patent lifetimes, governments should pay urgent attention to this matter and take steps to extend patent protection periods in such cases, especially in the pharmaceutical industry.

Thus, from the evidence presented in this section, there can be little doubt that, in some areas at least, regulation has caused significant delays in the commercialization of innovations. As a result it has added significantly to innovation costs and has in some cases resulted in a decrease in the patent protection period of new products and hence reduced their potential profitability. Further, the evidence suggests that regulation-induced lags are increasing, which must inevitably result in a reduced rate of innovation in those areas affected.

In areas where innovation is liable to affect worker health and safety or the environment, it might reasonably be thought that those likely to be affected would have a 'natural right to know' about the innovation and its potential impact on them. Attitudes towards the disclosure of information on, for example, environmental issues, however, vary greatly from country to country. In the United States (with its Freedom of Information Act), and in Sweden, information is generally made readily available; in Canada and in the United Kingdom, in contrast, administrative discretion and secrecy are great, and information flow is restricted. From the point of view of society at large, the former system is undoubtedly preferable. From the viewpoint of the innovator, who might be faced with vociferous, sometimes hysterical and possibly uninformed opposition, benefits from the free flow of information are less certain.

In the US chemical industry a great deal of concern is currently being expressed about the impact on business confidentiality of the Toxic Substances Control Act. Similar concern is being expressed concerning the forthcoming Sixth Amendment within the EEC. Among the responsibilities of the Administrator under TSCA, those affecting confidentiality are:

— requiring the process industries to provide substantial business and technical information about the production, distribution, use, exposure and health environmental and ecological effects of new chemicals;
— requiring a pre-manufacturing review of new chemical substances and significant new uses.

These clearly represent a serious threat to chemical companies in protecting crucial business information concerning innovative new chemicals, and will, it is feared, pose a significant disincentive to chemical innovation in the United States.

Finally, there exists a great deal of data from the United States, and in the case of the pharmaceutical industry also from the United Kingdom, to suggest that the high cost of regulatory compliance in some areas is reducing both the level of fundamental research undertaken by industry, and the amount of R & D devoted to the generation of new products and processes (see Rothwell, 1979). In the light of the discussion in Chapter 3, which suggested the need for a new 'push' of basic innovations to carry the world economy out of the current recession, this should be viewed by governments, and particularly the US government, with a great deal of concern.

REGULATION AND SIZE OF FIRM

Throughout the literature on technological innovation and regulation the question of differential impact according to firm size continually arises. If regulations significantly alter the relative comparative advantage between small and large size firms in a particular sector, then it will affect the size distribution of firms within that sector. The impact of this structural change on industrial innovation then depends on the relative contribution large and small firms make to technological innovation. If, in a particular area, small firms are consistently more innovative than their larger counterparts, then clearly a move to larger average firm size will reduce the rates of innovation, and vice versa (see Chapter 10). Clearly in those sectors in which small firms do make a major contribution to innovation, any reduction in their numbers will affect future rates of innovation.

It is in the area of regulatory-induced cost increases that small firms are liable to be affected to a greater extent than large firms and, according to Weidenbaum (1978), government regulation tends, often unwittingly, to hit small businesses disproportionately hard.

According to Hill (1975), commenting on the chemical industry, regulation favours large chemical firms because they can spread the costs of testing to meet regulatory requirements over a large number of products. They can also influence the development of the standards in the political process. As we have seen, regulation can force innovation and, as Hill goes on to point out, if the effect of regulation is that continued profitability is dependent upon a firm innovating more than it has historically done, small firms will form larger units or leave the industry.

A related problem is that of market size. In areas such as pharmaceuticals and pesticides small specialist firms, and large firms operating in small specialized markets, are likely to be disadvantaged through government regulation. In the first case, few small firms can afford the cost of testing new drugs or pesticides (even if they succeed in meeting development costs); in the second case, the high cost of testing is likely to make small markets uneconomic.

Finally, over-stringent regulations might (and there is some limited evidence to suggest that they do) adversely affect the creation of new small firms, which would pose a barrier to the generation of new business and hence to the generation of new employment opportunities, both particularly unfortunate in today's economic climate.

THE GENERAL CLIMATE FOR INDUSTRY

It was clear from a review of the US, and in some areas the European literature, that industry, especially US industry, feels that society at large, and the legislature in particular, is becoming increasingly hostile to its operations and that this hostility manifests itself through an ever-increasing volume of regulations of increasing severity. Whether this belief is justified is, of course, a matter for debate. Nevertheless this belief *is* widespread among industrial managers in the United States who *do* feel that their freedom of action is continually being eroded.

Innovation is a risky business, the outcome of which contains a high inherent degree of uncertainty, and regulation is clearly *perceived* by managers as increasing both innovative risk and uncertainty. The financial costs to industry of regulations, the diversion of R & D resources involved in compliance, and the time taken in simply meeting the form-filling requirements of regulatory bodies all place an added and unwelcome burden on would-be innovators. Now, while regulations are absolutely necessary to the wellbeing of society, and while industry, like everyone else, must accept some controls on its conduct, over-regulation – often the result of over-reaction to specific incidents by vociferous interest groups – might, in the long term, act to the disbenefit of society. At a time of growing energy shortages and potential raw material depletion, increasing competition in traditional areas from newly industrializing nations, and high levels of unemployment in the advanced economies, innovation is of increasing importance to the maintenance of high standards of living in the advanced western nations. This is evidenced by the increasing emphasis of western governments on instigating measures to stimulate and assist industrial innovation.

Clearly if industry is to be vigorously innovative, then means must be found to protect the health and safety of workers, the interests of consumers and the welfare of society at large via regulation, while at the same time maintaining a climate that is conducive to entrepreneurship and innovative endeavour. In the United States at present this does not appear to be the case, and there are, unfortunately, indications that – at least in the eyes of industry – Europe is moving in the same direction.

IMPLICATIONS FOR GOVERNMENT POLICY

Before discussing the implications of the above regulation-related issues for government policy, it is worth while making the point that the whole area is very much a political one, with pressure groups sometimes having as much influence in determining the nature and pace of regulation as governmental agencies. Also, the adverse regulatory climate described above in the United States is not at all typical of other advanced nations: here, partly as the result of industry's vigorous reaction against regulations, the government has adopted an 'adversary' approach to regulation formulation and implementation. In Sweden, in contrast, with government, industry and society at large generally agreeing on the need for regulations there exists a 'consensus' approach. In the United Kingdom, industry and government appear to act in a rather 'hand-in-glove' manner, with little recourse to the general public, producing regulations often less stringent than their counterparts in the United States and Sweden. In Japan, where industry–government cooperation is the norm, regulations have perhaps sometimes been less rigorously implemented than in other advanced nations. Export-oriented Japanese manufacturers have, however, been quick to respond to, and even to anticipate, new regulatory requirements in other countries. Despite these national differences, it is possible to describe a number of approaches governments can take in all the advanced market economies to alleviate the possible adverse effects of regulations on industrial innovation, and possibly to utilize regulation to stimulate innovation. Several of these approaches are discussed briefly below.

Economic Incentives and Economic Assistance with Compliance

Rather than governments imposing rigid standards, which are both legally and administratively enforceable and which must be met, or absolute thresholds of performance which must not be exceeded (the case with EWHS regulations in particular) the satisfaction of which can have a high R & D resource opportunity cost, it has been suggested that economic incentives and disincentives are preferable since they provide industry with greater choice in determining how to bear regulatory-induced costs. The use of economic incentives and disincentives is essentially an attempt to promote allocative efficiency through monetary incentives; it recognizes market effects of health and safety risks and environmental damage such that producers of goods and services absorb or pass on to the consumer the social costs, as well as their private costs, of production. Examples of this approach to regulation include pollution charges, emission offsets (whereby the normally prohibited new source of pollution is permitted in exchange for a greater pollution reduction elsewhere), exchangeable or marketable pollution rights among firms or industries, non-compliance fees, negotiated discharge quotas and various proposed programmes for pollution credits and subsidies for pollution abatement granted in exchange for investment in innovative technology for changes which reduce net pollution.

It has been argued, in favour of the economic incentives approach, that because market forces will cause the most efficient allocation of resources if market costs reflect net social costs, they have a better chance of promoting economic efficiency in the use and depletion of society's resources. However, to the extent that that regulation is in support of social policy, considerations of economic efficiency are only one of many factors in the choice of a policy tool.

The instrument of pollution charges is an important part of environmental policy in, for example, the Netherlands and France. This is based on the belief that, provided these charges are correctly calculated, they will not only act as an incentive not to pollute, but will also provide the state with financial resources for further pollution control.

One important political problem with the economic incentives approach is that it might be seen as providing industry with the ability to 'buy' the right to pollute. It also has an appearance of inequality in that it seems, in particular, to provide large corporations with a licence to pollute.

Indirect incentives usually exist alongside direct methods of control, although the balance between the two varies from country to country. In France and the Netherlands, for example, pollution charges predominate. In other countries these are used only occasionally; for example, Norway imposes a tax which relates to the sulphur content of fuels (Eva and Rothman, 1979).

There are, of course, instances where regulation must of necessity take a direct form, either because certain mental, health or safety effects are unacceptable even if their social costs were paid by the institution responsible — in this case the social and economic costs to society from non-regulation below some minimum direct regulatory threshold of, for example, a very toxic substance or a carcinogen, are too high — or because the administrative mechanism necessary for implementation of the economic incentives approach may be too complex and costly.

As well as offering economic incentives not to pollute, or at least to keep pollution to a minimum, a number of governments offer economic assistance with regulatory compliance and incentives to develop non-polluting processes. The European Commission, for example, has established guidelines for governmental support of non-polluting investments, and recently the Dutch government proposed to parliament to make grants available for 15 per cent of the cost of investment in anti-pollution developments. During the five years following the establishment of the Swedish Environmental Protection Agency, it made grants available for 25 per cent of the costs of investments in anti-pollution activities.

Since 1970 the Japanese government has laid some stress on the implementation of anti-pollution measures, and has explicitly recognized that the costs of such measures can place a particularly severe burden on small and medium-sized enterprises (SMEs). The Small Business Finance Corporation and the People's Finance Corporation can offer finance to SMFs for pollution-prevention equipment. The Environmental Pollution Control Service Corporation fosters the construction of joint anti-pollution facilities among SMEs. There are also anti-pollution equipment leasing schemes for smaller firms. Other measures include tax relief and guidance and consultation for SMEs carrying out anti-pollution development or pollution-related factory relocation projects.

In the United States, there are two major provisions in the Revenue Code which attempt to reduce the cost of complying with pollution-control regulations. These grant deductions and credits for investments in pollution-control hardware, and allow certain tax exemptions for municipal bond financing of pollution-abatement facilities.

Ashford (1979), however, believes that tax laws can bias compliance technology in a number of ways. In the first case they can encourage hardware investments exclusively, since no benefit is allowed for operating charges. Second, the requirement that changes be 'non-significant' encourages incremental or add-on changes rather than major process change. According to Ashford the provisions should be critically reconsidered with attention to the difficult tradeoff they pose between possibly penalizing innovations by decreasing the cost of incremental, add-on technology, and the large-scale subsidy they would represent in order to encourage more radical technological improvements.

Federal grants are also available in the United States for assistance with constructing municipal waste-water treatment facilities. According to the Denver Research Institute report (Boucher *et al.*, 1976), however, the EPA's grant programme in this area, because of its terms of reference, can create a considerable disincentive to innovate in waste-water treatment since the newer systems, which are primarily chemical or biological and thus have lower capital but higher operating costs, are economically less attractive because the grant programme, while providing capitalization funds, cannot provide funds towards operating costs.

Finally, in the United States the Small Business Administration make or guarantee loans for pollution control-related investments precipitated by regulatory requirements. Financial assistance with compliance might, especially in the case of small firms, be extended to areas of regulation other than pollution control.

Technical Assistance with Compliance

As well as offering financial assistance with compliance, governments can also act to reduce the technical risks and help to alleviate problems associated with the diversion of R & D resources from business innovation, associated with compliance. This might take the form of grants to collective industrial research organizations to perform compliance-related research; or it might take the form of assisting groups of firms to establish collaborative compliance-oriented laboratories. However, the latter approach might encounter problems in the United States associated with anti-trust regulations.

Time for Compliance

There are two main aspects to this question. The first is that if the time for compliance is too short, compliance costs are particularly onerous since they are imposed over a relatively short period. The second is that regulatory time pressures can lead to non-optimal technical solutions; the point is, if lead-times are too short, then insufficient time is available to develop long-term innovation solutions, and stopgap solutions may be found that will require further development to achieve optimality. This is clearly economically inefficient, but not necessarily a barrier to long-term compliance innovation. Ashford, Butler and Zolt (1977) have addressed the problem of timing and suggest that a possible solution — from the point of view of facilitating innovation — might lie in the timing, time-phasing or delaying of standards. Ashford, Butler and Zolt further suggest, in those cases where important compliance innovations — especially those involving relatively major changes in existing technology — could take from five to ten years to develop, that extension of the time period between standard promulgation and full compliance (that is, timing) could serve as a means of encouraging innovation.

From the point of view of the governmental regulator, whose major aim is normally not to stimulate innovation but to achieve compliance for other ends, time-phasing might involve unacceptable social costs. Thus, in certain areas (safety, the environment, for example) rigid compliance schedules might be necessary; in other areas — for example, with economic regulation — the regulator may be willing to adopt greater flexibility towards the timing of regulations.

The Use of 'Performance' Standards

It has often been asserted that performance standards are preferable to specification standards or design characteristics as a spur to compliance innovation because they allow for greater latitude in determining how to achieve the regulatory goal, and governments might consider adopting this approach to regulation. In practical terms, specification standards often make compliance innovation difficult because of agency reluctance to grant variances. For example, the Centre for Policy Alternatives chemical industry study (Ashford, 1979) showed that companies with new compliance technologies superior to what the regulation had specified experienced difficulty when they tried to persuade the regulatory agencies to allow them to use the alternative.

Hill (1975), on the basis of his survey of the chemical and allied products industry, agrees that in theory performance characteristic standards allow for any product or process components as long as they give the desired result. However, the choice between performance and specification standards cannot be made on the basis of the innovation consequences alone, and Hill hypothesized several circumstances in which design characteristic standards might be more appropriate than performance standards:

- regulations are already known, and if ascertaining the performance characteristics for the components in every case would be unnecessarily expensive or burdensome, then design standards might be appropriate;
- in some situations, for policy reasons, it may be necessary to know the performance characteristics of the components of a process. If the performance characteristics of certain components which could be required by design characteristics
- the result of the use of specific components is known and it is difficult or impossible to measure the effects of using other components (too high uncertainty);
- the use of a component, because of its own dangerous or other characteristics, cannot be justified;
- where, because of the danger of unknown or unanticipated effects, only approved non-active ingredients as well as active ingredients might be used in drugs licensed for manufacture.

Finally, a number of examples taken from two very different industry sectors and types of regulation suggest strongly, from the point of view of *innovation*, that performance standards are definitely preferable. In the first case, the EPA requirement for the use of activated carbon in air pollution control eliminated any incentive for firms to develop potentially better methods (Boucher *et al.* (1976)). In the second case, the Federal Communications Commission focuses on the end service and leaves the means of achieving the required quality of service to the telecommunications industry in the United States; as a consequence, this had resulted in a great deal of compliance innovation (Gillette, 1977). In other words in the telecommunications industry, from the point of view of stimulating innovation, it is better to simply specify performance – and leave the means of compliance to the communications company – rather than to specify the technical means to achieve the stipulated performance.

Forward-Looking Regulation as a Stimulus to Innovation

It has been suggested that if regulations were formulated in such a way that they reflected anticipated technological feasibility, rather than simply relying on currently available technology, then this would act as a spur to compliance innovation. This could, of course, place regulatory agencies in an impossible situation in anticipating 'technological feasibility'. It could also lead to the formulation of standards which, because of unforeseen technical problems, might be impossible to meet.

This proposition basically reflects a misunderstanding of the aims of regulation, which involve the control of a particular situation for the benefit of society, and do not generally include the stimulation of industrial innovation. That is not to say that regulations cannot, or should not, be formulated with the possibilities for radical compliance innovation in mind, and this might be a prime area for government policy consideration.

Regulation Formulation and Implementation

There is no doubt that much of the uncertainty over regulations in industry could be reduced if the regulation formulation and implementation processes were improved, and these are clearly areas in which government action could have a significant impact. There are a number of ways in which these processes might be improved, one being greater interaction between industries and government agencies during regulation formulation, and the establishment of efficient channels of communication to facilitate the continuous monitoring of regulatory impacts, both positive and negative.

There seems little doubt that the exchange of technical information between both parties would be mutually advantageous. For example, if the regulatory agency is fully aware of recent advances in industrial technology, then more forward-looking regulation might be formulated in the light of these. Certainly innovation might then be promoted, as technical personnel from industry interact with their technical counterparts in the regulatory agency in the knowledge that they had some influence to help shape the direction of regulation and of the technology necessary for compliance. Technical personnel in regulatory agencies might also assist firms, especially smaller firms, faced with regulation-induced technical problems. There could, however, be legal problems associated with this, especially in the United States; in the case of environmental regulation, for example, agencies offering direct technical assistance to industry might be faced with citizens' suits in environmental cases.

On the other hand, realistic and meaningful standards might more often be established if the technical strengths of regulatory bodies themselves were increased.

Perhaps the most cost-effective means of achieving this would be the use — as in the United Kingdom — of lay experts in the regulation formulation process. In this way, a comprehensive body of technical expertise could be assembled with respect to each specific regulation.

It is of prime importance that regulations should be formulated as clearly and as unambiguously as possible and governments — particularly the US government — should also take pains to ensure uniform interpretation by either local or state enforcement agencies. Much of the uncertainty currently associated with the different local interpretations of some regulations could thus be avoided.

Finally, regulations, should, where practicable, have maximum flexibility with respect to varying local circumstances, to changes in knowledge concerning the nature of technological impacts, and to advances in technology. This responsiveness to change is most likely to result in high rates of compliance and associated innovations.

References

Allen, T. J., Utterback, J. M., Sirbu, M. A., Ashford, N. A., and Hollomon, J. H. (1978), 'Government influence on the process of innovation in Europe and Japan', *Research Policy*, 7, 2, April.

Ashford, N. A. (1979), *Environmental/Safety Regulation and Technological Change in the US Chemical Industry*, Report to the National Science Foundation, Centre for Policy Alernatives, MIT, March.

—— Butler, S. E., and Zolt, E. M. (1977), *Comment on Drug Regulation and Innovation in the Pharmaceutical Industry*, HEW Review Panel on New Drug Regulation, Washington, DC, 10 February.

—— and Heaton, G. R. (1979), 'The effects of health and environment regulation on technological change in the chemical industry: theory and evidence', in Hill, C. T. (ed.) *Government Regulation and Chemical Innovation*, American Chemical Society.

Boucher, W. I., Anderson, M., Beckett, S., Culberson, L., and Strong, P. (1976), *Federal Incentives for Innovation*, Report R 75-05 for Denver Research Institute, January.

Bureau of Medical Devices (1978), 'Economic impact assessment of final fuelmaking good manufacturing practice regulation for manufacture, packing, storage and installation of medical devices', FDA, June.

Capron, W. M. (1971), (ed.) *Technological Change in Regulated Industries*, Washington, DC, Brookings Institution.

Eva, D. and Rothman, H. (1979), 'Control of the environmental impact of technology', in Johnson, R. and Gummet, P. (eds.), *Directing Technology*, London, Croom Helm.

Feinman, S. and Fuentevilla, W. (1976). *Indicators of International Trends in Technological Innovation*, Report for Gellman Research Associates to the National Science Foundation, NSF–C889, April.

Gabrowski, H. G. and Vernon, J. M. (1976), 'Structural effects of regulation on innovation in the ethical drug industry', in Massan, R. T. and Qualls, P. D. (eds.), *Essays on Industrial Organization*, Cambridge, Mass., Ballinger.

Gellman, A. J. (1971), 'Surface freight transportation', in Capron, W. E. (ed.), *Technological Change in Regulated Industries*, Washington, DC, Brookings Institution.

Gerstenfeld, A. (1977), 'Government regulation effects on the direction of innovation: a focus on performance standards', *IEEE Transactions Engineering Management*, EM–24, 3, August.

—— (1978), 'Technological innovation and government regulation: examples from the building construction and pharmaceutical industries', paper presented at the National Conference on the Advancement of Research, USA, September.

Gillette, D. (1977), 'How regulations encourage and discourage innovation', *Research Management*, March.

—— (1979), 'Interactions between telecommunications innovation and regulation in the United States', Six Countries Programme/NSF Workshop, The Hague, June.

Greenberg, E., Hill, C. T. and Newburger, D. J. (1977), *The Influence of Regulation and Input Costs on Process Innovation: A Case Study of Ammonia Production*, Washington, DC, Washington University, NSF–RDA 75–23266, June.

Hill, C. T. C. (1975), *A State of the Art Review of the Effects of Regulation on Technologial Innovation in the Chemical and Allied Products Industries*, Washington, DC, Washington University, February.

Lederman, L. L. and Morrison, R. E. (1979), 'Environmental and worker health/safety regulation and technological innovation', Six Countries Programme/NSF Workshop, The Hague, June.

Lester, R. K. (1978), *Nuclear Power Plant Lead-Time*, New York, The Rockefeller Foundation and London, The Royal Institute of International Affairs, November.

Little, Arthur D., Inc. (1973). *Barriers to Innovation in Industry: Opportunities for Public Policy Changes*, Executive Summary Report, Washington, DC, NSF Contract, NSF–C748.

Manners, G. E. and Nason, H. K. (1979), 'Regulation and innovation: symbiotes or antithets?' Six Countries Programme/NSF Workshop, The Hague, June.

Peltzman, S. (1973), 'An evaluation of consumer protection legislation: the 1962 drug amendments', *Journal of Political Economy*, **81**, 1049–91.

Rothwell, R. (1977), 'Characteristics of successful innovators and technically progressive firms', *R & D Management*, **1**, 3.

—— (1979), *Industrial Innovation and Government Regulation*, report to the Six Countries Programme on Aspects of Government Policy Towards Innovation in Industry, and the National Science Foundation, PO Box 215, Delft, Netherlands, December.

Rubenstein, A. H. and Ettlie, J. E. (1979), 'Innovation among suppliers to automobile manufacturers: an explanatory study of barriers and facilitators', *R & D Management*, **9**, 2, February.

Sarett, L. H. (1974), 'FDA regulations and their influence on future R & D', *Research Management*, March.

Schweitzer, G. (1977), *Regulation and Innovation: The Case of Environmental Chemicals*, Cornell University, February.

Steward, H. F. (1977), 'Public policy and innovation in the drug industry', in Black, Sir Douglas and Thomas, G. P. (eds.), *Providing for the Health Services*, London, Croom Helm.

US Department of Commerce (1976), *Survey of Current Business*, Bureau of Economic Analysis, July, p. 15, chart 6.

US Office of Technology Assessment (1978), *Changes in the Future Use and Characteristics of the Automobile Transportation System*, Washington, DC.

Weidenbaum, M. L. (1978), *The Costs of Government Regulation of Business*, Washington, DC, US Government Printing Office.

Weiss, M. (1978), *The Impact of Environmental Control Expenditures on the U.S. Copper, Lead and Zinc Mining and Smelting Industries*, National Economic Research Associates, Inc., January.

Williams, R. (1977), *Government Regulation of the Occupational and General Environments in the UK, the US and Sweden*, Ministry of Supply and Services, Canada (Catalogue No. 5521-1/40).

9. THE ROLE OF THE SCIENTIFIC AND TECHNOLOGICAL INFRASTRUCTURE

INTRODUCTION

In most of the advanced market economies the scientific and technological infra-structure plays an important role in the performance of national research and development work. This is illustrated in Table 9.1, which lists the contributions of industry, public and non-profit-making organizations and higher education (the latter two categories comprising 'the infrastructure') to the performance of R & D work in the EEC countries, the United States, Japan and Israel during 1967 and 1975.

Table 9.1 Contribution of the various sectors to the performance of R & D work in 1967 and 1975

	Industry		Public & non-profit-making institutions		Higher education	
	(As a percentage of national R & D expenditure)					
	1967	*1975*	*1967*	*1975*	*1967*	*1975*
Germany	64	63	16	17	19	20
France	51	60	34	25	15	16
Italy	51	56	21	22	28	22
The Netherlands	58	54	19	23	23	23
Belgium	53	64	11	10	37	26
United Kingdom	64	62	28	29	8	8
Ireland	34	31	51	53	15	16
Denmark	37	41	30	27	33	31
EEC	59	60	25	22	17	18
United States	71	68	18	19	11	13
Japan	54	57	14	15	32	28
Israel	—	24*	—	16	—	60*

*1974
Source: EEC (1979), *Analysis of the Research and Development Potentials of Member States of the European Community*, Directorate General for Research, Science and Education.

The significance of the infrastructure varies considerably between countries, being relatively high in Israel, Ireland and Denmark (76, 69 and 58 per cent of total R & D respectively in 1975) and relatively low in the United States (32 per cent of total R & D in 1975). This pattern might at least partially reflect a lack of industrial R & D strength in the smaller countries, Israel, Ireland, and Denmark – they are also countries in which agriculture plays a very significant role in the national economy, and both Ireland and Denmark spend a greater percentage of industrial R & D in the agricultural and foodstuffs industries than any of the other EEC member countries. Agriculture is, of course, essentially a non-competitive area in which government-funded organizations play the major role in the performing of national R & D.

Despite national differences, indications are (see Chapter 5) that governments in the advanced economies are laying increasing emphasis on utilizing the infrastructure as an adjunct to national innovation policies. This is evident even in the United States, where President Carter's Domestic Policy Review (1979) included statements concerning the need to improve university–industry interactions and the intention to establish government–funded collective industrial research organizations.

This chapter will deal with two specific aspects of the scientific and technological infrastructure, namely universities and collective industrial research organizations. It will also give a description of the problems that some of the larger and older national R & D establishments are faced with in their efforts to serve industry and government with respect to innovation.

UNIVERSITY*–INDUSTRY INTERACTION

The primary function of universities is, of course, one of education, and it is undoubtedly true to say that the 'production' of large numbers of highly trained technical specialists has been crucial to the economic progress enjoyed by the advanced western nations for many years. Universities also make a significant contribution via the performance of fundamental, undirected research which becomes widely diffused and opens up new possibilities for economic development. It is increasingly being mooted, however, that universities should be of greater *direct* utility to industry and be more involved in industrial technical problem-solving and innovation. This chapter will briefly present data which indicate the level of university–industry interactions — mainly in the United Kingdom — and comment on the utility of university chemistry research to industry. It will then outline a number of recent initiatives, designed explicitly to enhance the utility of universities to industrial firms.

University Research and Industry

A very detailed study conducted several years ago (Langrish, 1974) attempted to determine the relationship between university research in organic chemistry, and the use by industry of the results of this research. The technique used was to study the institutional origins of abstracts produced by the *Journal of the Society of Chemical Industry*, a journal which for 80 years or more has produced abstracts of the world's literature that might be of relevance to industrial chemists. The results of this exercise are shown in Table 9.2, which shows that there has been a marked change over time in the main institutional sources of abstracts, from European university (mainly German) in 1884, to American industry in 1952. It can be seen that, since the end of the nineteenth century, foreign industry has been the major source of inputs with, in 1952, UK industry being the second most important source; UK university has consistently been the least, or the second least, important source of inputs.

*University is here used as a shorthand for all institutions of higher education, such as polytechnics.

Table 9.2 Change with time of institutional sources of abstracts in *Journal of Society of Chemical Industry* for industrial areas connected with organic chemistry

Year of journal	1884	1889	1917	1935	1952
Institutional source	%	%	%	%	%
US industry	–	4.8	14.5	38.1	53.8
UK industry	8.8	17.3	6.2	9.3	19.0
European industry	23.5	44.7	52.4	24.1	13.6
Other industry	–	1.0	0.7	0.5	0.9
Total industry	32.3	67.8	73.8	72.0	87.4
US government	–	1.0	1.4	1.9	3.6
UK government	–	1.0	–	0.5	1.1
European government	5.9	1.9	2.1	3.4	1.3
Other government	–	1.0	2.1	0.5	1.1
Total government	5.9	4.8	5.5	6.3	7.2
US university	3.0	1.0	1.4	1.9	2.6
UK university	–	7.7	6.2	0.8	0.7
European university	58.8	18.7	13.1	15.3	0.2
Other university	–	–	–	3.7	2.0
Total university	61.8	27.4	20.7	21.7	5.5

Source: Langrish (1974).

Langrish (1974) offered two alternative hypotheses as to why the importance of university research has apparently declined:

— industry has increasingly taken over its own research;
— a new branch of science is only useful to industry in its early days. For example, the early days of astronomy as a science were linked with economically important attempts at improving navigation, but it has hardly been useful since then.

He then states:

The relationship between university research and industry may well be a function of the degree of development of the area concerned. Once a new area has been established, the aim of science is to understand; the aim of technology is to make it work, and industry has been very successful at making things work without too much reliance on understanding.

It might be, therefore, that in certain areas of science the role of universities is to make the initial fundamental breakthrough (atomic fission, for example), followed by many years of basic research to understand the *nature* of the process; the role of industry is commercially to utilize the breakthrough, concentrating on understanding and harnessing its *effects* while being, in the early days at least, largely unaware of their causes.

It might be, however, that due to severe shortages of technical specialists in some areas (such as microelectronics), and with the relationship between scientific discovery and technological innovation becoming closer in others (such as biotechnology), the need today is for universities and industry to move closer and work together on economically oriented developments. Certainly, with the rapidly increasing cost of industrial R & D, coupled to generally reduced rates of profit in industry, it might be argued that the great wealth of scientific and technical expertise contained within universities, as well as their large quantities of specialist equipment and facilities, should be made more readily available to industry to enable it to capitalize more directly on this considerable publicly funded resource. Because of the fundamental nature of much of university research, universities are also potential spawning grounds for the radical innovations of the future. Nevertheless, it must be accepted that the role of universities is, and must continue to be, primarily one of education.

Universities and Industrial Innovation

Several studies have been undertaken in the United Kingdom which looked at, among other things, the sources of ideas which resulted in successful technological innovations. The most important of these considered a sample of 1667 important innovations produced by UK industry between 1950 and 1970. The sources of the initial idea leading to these innovations are shown in Table 9.3 (Rothwell and Townsend, 1973), which shows that industry is the major source of its own ideas, foreign industry second most important, and universities supply only a small number of ideas leading to innovations (2.5 per cent).

Table 9.3 Sources of innovation ideas

Origin of initial idea	Number	Percentage
In-house industry	896	53.74
University	42	2.52
Government defence	21	1.25
Government civil	94	5.63
Research associations	70	4.20
Related industry	19	1.14
Unrelated industry	100	6.00
Independent individual	21	1.25
Parent company abroad	175	10.50
Abroad	211	12.66
Under licence from abroad	18	1.08
TOTAL	1667	100.00

Source: Rothwell and Townsend (1973).

Chapter 10 suggests that, because of their lack of in-house technical expertise, it is generally small and medium-sized manufacturing firms (SMEs) that have the greatest need for external technical assistance. It is interesting, therefore, to discover whether the interaction between universities and industry is a function of firm size.

Figure 9.1, taken from a report by the UK Universities and Industry Joint Committee (1970), shows the various ways in which companies use university R & D by size of company. It shows a marked pattern; that is, on all the measures of contact between industry and academia, small firms had by far the fewer contacts. Further, out of 403 firms employing less than 200, 75 per cent had no contact with universities; out of 96 firms with greater than 5000 employees, only 9 per cent had no contact with universities.

A correlation analysis on the data showed that a higher proportion of university-trained scientists in the senior management of smaller-sized companies meant a

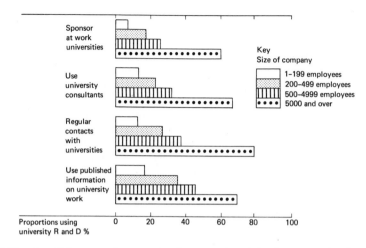

Fig. 9.1 Ways in which companies use university research and development — by size of company. Source: Universities and Industry Joint Committee (1970)

greater likelihood of contact with universities. However, since small firms generally employ fewer (if any) technical graduates than do their larger counterparts, this is clearly an area for concern, especially since the need of SMEs for external technology from universities is so great in a world of rapid technical change.

Planning for Increased University–Industry Interaction

If governments want universities to play an increasing role in helping industry to meet future technical requirements, then they must take positive steps to encourage them to adopt a more active stance towards industry. It might be that financial incentives can be offered to universities to mount courses with a vocational bias such as those offered by the polytechnics. It might be that more universities can offer 'sandwich' courses, during which students spend a specified part of their time working in industry. These are, however, medium to long-term measures relating solely to the increased use by industry of university graduates. Of more immediate concern, and of more central interest to this book, are those steps governments and universities can take to stimulate the more frequent use by industry of existing university technical expertise and equipment. Steps currently being taken by governments and universities in several countries to achieve this aim are outlined below:

Industrial Liaison Offices

A number of governments have established industrial liaison offices at universities, whose function is to increase the use by local industry of university facilities and expertise. This is a positive step which should go some way towards increasing industry's awareness of the technical potential available in universities, and should be of particular interest of SMEs which generally lack in-house technical expertise. Such a scheme was in existence with Department of Industry support, in the United Kingdom, but was officially discontinued some five or six years ago. However, since 1970, 45 universities and polytechnics in the United Kingdom have set up offices for industrial liaison from their own resources.

Probably the most significant government scheme in this area is in France where, since 1972, twenty industrial liaison officers have been appointed, one to each region. Their brief covers not only the promotion of university–industry contacts, but also includes the promotion of projects from other sources. Since the scheme's inception, more than 2000 projects to develop and launch innovations have been instigated, including a total investment of about 100 million francs.

Finally, in Sweden information liaison officers have been installed at all eight universities since 1970, and the recent white paper on innovation by the Dutch government envisages similar liaison officers at the three Dutch technical universities.

Before going on to describe other forms of linkage between universities and industry, it is worth while taking some space to describe something of what is currently known about patterns of communication during the technological innovation process. This has implications for both university–industry interactions, and for the interactions between industry and collective industrial research organizations.

Perhaps the most significant results in this area are those arising from the work of Allen at MIT (1977). From a wide range of studies, Allen identified certain key individuals within the firm who were particularly efficient 'transceivers' of scientific and technological information; these he christened 'technological gatekeepers'. The presence of a technological gatekeeper was significantly correlated with the superior performance of R & D project teams. Other researchers have also emphasized the key communication role played by individuals in the innovation process (Holland, 1972). Further, a wide variety of innovation studies have emphasized the dominance of *informal* communication channels during innovation, again pointing to the crucial function of individuals as communicators (Rothwell and Robertson, 1973).

Other studies have emphasized the different communication habits of scientists and engineers (Allen, 1966). Scientists tend to look mainly to the primary literature (journals) and they form 'invisible colleges' among their peers: they appear to be little constrained by the bounds of the firm. Engineers, on the other hand, look more to secondary literature (textbooks, trade publications) and draw very much on their own personal experience; they are very much bound by the firm in which they work.

A useful way to come to understand the differences between scientists and engineers is to view both science and technology as information processing systems. The input of both science and technology consists of verbally encoded information. The output, however, differs – in the case of science it consists of processed verbally encoded information, while in the case of technology the main product is physically encoded information, often hardware. In other words, the input and output of the science information system are both verbally encoded information of the same nature. There exists, however, a basic incompatibility between input and output of the technology system, a system that transforms 'ideas and information into hardware'. It goes without saying that the transformation processes in both systems are distinctly different. A second important difference is the fact that engineers work for organizations that compete with others, often on the same market. Scientists, on the other hand, produce ideas that are to be exposed to the scientific community; to 'invisible colleges'.

The organizational implications of the differences between the science and technology system are far-reaching and can be summarized as follows: A scientist pursues great professional autonomy and selects the problems to be studied more or less himself, this being a basic requirement of the science system. A scientist communicates with his 'invisible colleagues' in various scientific institutions who all belong to his scientific community. Communication is usually on paper, and a scientist therefore values highly publication of research results. Scientists work in loosely structured organizations, to which they belong administratively. Functional contacts, however, are usually outside these organizations. Furthermore the rewarding systems for scientists is outside their administrative organization. It is in fact the scientific community, which determines the professional qualifications, status and rewards of a scientist. The implications for engineers are rather different. Engineers work on hardware that will determine the company's future success. Engineers should refrain from early publication of results as the company may lose its lead in a specific R & D area and consequently its competitive advantage in the market. Furthermore, engineers work together in groups in one company, and usually communicate through personal contacts with fellow engineers in the same company. The hardware on which they work is not their own choice, but is determined by the company's interests. Moreover, the vast majority of engineers are employed by rather bureaucratic organizations with well-defined missions. This demands from an engineer a high degree of identification with the organization for which he works. Finally, the rewarding system of an engineer is the organization for which he works.

What are the implications of the above for university–industrial liaison officers? The role of liaison officers will vary between a formal database and an informal 'go-between'. It is likely, however, that neither of these roles will be really satisfactory. When acting as a formal database, the informal aspects of technology transfer with its emphasis on very personal contacts will be neglected. When acting as an informal go-between, it is unlikely that one, or even a few, officers per university will be sufficient; informal communication is labour-intensive and can be highly time-consuming if it is to be effective.

Three aspects should be kept in mind when considering the role of the liaison officers. First of all the willingness of individual scientists at various university departments to cooperate with liaison officers who are formally appointed. Secondly, the willingness of scientists to work for, or at least supply information and advice to, organizations that pursue entirely different objectives from a university. (We refer to the previously described difference in characteristics between the science and the technology information-processing systems and between the attitude of scientists and engineers.) Thirdly, as technological transfer is a highly intensive process between people it will be obvious, as mentioned above, that with the appointment of one or a few officers the problem of transfer of knowledge will not be solved; probably a much larger and more informal network is needed.

In our opinion it is questionable whether formal liaison officers alone are a real solution to the problem of transfer of knowledge between universities and industry. A much more effective means can be found for example in Germany where universities have their own institute for applied research, which carries out applied research and development on the assignment of industry. These institutes are located in the same buildings as the university. Scientists and engineers can meet frequently and yet pursue their own objectives, and scientists can even be temporary advisors to certain applied research projects. The great advantage of this type of organization is, on the one hand, that science and technology remain separate information processing systems, each having its own characteristics and objectives, and yet, on the other hand, because the systems are physically interwoven, scientists and engineers can communicate very effectively on an *ad hoc* and informal basis. For the Netherlands too a well-functioning example can be cited, the institute called the TH–TNO Institute of Applied Physics, set up by the Technical University of Delft and the Organization for Applied Scientific Research TNO.

The above should not be taken to suggest that university–industrial liaison officers should not be used. Rather it suggests that they should be part of a broader system which is capable of fostering frequent and informal contacts between university and industrial researchers, and especially between scientists and engineers. A number of initiatives which are currently attempting to go some way towards achieving this broader, more effective, transfer are described below.

University Innovation Centres

From the results of a number of background studies in the United States, the National Science Foundation reached the conclusion that innovation was inseparably linked with entrepreneurship, and that there was a trend in the United States towards a decreasing number of entrepreneurs. Innovation centres (ICs) were conceived as vehicles within universities for stimulating technological innovation and for increasing the entrepreneurial tendencies of graduates as they pursued their careers. The ICs were designed to offer both formal education and practical experience in invention, innovation and entrepreneurship. Other objectives were to provide support for the independent inventor or entrepreneur, increase non-federal investment in R & D, and accelerate the commercialization of university inventions. In 1973 three ICs were established at different universities.

Special provisions were included in the NSF/IC agreements that encouraged ICs to derive income from their activities; for example, both inventors and the ICs could share in rights to patents developed during the course of centre activities.

The success of the IC experiment can be gauged from the following figures. To date the three ICs have between them:

— participated in the creation of over 30 new ventures, of which 23 have achieved sales of over $30 million;
— resulted in approximately 1000 new jobs;
— generated over $6 million in tax revenues (for a total NSF outlay of $3 million);
— exposed over 2000 students to instruction and/or experience in the entrepreneurial, invention and innovation processes;
— assisted in the evaluation of over 2000 ideas for new products.

Similar structures are currently being established in Canada and the Republic of Ireland.

NSF Technology Innovation Programme Experiments

A second NSF initiative to improve university–industry interaction is the Technology Innovation Programme (TIP), which is directed toward shortening the time between university research results and commercial utilization (Wetmore, 1980).

A major TIP project builds upon the research results in programmable automation assembly from the University of Massachusetts, the Stanford Research Institute, and the Charles Stark Draper Laboratory, Inc. The cooperative project funds Westinghouse and the researchers to analyse ways in which the research results could be cost effectively applied in developing an experimental automated programmable assembly system for batch assembly which represents some 75 per cent of US manufacturer assembly operations. The work to date has already shown that this university–industry interaction increases the rate of technology transfer and increases both the effectiveness of the researchers and the ability of industry to utilize the research results.

The current phase of this project is experimenting with a fully integrated experimental assembly system which will provide significant information necessary for adoption throughout the batch assembly sector of industry and will significantly reduce the risk, financial and technological, normally associated with the initial application of research results.

Since few companies will undertake an innovation without having a reasonable assurance that the innovation will be reliable, cost-effective and capturable, an experimental test in an industrial setting is an effective means to obtain industry acceptance. Moreover, universities do not normally perform the types of tests that develop data necessary for industry acceptance. Thus, an experimental project with a firm is frequently the only means to provide the data necessary for industry-wide acceptance of an innovation.

University Companies

The data listed in Table 9.3 are now several years out of date, and there is some evidence to suggest that during the 1970s British universities increasingly began to establish 'companies' or commercial activities relating to industry. According to a recent article, 'at least 33 universities or university colleges in the United Kingdom have a declared interest in specific university–industry liaison activities as a formal part of the function of the university. A number of others interact with industry on an informal basis via academic staff consortia or individual staff who operate private companies' (Smith, 1977).

Table 9.4 lists some of the genuine 'company' activities that are currently in progress.

Table 9.4 Some universities with commercial activities

University	Commercial activity
Bath	South Western Industrial Research Ltd (SWIRL)
Cardiff	Cardiff University Industry Centre (CUIC)
Cranfield	Cranfield Unit for Precision Engineering (CUPE)
Dundee	Centre for Industrial Research and Consultancy
Lancaster	ISCOL Ltd (International Systems Corporation of Lancaster)
	LANCORD Ltd (Lancaster Operational Research)
	ULDECO Ltd (University of Lancaster Developments)
	Enterprise Lancaster (joint project)
Leeds	University of Leeds Industrial Services Ltd (ULIS)
London	QMC Industrial Research Ltd (QMC-IRL) and two subsidiary companies
Loughborough	Loughborough Consultants Ltd
Newcastle upon Tyne	Design Unit
	Marine Industries Centre
North Wales	Industrial Development (Bangor)
Salford	Industrial Centre of Design and Manufacturing Engineering
Southampton	Seven specialized design and advisory units

Source: Smith (1977).

The Teaching Company

An interesting experiment has recently begun in the United Kingdom at Manchester University, the so-called Teaching Company Scheme, which is jointly backed by the Science Research Council and the Department of Industry. Under this scheme, instead of taking higher degrees by working solely within the university laboratory, graduate engineers become 'associates' in partnership with a particular company (there are now eleven of these). They perform most of their work within the company on a specific project (often in production engineering), and ultimately take a higher degree based on this work. The aim of the scheme is to bridge the gap between university and industry, raise the level of industrial technology and make an industrial career more attractive to graduates. Similar schemes are underway in three or four other universities. They should be of particular interest to SMEs who might acquire a high level of technical expertise at very low cost.

University Industrial Parks

In a number of countries industrial parks have been established adjacent to university campuses. The aim of this setup is to provide for firms quick and easy access to university expertise and facilities; in some instances firms are wholly or partly owned by the university. University industrial parks are particularly well suited to small, high technology-based companies.

DISCUSSION

In all the major industrial nations, universities and other institutions of higher education between them constitute a formidable reservoir of technical knowledge and specialized research facilities. Any assessment of the *direct* input such establishments make to industrial innovation must, however, necessarily underestimate their total contribution. This is because they make a significant *indirect* contribution via both the generation of a wealth of fundamental scientific and technical knowledge, much of which gradually diffuses throughout the economy, and via the provision of qualified manpower for industrial R & D. Nevertheless, the direct contribution of universities to industry is probably a good deal less than it might be in most advanced countries.

There exists some evidence to suggest that universities are generally becoming increasingly aware of their potential usefulness to industry, and are taking positive steps to plan for increased university–industry interaction. It might be that government can help here with the provision of cash for the establishment of industrial liaison centres at all universities, and perhaps even with the provision of workshop facilities in which university personnel can develop promising new ideas to the prototype stage. Governments might also offer financial incentives to firms, and especially to SMEs, to contract out R & D work to universities, which should go some way towards increasing academic staff's involvement with, and awareness of, the problems of industry.

Universities do not only provide scientific and technological advance and assistance to industry, but many also offer postgraduate and post-experience education and consultancy in subjects such as management, marketing and business studies. These non-technical services undoubtedly have significant potential for increasing the general quality and performance of industrial management although, unfortunately, such courses appear to be patronized mainly by large firms, with small firms being much less represented. This again, might be an area for governmental support through, for example, offering sponsored, or subsidized, places for small-firm managers.

There are marked national differences in the degree of interaction between universities and industry, which have both an historical and cultural basis. There is, for example, a long tradition of interaction on technical matters between universities and companies in Germany. In the United States there is a strong tradition of management consultancy. In the United Kingdom 'ivory-towerism' appears to have dominated (outside the polytechnics), although there are indications that this is changing. What is apparent, however, is that the trend for governments to attempt to increase industry's utilization of university resources – both intellectual and physical – is today rather strong and quite widely established.

There is, as emphasized in Chapter 11, a growing need in many countries for the retraining of displaced workers in new disciplines demanded by the rapid diffusion of new technology, notably microelectronics. It would seem crucial that universities should increasingly become involved in this aspect of education, and in adult education generally as economic, social and technological changes place greater demands on workers, managers and government decision-makers for both higher level and new skills. The generally projected reduction in numbers of school-leavers of university potential should facilitate the necessary adjustments within the various university structures.

COLLECTIVE INDUSTRIAL RESEARCH

Although collective research can take a variety of forms, collective industrial research as discussed in this chapter is defined as: 'Including all establishments and activities designed to promote technical progress in a branch of a particular industry sector or in a particular scientific or technical discipline which is being developed in industry'. The systems of collective industrial research, as defined above, in eight advanced market economies, are set out briefly in Table 9.5.

Not all industries, of course, subscribe to collective industrial research, although this varies to some extent with the local industrial environment, such as pharmaceuticals in the United Kingdom, chemicals in Belgium and electronics in France. Strongly competitive topics are generally anti-collective research, particularly where technology is an important factor in competition. Indeed, Wolek (1979) has indicated a reverse relationship between 'R & D importance to an industry and its cooperative support of R & D'. The presence of multinationals or large dominating organizations in a sector can also preclude collective research activities. In most countries collective industrial research organizations exist to service the traditional, and often highly fragmented, sectors of industry.

Despite lack of total sectoral membership indications are that collective industrial research is generally on the increase, and that there is an increasing awareness of its potential usefulness to industry at a time of rapid technical and economic change, especially on the part of governments. While governmental involvement in determining the rate and direction of collective research varies a great deal from country to country (negligible in the United States, high in Japan), there appears to be a growing awareness of its utility as an area of government industry policy. In a number of countries, notably West Germany, Sweden and Japan, collective industrial research is in particular an important component of government policy towards small and medium-sized firms.

Table 9.5 Summary of collective industrial research efforts in eight countries

Country	Collective research organizations	Manpower employed	Expenditure on collective research	Percentage of total industrial R & D expenditure	Source of funding
France	22 industrial technical centres	5239 (1976)	850 million francs (1976)	5	7% (1978) Public financing 59% parafiscal taxes and voluntary subscriptions 34% own resources (private contracts etc.)
Japan	18 government centres; 187 local centres	4115 (1976) 6115 (1976)	29 760 million yen 31 000 million yen	1.0 1.1	100% government funding 90% local authority; 3–9% M.Y. 1–7% industrial services
	5 semi-public centres	262 (1976)	2765 million yen	0.1	50–90% direct or indirect subsidies Approx. 30% from testing and services. Less than 10% voluntary industry funds
Netherlands	TNO Organization for Industrial Research	1700 (1978)	18.5 million dutch florins (1978)	Approx. 5	33% government stimulation subsidy 67% industry contributions

Republic of Ireland	IIRS and Agricultural institute	1240 (1979)	£19 million	—	IIRS: 37% fee-paid consultancy 63% government grant Agric. Inst.: 100% government grant
Sweden	23 cooperative research institutes	—	£14 million	—	50% government funding via STU 50% industry contributions
United Kingdom	42 research associations	4718 (in 37 RAs) (1975)	£70 million (42 RAs)	3.2	33% subscription income 2.66% statutory levy 27.3% government funding 33% industry contracts and contributions 5.16% information services etc.
United States	100 cooperative research organizations	—	$125 million (1976)	Approx. 1% of industrial non-military R & D	20% government contracts 80% industry subscription and contracts
	4 proposed generic research centres	—	Initially $6–8 million		Initially mainly government funding reducing to 20% after 5 years
West Germany	63 collective research institutes	3500	277 million Deutschmarks	3%	75% membership fees 25% governmental support

While collective industrial research organizations have, in the past, been concerned in the main with technical problems of industry, it is clear that they are moving increasingly towards the provision of non-technical services, based on a growing awareness of the importance of such economic factors as management and marketing to the successful development, adoption and commercialization of new ideas. This is especially true where product development is concerned, and there is a clear trend towards greater involvement of collective research organizations in the development of new products in most of the countries listed in Table 9.5.

Finally, there is a trend towards undertaking more 'generic' research — notably in microelectronics — and recently established, or proposed, collective industrial research organizations in several countries have been primarily of the generic type.

Below a number of common problems of collective industrial research are discussed, and some recent trends in the services offered by collective industrial research organizations in several countries are described. Some generally observed trends are highlighted. (For a description of the organization and financing of collective industrial research in eight advanced market economies see Rothwell (1980).)

Collective Research: Some Critical Issues

Collective research is organized and financed in a variety of ways in different countries. Despite these national differences, however, there are a number of important issues common to collective research in all countries. The most critical of these issues are discussed briefly below.

Funding of Collective Research

Clearly the mode and level of funding of collective research will have a significant impact on both its effectiveness and its orientation (long-term or short-term; orientation towards fulfilling the needs of industry, etc.). The three main modes of *base* funding for collective research, are:

— subscription income from industrial membership;
— compulsory levy (such as parafiscal tax);
— direct government grants.

Other sources of finance are:

— government contracts;
— voluntary contributions;
— contract research, either for a single firm or on a multi-client basis.

In most cases, base funding derives from a combination of two or more of the above sources, and government support is often linked to specific projects or programmes. The different modes of base funding each have marked advantages and disadvantages. A high base level of support, from whatever source, has the advantages of enabling the collective research organization to instigate comprehensive programmes of research (as opposed to individual projects) and to undertake more fundamental, long-term research to meet the future needs of industry. On the other hand, it can lead to research for its own sake, often with little relevance to the more urgent current needs of industry. It can also result in a general climate of complacency within the collective research system. Direct government grants have the advantage of providing funds to cover the high cost of services to small firms, many of which might otherwise not receive assistance.

In a number of countries contract research provides an important component of funding for cooperative research. This often relates to product, rather than process, development, and in either case should increase the awareness in co-operative research organizations of industry's needs. Governments also provide contract support for specific research programmes or projects, which is in some cases linked to stated industry needs coupled to direct industry cash support (for example, the Netherlands' government stimulation subsidy, TNO). In other cases it is in the form of a direct grant for a specific piece of research, which is often defined by the government funding agency (for example, research requirements board system in the United Kingdom). One of the disadvantages of the latter system is that it can result in a strong focus on short-term research; an advantage is that it provides funding for research directed towards clearly defined industry needs.

A statutory levy (such as the parafiscal tax system employed in France) has the advantage of guaranteeing all firms in an industry membership of a collective research organization. It can, however, result in some resentment on the part of firms who feel that they are not receiving value for money. This resentment is compounded by the fact that some sectors which escape the parafiscal tax nevertheless benefit from the collective research (the automobile industry in France, for example). Too high a level of statutory support can also result in complacency, lack of creativity and the formulation of programmes remote from the needs of industry. However, because of the nature of the parafiscal tax, receipts can vary significantly from year to year, which introduces a degree of uncertainty into the system.

The question of level of base support leads to the more general question of the threshold of resources for effective operation. According to Brousse (1979), for example, '50 per cent of resources from parafiscal tax constitutes a minimum below which it is dangerous to drop without running the risk of transforming the Centre into a design office', and Erngren (1979) has pointed out that in Sweden 'the present institutes are usually too small to cope with the increasingly necessary marketing of the work produced by the institute'. Certainly evidence has been presented which suggests that there is a threshold level below which collective research organizations cannot operate effectively, and that this is an area for government intervention (Rothwell and Zegveld, 1978).

Collective Research and Government Policy

Collective research clearly represents a useful adjunct to government industrial policy, and it is often explicitly employed as such. The degree to which governments influence collective research programmes depends largely on the level of government financial support and the means by which this support is administered. In general, it seems that government support, linked to an overall industrial strategy, can have an integrative effect on an otherwise often fragmented research system.

In the Netherlands individual ministries provide funds to TNO for research in areas of special relevance to government policy. In Sweden, the government, via STU, has a strong say in determining the research programmes of the various collective research organizations. In France, in contrast, governmental involvement in determining directions of collective research is relatively small and largely negative via a veto. In the United Kingdom governmental direction of collective research is achieved via the research requirements boards which fund selected projects and programmes in research associations. While collective industrial research in the United States is largely uncoordinated, with virtually no governmental involvement, in West Germany it is closely linked to government policy, and indeed policy towards small and medium-sized firms is implemented largely through the industrial research associations.

Perhaps the closest integration of collective research to government policy occurs in Japan. Research performed in the government centres, which are attached to specific ministries, is predominantly of a medium to long-term nature and reflects national needs as defined by the ministries. The local and semi-public centres, albeit funded primarily through local sources, nevertheless reflect the strong governmental bias towards assisting innovation in small and medium-sized firms: their research programmes, are generally indirectly influenced by the Japanese Ministry for Trade and Industry (MITI) along paths relevant to central government policy.

One of the major potential problem areas associated with the utilization of cooperative research as an arm of governmental policy is the involvement of government representatives in the decision-making process. There are two aspects to this. The first lies with the possible bureaucratization, and consequent slowing down, of the decision-making process. The second relates to the question of the level of governmental understanding of the needs of industry and the competence of governments to take strategic decisions concerning the future direction of co-operative research. On the other hand, it is probably true to say that in areas such as energy, health and the environment, governments *should* take the initiative in instigating programmes of cooperative research in line with central policy.

In general terms it would seem sensible for collective research organizations to be involved in implementing policy initiatives involving areas of high technical risk, programmes of long-term research, and major programmes of industrial re-generation and restructuring, especially when they involve the adoption of new technologies. A government-backed scheme for accelerating the use in traditional industries in West Germany of microprocessors is a good example of this.

Finally, where collective research is largely decentralized as in Japan, for example, it would seem particularly well suited to the implementation of regional policy.

Programme Selection and the Decision-Making Process

While governments can influence national trends in collective research, generally it is true to say that programme decisions are taken primarily by the collective research organizations themselves. In many cases the decision-making committee will contain strong industrial representation, although this varies from country to country. The major advantage in having a significant industrial representation is that it does − or should − ensure relevance of the research to the needs of industry. On the other hand, it might result in a focus on short-term problem-solving activities to the detriment of longer-term research.

A major problem of committee decision-making − often involving a number of committees sequentially − is that programmes involving a relatively high element of risk are likely to be rejected. As a consequence, programmes can easily involve simply adding minor changes to existing technologies or products, and opportunities presented by new areas of research can be lost. In those cases where income derives from a parafiscal tax, Gaudin (1980) has suggested separating the function of management of the research organization from that of management of the levy. This, he contends, can help overcome a tendency towards introspection and lack of relevance on the part of organizations funded via statutory levies. Moreover, the levy should be administered via committees, with respect to which the following two conditions should be met:

— they must be subject to mandatory renewal, thus avoiding the creation of a group of *apparatchiks*;
— the amount of money each committee can manage should be limited, thus preventing it being tied down in dealing with a large number of often minor requests for support and assistance, to the detriment of more strategic issues.

Collective research institutes need to formulate an explicit, long-term strategy to guide programme selection, which must be based on both current and future technical needs to meet current and future market requirements. It should, however, be flexible and responsive to important, and perhaps unforeseen, changes in technology, the economic climate and market needs. It must be subject to guidance and to regular evaluation concerning its continued worth and relevance. Evaluation of collective research is, of course, inherently difficult, and indeed there are few examples of this, although some attempts have been made in the United Kingdom, West Germany and France.

Thus, we see a need for strategic thinking on the part of decision-makers in collective research institutes, and for the formulation of research programmes relating both to government policy and to industry's future as well as current needs. At the same time, collective research organizations should be responsive in solving the day-to-day problems of industry. It is a question of striking a balance between strategic objectives and of reacting to current needs, which requires a difficult combination of central direction of research coupled with flexibility in the provision of technical and advisory services.

Finally, probably the major problem of decision-making with respect to instigating short-term programmes or projects is the time it takes to reach a conclusion. In West Germany, for example, this can take as long as fifteen months which is often too long for companies requiring rapid solutions to today's problems. This is a consequence of the rather cumbersome, centralized decision-making processes of the AIF. In the United Kingdom, where decisions are taken at the level of the individual research association, they are usually made within about six months. In Sweden, periods as short as six weeks are common, especially for relatively minor projects involving small firms.

Interaction Between Collective Research Organizations

In most countries collective industrial research is organized on a sectoral basis, each institution working on often highly specific problems relating to its parent industry. A number of problems, in contrast, are shared across many industry branches and the solution to these might be outside the competence of a single industry-based collective research organization. In areas relating, for example, to health, safety and the environment it would appear sensible for a number of institutions to pool their resources, thus adopting an integrated approach to common problems and avoiding a great deal of duplication of research. The same applies to widely used technologies, such as electronics. In general, interaction between industry-based collective research organizations is quite small in most countries.

This raises the question of whether, in certain fields, 'generic' research organizations are the most appropriate. In the United Kingdom, for example, the establishment of a single research association to deal with problems of the use of microprocessors might be more efficient than a highly fragmented effort in each of the 42 existing research associations. Proposed, new, government-backed collective research centres in the United States are to be of the generic type. A possible disadvantage of this kind of organization is that, lacking identification with a particular sector, it could experience difficulties in establishing intimate contacts with companies. On the other hand, the range of potential contacts is very much greater, encompassing a large number of industry branches.

In several countries collective industrial research organizations often enjoy close collaboration with other collective research institutions, such as government research laboratories, universities, etc. This is the case in Sweden, especially with the more recently established collective research organizations which themselves contain no research facilities, but which subcontract research to, among others, the universities. In West Germany close contact is also maintained between centres of collective industrial research and others — for example, Fraunhofer Gesellschaft (FGS), and research is often contracted out to external laboratories. In Japan there is some contact between the various technical centres and universities on an educational, rather than on a shared research, basis. In the United Kingdom interaction between research associations and universities is rare. This is clearly unsatisfactory since universities are repositories of a wealth of technical and scientific expertise and equipment and perform much of the country's more fundamental research which, via the intermediary of a research association, could be linked more directly to the needs of industry. In Israel, in contrast, where a high percentage of national R & D is performed in universities, collective research organizations are explicitly seen as the main link between universities and industry.

One way of increasing the interaction between diverse industrial collective research organizations is to bring them together in a single 'umbrella' organization. This can be achieved organizationally as with the AIF in West Germany, or both organizationally and physically like the TNO organization in the Netherlands. The advantage of the latter system is that direct communication between researchers and decision-makers is made easy; it also facilitates the establishment of common laboratories for performing long-term research and joint programmes of generic research.

While such a system can work extremely effectively in a a small, low-population country like the Netherlands, it would be unlikely to operate well in larger, more populous countries where greater emphasis would need to be placed on decentralization and the regionalization of facilities. This is particularly important when dealing with small firms.

Identification of Users

A crucial problem facing collective industrial research organizations is that of identifying firms which might benefit from their services, and then convincing them to use these services. Probably about 5 to 10 per cent of firms in a sector will be active innovators and will have been involved with a collective research organization at one time or another; between 25 and 40 per cent will have the potential for innovating, but need help in this; the remainder, because of their structure, management style, or whatever, will lack the ability to innovate, and there is little that can be done to change this. From the point of view of the collective research organization the second group is most important, and it is into identifying these firms that the major effort should go. Since the group is quite large, it is unlikely that the research organization could identify and directly contact all its members. Consequently, programmes aimed at this group should have a demonstration component, so that the benefits of both innovation and the use of collective research can be brought to other members' notice.

Most collective research organizations operate in highly fragmented industries composed of a relatively few large, and very many small, firms which presents them with very real problems. For example, outside those countries that employ levies, membership is likely to comprise mainly of the larger firms in the sector, which then dominate the programme selection process. Small firms often see 'programmes' of research as being less relevant than individual projects, often because of their more general nature, and also because of their long-term perspective. Certainly small firms require a speedy solution to their problems — especially those concerned with product development — and are unwilling, and frequently unable, to wait while the wheels of bureaucratic decision-making grind slowly to a conclusion. Thus, while it is clearly necessary to establish comprehensive programmes of collective research, it is also necessary to maintain a high degree of flexibility with respect to individual problems for small firms.

The particular problems of small firms are, of course, widely recognized and collective research in several countries, most notably in Japan and West Germany, is biased firmly towards solving them. Some collective research organizations also discriminate in favour of small firms by linking subscription rates to either turnover or employment.

Because of the limited ability of small firms to pay for contract research, services to them tend to be extremely costly to the collective research institute. This is an area in which governments can — and some do — help by providing funds specifically for services to small firms. Ideally these should cover the initial project definition and the final technology transfer phases, as well as the actual technical problem-solving.

Finally, the encouragement of multi-client work for groups of small firms with common problems has potential for increasing their utilization of collective research. Such a scheme has been tried in France, where its implementation was fraught with great difficulty.

Collective Research versus Contract Research

Not surprisingly the bulk of the research undertaken by collective industrial research organizations is of a 'collective' nature, designed to solve problems common to the majority of member firms. This might be concerned with establishing standards, improving overall efficiency or helping industry cope with new regulations; it more often relates to process, rather than product, development. Increasingly, however, collective research organizations are becoming involved in 'contract' research for individual firms — or relatively small groups of firms — often in the area of new product development.

Contract research can raise very real problems associated with confidentiality, proprietary rights over research results and especially patents. On the other hand, contract research can bring new people into the collective research organization, and greatly increase its awareness of industry's more pressing needs, and it seems desirable that collective research institutes should be involved in both kinds of activity. Contract research would certainly appear more appropriate in the case of small firms which most often need rather rapid solutions to specific problems.

Information Dissemination

There are a number of aspects to the question of information flows between collective research organizations and industry. In the first place, there is the problem of making firms aware of the range of services the research organization has to offer. Secondly, there is the need for collective research organizations to be aware of the current and future needs of the firms they are attempting to service, including general technical, economic and market trends that are likely to affect them in the future. Thirdly, there is the question of the dissemination of information concerning standards, regulatory requirements, etc., including signposting services. Finally, there is the question of the final transfer of research results to potential user firms.

The latter aspect is particularly crucial in fragmented industries characterized by many small firms. These not only need the information, but require it to be 'translated' into a language they can understand. The process of technology transfer to small firms can, if it is to be achieved satisfactorily, be labour-intensive, involving the employment of 'brokers'. The broker system has the added advantage of increasing the degree of feedback from industry to the research organization.

Where government funds are involved, it seems sensible that contracts should explicitly include an allowance for achieving technology transfer. This is particularly appropriate as an adjunct to small-firms policy.

Finally, do-it-yourself laboratories of the type established at TNO in the Netherlands have great potential for stimulating information flows and establishing strong personal contacts between members of collective research organizations and user firms.

Quality of Staff and Staff Mobility

An important question here is that of the quality and mobility of staff in collective research institutes. Many of the more senior staff, for example, will have been with the organization for many years and will often tend to be conservative in their attitudes towards research and to other services offered. It also seems that the 'image' of collective research, especially in traditional areas, is such that organizations experience difficulty in attracting high-quality researchers. Certainly there exists a general problem of inducing change in some of the long-established collective research organizations, which must act to their disadvantage at a time of rapid technological and economic change.

The general trend towards more contract research might help to overcome a number of these problems. It can provide the possibility of offering short-term contracts to researchers, thus ensuring some staff turnover. It can also result in a greater interchange of staff between collective research organizations and industry. In the United Kingdom it has resulted in the employment of more researchers with industrial experience rather than those with a purely academic background.

Range of Services

Most of the work of collective industrial research organizations has traditionally been concerned with solving the technical problems of industry. The bulk of the literature on the industrial innovation process, however, has emphasized non-technical causes for innovative failure. Partly as a result of these innovation studies, and partly based on their own experiences, collective research organizations have increasingly offered a range of non-technical services. These 'economic' services include the training of researchers and managers, advice concerning general reorganization and rationalization and advice on marketing techniques and market trends. As the next section shows, the provision of economic services is generally on the increase.

Some Trends in Collective Industrial Research

A number of the more significant issues and problems associated with the organization, planning and implementation of collective industrial research were discussed above. There problems are, of course, generally recognized in most countries, which have recently taken a variety of steps towards their solution. A number of the more important of these initiatives are described below.

Belgium

In Belgium a Technical Advisory Scheme has been initiated in order to increase the utility of collective research to small and medium-sized firms (SMEs). With this approach the cost of the initial contact and advice is borne totally by the Belgian government. It involves the collective research association adopting an active stance towards contacting SMEs via the direct personal contact of a broker.

France

Perhaps the major initiative in collective industrial research in France was the decree of July 1979 which instituted an 'innovation grant' for the motivation of SMEs to more frequently utilize the services of the industrial technical centres. Under this scheme a government grant is available to cover 25 per cent of the costs of the project.

Based on a variety of studies, a number of recommendations have been made at governmental level to improve industrial utilization of the technical centres. These include:

— periodic review of provisional tax rates;
— regrouping of centres to avoid duplication of research effort and to enable smaller centres to jointly achieve a critical size level;
— creation of *generic* research centres;
— increased regionalization of services. This involves: (a) regional industrial liaison offices (already established), for better links between universities, technical centres and industry; (b) regional agencies for scientific and technical information, some of which will be established at the technical centres, others at chambers of commerce, universities and engineering schools; (c) in addition, the government has decided to decentralize the administration of financial aid for industrial innovation;
— encouraging the development of contract research by the technical centres in order to improve their relations with industry;
— encouraging the development of economic and market studies within the technical centres;
— encouraging new areas of research, notably in pollution control, energy conservation, raw materials conservation and working conditions;
— involving technical centres in a scheme for the rapid transfer of new technologies (telemetrics, microelectronics, new materials) into industrial use via technological advisers, regional support centres and national support centres;
— improving the administration of collective research by including on the boards of the technical centres representatives from SMEs, the outside scientific and technical world and consumers.

Japan

The collective industrial research infrastructure in Japan is both long established and comprehensive. The only notable trend is the attempt to foster greater collaboration between industry, universities and the various technical centres. The recent establishment of the semi-public centres represent an attempt to find at least a partial solution to this problem.

The Netherlands

Recent trends within TNO, the Dutch 'umbrella' collective research organization, include:

— increasing interest in non-technical services such as organization, pricing policy, social implications of industrial activities in regard to, for example, energy, the environment, work conditions, automation and health care.
— in order to satisfy the particular demands of SMEs, there will be a move towards research projects rather than research programmes, the latter often seeming too vague and lacking in relevance.

It seems probable that government involvement with TNO will increase. This was indicated in a recent government white paper on innovation which explicitly included recommendations concerning TNO:

Main points of policy in relation to TNO:
(a) Vigorous continuation of the reorganization of TNO, so that it can function as a whole and take action to help solve the multidisciplinary problems faced by the government, industry and other social groups;
(b) Maintenance and development of selected expertise useful in industrial R & D work;
(c) Increased orientation towards users and improvement of the quality of the services provided by TNO;
(d) More understanding of research needs, now and in the future: collaboration with, and demarcation of responsibilities in relation to, other R & D organizations (universities, technological universities etc.) on this matter;
(e) Strengthening of special links with other parties involved in the provisions of advice and information on innovation (technological universities, the Industrial Consulting Service RND), regional development companies, in management consultants, the Central Institute for small and medium-sized firms (CIMK);
(f) Drafting of medium-term programmes for policy-linked research to aid industry, government and social groups; establishing the mechanisms for effecting a patents policy that stimulates innovation both for TNO itself and as a service available to other organizations;
(h) Better use of the knowhow available at the TNO for educational purposes in suitable cases;
(i) More internal and external mobility for scientists and engineers;
(j) More direct linking to users of part of the government expenditure on TNO;
(k) Improved use of existing knowhow and expertise;
(l) Increased orientation of TNO and the other large research organizations (ECN, NSP, etc.) to their 'markets';

(m) Introduction of a regional system of 'transfer points' at the technological universities, the Industrial Consulting Service (RND) and the Industrial Service Centre (IDC) of TNO. The aim is to create close contacts and thus to make the know-how available in this country more accessible, through clearly recognizable outlets, in particular to small and medium-sized firms.

Republic of Ireland

A recent trend in collective research in Ireland is the establishment of a research facility in solid-state electronics in University College Dublin to work with that rapidly expanding sector of industry. A special programme of expansion in the engineering and computer science faculties of several universities is geared to producing specialist manpower, but related research work is also increasing.

Sweden

Current and likely future trends in collective industrial research in Sweden are:

— the present cooperation between industry and the government as regards joint financing of R & D will continue;
— cooperative research in Sweden will be dominated by existing institutes, but further new *interdisciplinary* institutes will probably be started;
— to a growing extent, *existing* resources at technical institutes, universities and industrial laboratories will be used for the implementation of the institutes' research programmes;
— governmental aid to the research programmes will be fairly large when new institutes are created but will be reduced successively, so that industry progressively takes over the responsibility for the activity;
— the government will continue to play a dominant role in the initiation of new cooperative research programmes;
— the government will use the institutes as a resource for the implementation of projects especially important to society (financed entirely by the government);
— the institutes will be 'opened' to smaller companies (experimentation activities with governmental aid are at present going on at six institutes);
— the technology transfer process as well as marketing activities will be stimulated through financial aid by the government. The institutes will generally become increasingly involved in 'economic' services;
— the use of 'brokers' in initiating contacts and providing advice to SMEs will be continued and perhaps extended;
— it is possible that a 'small enterprise institute' will be established, common to all sectors, to tackle such problems as product design and product marketing;
— regionalization (decentralization) of services, especially to small firms, will be continued;
— the current trend towards providing 'product development' assistance, financed directly by individual companies, will continue.

United Kingdom

There is a marked trend among an increasing number of research associations towards the provision of non-technical services. These include information dissemination, management and other training, and economic advisory services such as marketing, forecasting and strategic planning. A trend also exists away from long-term cooperatively funded basic research and towards direct-fee work of all types, both for individual companies and small groups of companies. Accompanying these trends has been an increasing emphasis on the employment of industrial personnel — rather than those with a purely academic background — to provide the wider variety of consultancy services offered.

Finally, while the emphasis in the past has been on process research, there exists evidence to suggest that research associations are becoming increasingly involved in product development for individual firms.

United States

To date cooperative industrial research in the United States has been highly fragmented and largely uncoordinated, and based mainly on industry-specific research organizations. Governmental involvement in programme determination has been negligible, although some contract research for government agencies has been performed. This situation is in the process of change following the President's Domestic Policy Review (1979), in which a number of government-supported, generic cooperative research centres were proposed. Thus, generic cooperative research is about to become an arm of governmental industry policy in the United States.

West Germany

It is, perhaps, in West Germany that the greatest number of initiatives have been taken to improve the utility of cooperative research to industry. These initiatives have, by and large, been concerned with assisting small and medium-sized firms.

New trends in collective industrial research in West Germany are:

- the provision, since 1978, of federal funds to assist the efficient transfer of results of collective research into SMEs;
- a movement towards more firm-specific contract research, as opposed to collective research;
- the appointment in 1978 of government-funded technological advisers to SMEs. This has been accompanied by the creation of a number of information brokers whose task is to generally increase the awareness in SMEs of the services available in collective research organizations;
- several collective research organizations have initiated and performed detailed studies on the development of future markets in a group of related new products or for new technologies (such as microelectronics and their use in the manufacture of watches and clocks);
- the VDI Technology Centre in Berlin, in collaboration with other research organizations, is attempting to provide R & D, knowhow and technology transfer assistance to SMEs in the microelectronics field;
- in 1976 a fund was established to support contractual research for SMEs in the laboratories of the *Fraunhofer Gesellschaft* (FGS).

DISCUSSION

The discussion of the complexities and difficulties of regulation, public procurement, and government subsidies given in this book clearly points to the overwhelming importance of in-house technical competence, the quality of the independent scientific and technical advice available to various government agencies and to the problems of policy coordination. Good high-level natural scientists and technologists are clearly essential but they are not enough. Indeed, it could be dangerous if they were to be a unique source of advice and policy formation. Competence in natural science and technology must be systematically related to other types of expertise in economics, social policy and politics. The development of this all-round competence is, of course, equally essential in industry, and in both sectors there is clear evidence of the development of management techniques, institutions and structures appropriate to the nature of these problems. It is to this general problem of 'infrastructure' that we now turn.

As in the case of policy towards subsidies there has been a change of attitudes towards scientific and technological infrastructures. While recognizing the large contribution made by government-financed laboratories and by universities to many areas of new technology, policy-makers in industry and government have been increasingly concerned by the inability of these infrastructural institutions to contribute to the resolution of policy problems. High quality R & D may of course be very useful but innovation involves far more than this. Social, political, economic and managerial problems associated with technical innovations cannot, as we have seen, be easily resolved, yet the pressures to find good solutions are increasing.

Clearly the universities have the major responsibility, as they have had for a long time, for educating scientists and technologists of the necessary calibre. Despite some hesitant steps, it may be doubted whether any of the universities yet live up to their name and fame in developing the capacity of engineers and scientists to get to grips with the social problems associated with technical change.

Again, although it can be shown that universities have usually been the source of many of the most original and creative ideas which have ultimately revolutionized whole branches of industry and technology, there is still room for some doubt as to whether the universities are succeeding in maintaining this quest for originality and for excellence in changed circumstances. New types of research organization may be needed in many areas of research and there are obviously financial and political pressures both within and outside the universities to substitute short-term lower quality research for the more challenging and difficult objectives.

However, these problems of the universities are not our central concern here. We are concerned more with the role of those institutions which stand in a more direct and immediate relationship with industry and government in policy formation. Here, the evidence is clear-cut; in all countries there has been a slow and halting recognition that R & D is not enough. This recognition is reflected in many ways.

First of all, there is a clear trend (although with many misgivings and hesitations) towards the acceptance of the need for government-financed research organizations to make use of various types of social scientists and management specialists; this is for their efficient internal functioning, the selection of research subjects, and for the execution of the services required by industry and government. The American non-profit institutes were ahead of Europe in this respect. Already in the mid-1960s a survey showed that institutes such as Stanford, Battelle and Mid-Western were employing on the average more than 15 per cent of social scientists on their professional staff. This reflected their already much greater involvement in policy problems of government and industry, and their recognition that the social and economic aspects of innovation had to be considered simultaneously with the technology. In a later stage this mean the incorporation of policy analysis instruments such as scenario-writing, technology assessment, risk-analysis, impact-analysis and modelling.

Secondly, in many government-financed national laboratories and other scientific and technological institutes, there have been organizational and structural changes designed to facilitate contact and communication with policy-makers in industry and government. Sometimes these changes affect the composition of governing bodies, and sometimes representation on various panels, committees, advisory groups and so on, but although very diverse in form they are all designed with a similar purpose – to strengthen the coupling between the various parts of the system and to increase the awareness and responsiveness within the government-financed infrastructure to contemporary economic, industrial and social problems.

Thirdly, there has been a clear-cut trend towards an increasing reliance on contractual arrangements for R & D and other scientific services, either to replace budgetary allocations or to complement them. Sometimes, as in the case of Eastern Europe and the Rothschild Report (1971) in the United Kingdom, there is an explicit philosophy of reliance on contract mechanisms and a deliberate reallocation of resources. In other cases there has been a more gradual and less explicit shift but the tendency has been apparent almost everywhere.

Fourthly, as organizations in the infrastructure have increasingly responded to this changing climate they have begun to accept new responsibilities and have changed patterns of organization. This has led to a new flexibility in the whole approach to problems of both government and industry policy for technical change. This new flexibility is already apparent in organizations such as TNO in the Netherlands, the Fraunhofer Institute in the German Federal Republic, the NRDC and Harwell in the United Kingdom, STU in Sweden, the CSIRO in Australia, all of which now accept very considerable responsibilities with respect to wider problems of innovation management, and are ready in varying degrees to take on a more active entrepreneurial role. Adjustment of government-sponsored R & D organizations towards the new environment can best be illustrated by the structural changes in the TNO organization that have currently been decided upon by the Netherlands government. Within the new structure TNO will undoubtedly be in a better position to pull together that capability from within the organization that will be required to provide answers to present-day societal problems including those of industry.

Finally, despite the myriad problems of collective industrial research, it is clear that it is definitely on the increase in most countries. To a large extent this is due, as discussed above, to a greater awareness on the part of governments of the potential utility of collective industrial research as an arm of government policy towards industry generally, and more specifically towards stimulating and assisting innovation; in particular collective industrial research is increasingly being used as a major component of government policy towards assisting small and medium-sized firms. It is also due to some extent to greater efforts on the part of collective industrial research organizations themselves to promote their services; they appear in many cases to be adopting a more positive stance and are actively 'marketing' their services in both industry and government.

While the modes of organization and financing of collective industrial research vary considerably from country to country, nevertheless there does appear to be a growing convergence in aims and practices. Certainly, a number of general trends in collective industrial research are observable internationally. The most significant of these trends can be summarized as follows:

- increasing strategic use by governments of collective industrial research as an arm of industry policy;
- greater emphasis on the provision of 'economic' services, such as management training, assistance with marketing, etc.: that is, collective research organizations are increasingly becoming involved in the complete process of innovation, rather than solely with the R & D end of that process;
- increased support from governments for the utilization of collective industrial research by SMEs, both by the provision of financial assistance for contract research and by the use of information brokers;
- the awareness within collective research organizations of their potential to assist SMEs — with or without governmental assistance — has generally also increased;
- there is a trend towards the performance of more generic research (notably in the field of microelectronics) and newly established, or proposed, collective research organizations in several countries have been of the generic type;
- collective industrial research organizations are generally performing a higher percentage of contract research for single firms or small groups of firms, rather than collective research for whole sectors of industry. This has resulted in a greater new product-orientation of research and a generally increased awareness of the problems and needs of industry;
- in a number of countries, services — especially to SMEs — are becoming increasingly regionalized;
- collective industrial research organizations in several countries are more and more involving other research organizations (universities, government research institutes) in their activities.

Thus, while the history and practice of collective industrial research has varied greatly from country to country (long-established and comprehensive in Japan; comprehensive with a strong bias towards small firms in West Germany; highly fragmented, with little government support or direction in the United States), attitudes, aims and practices are converging. While this is partly due to the fact that the advanced nations face similar economic and industrial problems, it is also a result of governments becoming increasingly involved in policies for industrial innovation, and in particular, of a growing awareness on their part of the potential utility of collective research as an important active component in these policies.

References

Allen, T. J. (1966), 'Performance of information channels in the transfer of technology', *Industrial Management Review,* 87.
—— (1977), *Managing the Flow of Technology*, Cambridge, Mass., MIT.
Brousse, A. (1979), 'Industrial technical centres in France', Six Countries Programme Meeting on Trends in Collective Industrial Research, London, November.
Erngren, B. (1979), 'Cooperative research in Sweden', Six Countries Programme Meeting on Trends in Collective Industrial Research, London, November.
Gaudin, T. (1980), 'Collective research is back', French Ministry of Industry.
Holland, W. E. (1972), 'Characteristics of individuals with high information potential in government R & D laboratories', *IEEE Transactions in Engineering Management*, EM-19, 2.
Langrish, J. (1974), 'The changing relationship between science and technology', *Nature*, 250, No. 5468, August.
Rothschild, Lord (1971), *A Framework for Government Research and Development* (Rothschild Report), London, HMSO.

Rothwell, R. (1980), *Trends in Collective Industrial Research*, Report to the Six Countries Programme on Innovation, TNO, PO Box 215, Delft, Netherlands, April.

—— and Robertson, A. B. (1973), 'The role of communications in technological innovation', *Research Policy*, 2.

—— and Townsend, J. (1973), 'The communication problems of small firms', *R & D Management*, 3, 3, June.

—— and Zegveld, W. (1978), *Small and Medium Sized Manufacturing Firms: Their Role and Problems in Innovation — Government Policy in Europe, the USA, Canada, Japan and Israel*, Report to the Six Countries Programme on Innovation, TNO, PO Box 215, Delft, Netherlands, June.

Smith, D. (1977), 'Contracts on the campus', *Physics Bulletin*, **28**, 2, December.

Universities and Industry Joint Committee (1970), *Industry, Science and the Universities*, London, CBI, July.

Wetmore, W. H. (1980), *The Industry Programme in the US National Science Foundation: Its Role in Stimulating Technological Innovation*, Washington, DC, NSF.

White House (1979), *The President's Industrial Innovation Initiatives* (fact sheet), Washington, DC, October.

Wolek, F. W. (1979), 'Cooperative research and development in the United States', in Baker, M. J. (ed.), *Industrial Innovation*, London, Macmillan.

10. SMALL AND MEDIUM-SIZED MANUFACTURING ENTERPRISES AND TECHNOLOGICAL INNOVATION:* THE ROLE OF GOVERNMENT

INTRODUCTION

Today, as in the past, support for small and medium-sized firms comes from many and diverse quarters. Historically we find two rather different approaches to the problem:

— the first approach, which has generally prevailed in most European countries and in Japan, takes overall economic, social and political considerations concerning the place of small firms as its starting-point, and considers a large range of measures aimed at strengthening their productivity and competitiveness. Among these measures we generally find some which are more specifically aimed at strengthening the technological capacity of the firms concerned and improving their position as utilizers of modern technologies;
— the second approach, which is based to a high degree on American experience, centres its interest mainly on the problem of the growth and existence of the small *innovative* firms active in industrial branches generally characterized by science-intensive technologies, fluid industrial structures and rapid growth rates.

Some countries have begun to develop a two-tier policy and build-up measures specially aimed at the small innovative firms alongside the wider measures aimed at the overall population of small firms. This development, however, is by no means general yet, or complete.

There is an important margin of uncertainty in the definition of the small industrial firm. Much of the literature in this area speaks of 'small and medium-sized' firms. The dimension of size may alternatively be number of employees, amount of capital, or annual sales; which dimension is appropriate will often depend on the nature of the industry. Numbers of employees cannot provide a useful comparison of size between firms in labour-intensive and capital-intensive industries. Sales are misleading when comparisons are made between industrial and trading firms. Some industries have their own specific size variable, such as 'sales area in m^2' in retailing. In general, we can say that definite cutoff points on a single dimension are only useful when making an analysis within a given sector of industry, but have less relevance when discussing industry as a whole.

In Europe the criterion of 500 employees or less has been used as a rough but convenient cutoff point, although in many sectors of industry this may already constitute a sizeable enterprise. The OECD has estimated that in the 1960s in almost all member countries enterprises employing less than 500 people continued to represent 50 per cent of net industrial output and 50 per cent of employment

---

*For a detailed discussion of this issue, and a comprehensive description of government policies towards SMEs in ten countries, see Rothwell and Zegveld (1978).

in industry. Some more recent data are: Italy (1971): 67 per cent, Holland (1973): 62 per cent, Belgium (1970): 67 per cent, Germany (1967): 52 per cent, France (1971): 49 per cent and Britain (1972): 32 per cent.

Although the measures taken by the respective governments on behalf of small and medium-sized enterprises differ from country to country, we can safely say that there is broad consensus regarding general policy objectives to support these firms.

GENERAL POLICY REASONS FOR SUPPORTING SMEs

Among the general policy reasons for supporting small firms are:

(1) The distribution of economic power through a system of small firms leads to a more favourable distribution of power in society in general. The existence of small firms has positive effects on political and social stability. Conversely, it is often held that excessive concentration of economic power has unfavourable and destabilizing effects in the long run.

(2) A high degree of market concentration leads to economic inefficiency. This argument can be interpreted in the static sense, to mean that monopoly power leads to misallocation of resources. It can also be interpreted in terms of dynamic efficiency. In this sense it can be argued that monopoly power leads to complacency, which in turn leads to a slower rate of technological progress than would otherwise be possible. It is argued, therefore, that small firms are a necessary competitive spur to existing oligopolists; that their existence is a proof that market entry is possible; and hence that the presence of small firms itself guarantees a certain market dynamism.

(3) A more widely held position considers that small firms are a necessary complement, rather than an alternative, to the economies of scale offered by large firms. Large-scale modern process industries, for example, cannot effectively survive without an appropriate 'hinterland' of small, user-oriented firms and an industrial fabric marked by a wide network of subcontracting relations between large companies and small firms.

(4) Another argument is that small firms should be valued more highly than their quantitative share of the market suggests, because their diversified products are better able to cater to the individual tastes of consumers at a time when the dominant technological regime, dictated by economies of scale, tends towards a culturally impoverishing reduction in variety. There are two aspects to this argument:

- It is argued that if the external costs to society as a whole of economies of scale are brought into the economic equation, it becomes clear that small firms should receive some sort of protection from governments. Although in the area of manufacturing there is leeway for letting the quality of the small firms products speak for itself, governments may help by improving the flow of information to consumers, and modify a situation too highly dominated by the marketing budgets available to large-scale producers;
- the second aspect to this argument is the claim that after two decades of technological development characterized by the exploitation of economies

of scale certain limits have now been reached in this respect, both in the area of consumer acceptance of mass goods that offer little potential for individual expression, and in that of technical opportunities for development. A change of technological regime from low-cost production and economies of scale to quality and individuality will in itself offer good opportunities to the small industrial firm.

(5) Small firms are sometimes seen as a buffer to sharp fluctuations in employment, although statistical data on this matter seem to be incomplete. However, the Japanese Ministry of International Trade and Industry reports in the 1977 white paper on small and medium business enterprises that during the recent recession a substantial decrease in employment was recorded in manufacturing corporations with 500 or more employees.

This was offset by an increase in employment in enterprises with one to 29 employees, chiefly in wholesale, retail, services and construction industries. However, a shift of employment from manufacturing to the service sector should not be mistaken for a shift to small industrial firms. In the United Kingdom Fothergill and Gudgin (1979) found that, during a period of severe industrial world stagnation in the 1970s, small manufacturing firms have been more buoyant than their larger counterparts. A related case is sometimes made for the superiority for small local firms over manufacturing divisions or branches of large firms, with headquarters elsewhere, in providing employment stability in underindustrialized regions. This position is based on the disappointing results of regional industrialization policies in a number of countries. While providing short-term relief of local unemployment when enticed by government subsidies to locate in the region, branch manufacturing plants were hardest hit when the recession came. Gronhaug, Frederiksen and Vatne (1979) have provided convincing evidence for this in the Jorpland and Rjukan areas of Norway.

It is also argued by some experts that government would do better to support local small firms because of their more even balance between direct and indirect labour and firmer commitment to local interests. This offers greater possibilities for a more balanced growth in the range of local skills.

(6) The quality of working life in small firms is sometimes said to have certain advantages over work in large firms. Relations are less impersonal, and there is a more direct relationship between an individual's effort and the final output of the firm. On the other hand employees of large firms are often better organized to protect their economic position, safety rules may be better adhered to, and, as the recent Japanese MITI survey found, more emphasis may be placed on participation programmes. It is clear that as yet no broad statements can be made on the quality of working life in small industrial firms as compared to large ones. Further analysis of existing data on job satisfaction, turnover, and health, as well as new empirical data would be welcome.

(7) Small and medium-sized manufacturing firms are to a large extent working in areas of traditional industry that are gradually being placed at a competitive level with industries in developing countries. Initially this was true for such sectors as textiles, shoes, etc., but now also the metal fabricating sectors of industry are challenged. There seems ample opportunity to make industries in developed nations more efficient from a standpoint of both current and future production.

TECHNOLOGICAL POLICY ARGUMENTS FOR SUPPORTING SMEs

The position of the small industrial firms with regard to technological change is a many-faceted subject. Depending on the type of small firm being considered, emphasis may be put on the role of the small firm either as a source of technical innovation or on the contrary as a barrier to the widest possible diffusion of the 'best' technical practices. Research has shown that a significant number of basic innovations have originated in small firms and that small firms often play an important role, especially in the United States, in industries characterized by a particularly high rate of growth and technological change.

On the other hand, many traditional industries with a low rate of growth are also characterized by a large number of small firms, unable to generate enough income to finance not only the R & D that might lead to higher productivity and new products, but also the new investments which would incorporate upgraded technologies. The arguments below will be principally those related to the role of the small firm as a source of new ideas and innovations. These arguments may be listed as follows:

(1) Technological change is best promoted in a system where the complementarity of small and large firms lies in the fact that the former are particularly adept as initiators of radical innovations while only the latter have sufficient resources for successful large-scale development.

(2) Research results showing the ability of small firms to produce radical innovations tend to suggest that in certain industry sectors, small firms are responsible for a disproportionately large share of radical innovations. If these findings are placed alongside Schumpeter's analysis that entrepreneurial activity is responsible for creating the new technoeconomic combinations on which the economic upswing is based, governments should be especially concerned at present about the vigour of small firms. From this standpoint these firms can be viewed as a genetic pool from which the successful technoeconomic combinations of the future will be selected.

(3) The place attributed to the contribution of small firms in technological innovation is brought out by the model developed by Abernathy and Utterback (1978, Chapter 3). This model distinguishes between productlines which are in a very rapid or 'fluid' stage of development, and more mature sectors characterized by 'specific' manufacturing technology. Firms in the fluid state are characterized by high rates of product innovation, competition on the basis of performance maximization rather than price, small size, loose entrepreneurial organization and the employment of general-purpose manufacturing technology with relatively skilled labour.

By contrast, as a productline matures, individual products become more and more standardized, almost a commodity; process change tends to predominate over product change; competition is primarily on the basis of cost minimization and minor product differentiation; the firm becomes much larger, more hierarchical with strong division along functional lines; production equipment becomes highly specialized; and product changes become more difficult. For mature firms working in oligopolistic markets, innovations consist primarily of small incremental process improvements.

An industrial structure marked by the presence of small high-technology firms may thus be considered to be simultaneously the cause and the consequence of productlines in the fluid stages of development.

(4) Calculations made by the National Science Foundation on the basis of its industrial R & D statistics suggest that in terms of innovation measured against dollar expenditure on R & D the small firms have had a much higher — although falling — productivity than their larger counterparts. The argument concerning the contribution of small firms to innovation seems, however, to require quite definitively a branch-level analysis, and the question of the contribution of small firms to invention and innovation is discussed in some detail below.

Almost all the reasons given above why governments should be interested in supporting SMEs except, perhaps, that relating to high current levels of unemployment, have been valid for at least the past decade. However, changes in both the world economic climate, and in rates of technical change, make it even more imperative that governments should support SMEs today.

Recent drastic increases in the cost of energy, higher raw materials costs and ever increasing concern with, and legislation on, the environment, imposed greater demands on the limited abilities and resources of small firms. (On the other hand this might provide SMEs with a wide range of new opportunities to innovate energy saving devices, new substitute materials and pollution monitoring and control equipment.) It might be that only with government assistance will many of today's small firms achieve adjustment to the changed circumstances.

It seems likely that it is at the front end of the product lifecycle that most innovation takes place, and at the tail-end of the cycle where production economies become more important. This means that SMEs in the advanced economies have a comparative advantage at the beginning of the cycle, whereas firms in the low labour cost developing countries enjoy a comparative advantage nearer the end of the cycle. This has implications relating to the international division of labour, and might pose a cogent argument for western governments to intervene to stimulate innovation in SMEs. Indeed, there is some evidence to suggest that, because technology is developing faster, this lifecycle is shortening. This means, however, that an increasing percentage of the total cost is becoming concentrated at the R & D end, which means in turn that the financial risk for SMEs is greater since more R & D expenditure is required more often. This poses yet another potent argument in favour of greater government support for SMEs today.

Because of the above factors it is becoming increasingly important for SMEs carefully to formulate explicit new product-marketing strategies. Also, due to recent high rates of inflation, and relatively large fluctuations in the international value of various national currencies, other management problems such as pricing cost control and rates of materials purchasing have intensified. It is, therefore, more important than ever that governments should assist in providing management and accountancy services and/or training to SMEs.

Finally, if lifecycles are shortening, and if rapidly changing economic and environmental conditions are imposing new constraints on industry, it is of even greater importance today for SMEs, most of which lack comprehensive R & D facilities, to gain *quick* access to the technology they require to enable them to respond to these changes. The point is, without this fast access to technology, SMEs are liable to 'miss the boat'. This has implications for the role of the government-supported R & D infrastructure, and in particular its need to adopt a more active stance.

ADVANTAGES AND DISADVANTAGES OF SMEs IN INNOVATION

Small and medium-sized manufacturing firms are said to enjoy a number of advantages in the technological innovation process, inherent in their small size. They are also seen to suffer a number of size-related disadvantages *vis-à-vis* their larger counterparts. Government policies towards SMEs should therefore be designed to assist them to overcome their inherent disadvantages as well as to capitalize on their advantages. A number of advantages and disadvantages of SMEs in the innovation process are outlined below.

Advantages

Marketing

This is an area where, in some instances, SMEs have a comparative advantage over their larger counterparts. They develop specific capabilities in certain technological areas, serving a narrow but sophisticated market; through close contact with customers they keep abreast of often fast-changing market demands and are able to react *quickly* and *efficiently* to both market and technological changes. They do not suffer from the bureaucratic inertia that often afflicts very large enterprises and thus enjoy the advantages of rapid, flexible response to demand shifts.

Dynamic, Entrepreneurial Management

Small high-technology firms are often controlled by dynamic, entrepreneurial characters who react swiftly to take advantage of new opportunities. Large firms, in contrast, often possess a management structure that stifles entrepreneurial endeavour. Indeed this has been recognized for some time in the United States, where a number of very large corporations have reorganized their new product development efforts along small-firm lines (Rothwell, 1975).

A second point is that entrepreneurs who have founded their company on a particular innovation are perhaps more amenable to undertaking subsequent high-risk innovation projects than managers in large companies which are often controlled by accountants who are averse to risk-taking.

Internal Communications

The efficient running of any organization requires good internal communications. Small firms often enjoy an advantage over large firms because of the ease with which they can organize internal communications. There is less need to establish sophisticated formal communication networks in small firms, where communication is most often of an informal reactive kind, and where it generally occurs very rapidly offering a fast response to internal problem-solving and in reorganizing to adapt to changes in the external environment.

Disadvantages

Manpower

Innovation, and particularly radical innovation, normally requires the use of qualified engineers and scientists. SMEs, which do not normally possess a formal R & D department, and which can afford to spend only small sums on technical developments, often experience considerable difficulty in attracting and financing on a permanent basis one or more qualified engineers and scientists. As the data in

Table 10.1 indicate both the absolute number and relative percentage of professionals in R & D employed by enterprises in West Germany with less than 500 employees declined considerably between 1964 and 1973 (Echterhoff-Severit, 1977).

Table 10.1 Professionals in R & D in West German enterprises by size of firm in 1964 and 1973

Size of firm (employees)	Year	Professionals in R & D	
		Number	Percentage of total
Less than 500	1964	576	5.2
	1973	390	2.1
500 to 1999	1964	1002	9.1
	1973	1728	9.3
2000 and more	1964	9472	85.7
	1973	16 397	88.6

The marketing of complex, high-technology goods often requires teams which include technically qualified members, as does the aftersales servicing of sophisticated equipment. This is a costly business, which can once again put SMEs at a disadvantage relative to large firms.

External Communication

To enable a firm to undertake the rational planning and assessment of innovation endeavours, a great deal of information is needed on a variety of subjects, such as the market situation, new technological developments, sources of technical assistance, government promotional measures, etc. Because of their lack of resources, SMEs are at a disadvantage in gathering and analysing such information. A recent survey in West Germany has shown, for example, that relatively few small enterprises attempted to forecast technological developments, a major reason being that they regarded gathering pertinent information as being too expensive; further, funds for hiring a qualified employee to perform this work were not available (Oppenländer, 1976). A second survey in West Germany showed, with respect to information on economic developments, that most smaller firms were similarly unable to gather and analyse data useful for their specific needs. Smaller firms also bemoaned the absence of publicly available data on probable developments of small sectors of industry or on specific markets, which would be more useful to them than standard macroeconomic projections (Newmann, 1973).

A crucial area in which small firms are disadvantaged *vis-à-vis* larger firms is in the gathering of scientific and technical information. In this respect small firms often suffer from a serious information gap, which is made worse through the inability of SMEs to establish comprehensive library and data retrieval systems and to send personnel to conferences and seminars. As a result of this small firms can become introspective, seeking ideas mainly from within and lacking awareness of new technical trends and opportunities. That small firms obtain a greater percentage of ideas for innovations from within than do larger companies is clearly demonstrated in Table 10.2.

Table 10.2 Sources of innovative ideas by firm size (1667 important innovations introduced into British industry between 1950 and 1970)

	Small (1-199)		Medium (200-999)		Large (1000 +)		Total	
	No.	*%*	*No.*	*%*	*No.*	*%*	*No.*	*%*
In-house	139	70.5	151	65.6	606	48.8	896	53.7
External	58	29.5	79	34.4	634	51.2	771	46.3

Mamangement Techniques and Practice

While small entrepreneurial firms often enjoy the advantages of dynamic open-minded management, SMEs in traditional areas of manufacturing sometimes suffer through possessing a 'Dickensian' management structure. In the latter instance, the firm is headed by an all-powerful autocrat, who refuses to listen to advice from his subordinates and who runs the firm entirely as he sees fit to do so. If this autocrat is suitably gifted, the firm thrives; if not, the firm declines, and there is little or nothing anyone can do about it. Even in the former case the firm will eventually run into trouble since it will have to face the problems of succession when the autocrat retires. In such companies, normal theories of management practice have little meaning, and it is difficult to see what can be done by government or anyone else to improve the situation.

Even in SMEs possessing democratic, consultative managers, problems can exist because of their lack of management expertise. This often manifests itself in an inability to plan properly for the future. In a time of accelerated technical, social and economic change, the formulation of a corporate strategy, and of plans to implement such a strategy, is essential. This is a particularly weak point in SMEs. As an indication of this, a survey in West Germany in 1974 showed that even in those firms having a formal R & D budget, only 11 per cent of these employing fewer than 200 derived it from a co-operate plan extending over several years; the comparable figure for firms employing 5000 or more was 53 per cent (Stroetmann, 1979).

Finance

Innovation is both costly and risky and small firms often experience constraints due to their lack of financial resources. Certainly few small firms can afford to spread the risk by embarking on several projects simultaneously. Large firms, in contrast, are able to diversify the risk through having a portfolio of projects at different stages of completion. SMEs also appear to experience greater difficulty than do large firms in raising capital for high-risk projects and particularly in raising longer-term capital (Waite, 1973).

Finally, marketing startup with new innovative products can be both difficult and costly. With certain types of equipment, such as farm machinery, the cost of market startup abroad can be prohibitive for many small firms since it involves actual demonstrations of the machine's performance on site, which is an expensive and time-consuming business beyond their financial capabilities.

Economies of Scale and the Systems Approach

In some areas economies of scale form a substantial entry barrier to small firms (such as automobiles, consumer durables). SMEs can, however, play a substantial role as suppliers of components and sub-assemblies to large manufacturers. If SMEs wish to enter these areas, they can only do so by offering highly innovative, individualistic products at the top end of the market (for example Sinclair Calculators, or Aston Martin automobiles).

A second size barrier is the growing need in some areas to offer integrated systems, and this is particularly true where turnkey projects are required. SMEs are unable to offer a fully integrated range of products which can put them at a great disadvantage *vis-à-vis* large firms.

Ability to Cope with Government Regulations

One area in which SMEs appear to be particularly disadvantaged is the relatively inordinately large impact they can suffer through governmental regulations (for a more detailed discussion of this issue, see Rothwell (1980)). There are a number of aspects to this: first of all, the mere existence of regulations is especially burdensome to SMEs; second, the cost of compliance can be prohibitively high to them; third, SMEs might not possess either the technical or the legal expertise, to cope with technically or legally complex compliance problems.

Weidenbaum (1978) has addressed the question of the impact of regulations on SMEs in the United States, where the rate of promulgation and severity of regulations has been particularly high (see Chapter 8): He states, for example, that the unit cost of meeting the form-filling requirements of a National Labour Relations Board election is small for the large firm ($101.60 for companies with over 1000 employees) and larger for the small firm ($134.60 for firms with fewer than 100 workers).

The American Chemical Society, commenting on the impact of TSCA on the US industry in 1979, mention the results of a report to the EPA which estimates that a small chemical company with annual sales of $100 000 would have its after-tax profit reduced by 13.3 per cent simply from the cost of preparing the mandated inventory of products and intermediates; the cost for a company with annual sales of $100 million would reduce after-tax profits by only 0.4 per cent.

In the United Kingdom SMEs suffer mainly through social legislation — and in particular, the Protection of Employment Act — and the sheer volume of legislation and official returns. A recent report for the Confederation of British Industry (1979) found that while managers in companies of all sizes found the time taken to comprehend and become familiar with the plethora of Acts and Orders promulgated in the previous five years increasingly burdensome, this was particularly so for SMEs. The latter found that much valuable management time that should have been spent on expanding and improving their business, was being expended on coping with this burden.

Another important problem is that of market size. In areas such as pharmaceuticals and pesticides, small specialist firms, and large firms operating in small specialized markets, are likely to be disadvantaged through government regulation. In the first case, few small firms can afford the cost of testing new drugs or pesticides (even if they succeed in meeting development costs); in the second case the high cost of testing is likely to make small markets uneconomic.

Thus, in some areas, the high costs of regulatory compliance acts to the particular disadvantage of existing small firms; it can also impose a considerable barrier to potential new entrants. Further, if because of rate-of-return regulation an Averch–Johnson type of effect occurs, then rapidly increasing capital intensity will pose yet another barrier to the entry of new small firms.

To conclude, while SMEs enjoy a number of advantages over large firms in the innovation process, such as flexibility, dynamic response to market shifts, entrepreneurial environment, they also suffer from a number of inherent disadvantages. These disadvantages are mainly related to scale, that is lack of cash and qualified manpower resources, inability to obtain economies of scale in production and distribution. This lack of resources means that SMEs are less able to accommodate the high risks involved in innovating than their larger counterparts.

Government policies towards SMEs should therefore be aimed at helping them overcome the disadvantages of small scale and at reducing the technical, financial and market risks to them in developing highly innovative, specialist products, in which area their comparative advantage over large firms generally lies. Assistance should also be made available to SMEs, to help them cope with problems of regulatory compliance.

THE ROLE OF SMEs IN INNOVATION

A great deal has been written concerning the innovativeness of SMEs in comparison to that of large companies. It has been argued, on the one hand, that large size and monopoly power are prerequisites for economic progress via technical change, while, on the other hand, it has been argued that small firms are more efficient at performing innovative activities and are, in fact, the major source of innovations. In this sections the relative contributions of SMEs to both invention and innovation are discussed.

Firm Size and R & D Expenditure

Innovations are generally the result of R & D endeavour, and it might be interesting here to briefly discuss the relationship between firm size and R & D expenditure. According to a detailed literature survey, empirical evidence indicates that for those firms that undertake R & D, innovational efforts tend to increase more than proportionally with firm size up to some point that varies with industry sector. Beyond some magnitude, size does not appear especially conducive to either innovational effort or output (Kamien and Schwartz 1975). It is important to note, however, that most SMEs do not engage in formal R & D (probably less than 5 per cent of firms employing under 200 perform R & D) while most large firms do so.*

Taking *company-financed* R & D only (as opposed to *total* R & D performed, which might include government-funded work), differences in R & D expenditure by size of firm become less marked (this, of course, relates to firms that *do* perform R & D). There are also large differences between industry sectors and in some sectors there is an inverse correlation between *research-intensity* — rather than absolute R & D expenditure — and firm size (Freeman, 1974).

*The following figures provide some indication of the *concentration* of R & D expenditures in large companies: In 1970, firms employing more than 5000 accounted for 89 per cent of all industrial R & D expenditure in the United States, 75 per cent in West Germany and 60 per cent in France. In 1961, firms in Britain with more than 10 000 employees accounted for nearly 60 per cent of industrial R & D.

Firm Size and Invention

Evidence concerning the relative contributions of firms of different sizes to *inventive* output is limited (for a detailed discussion of this issue see Soete, 1979). Table 10.3 lists the results of several studies on the frequency of major inventions by small firms or independent inventors; it suggests that small firms and independent inventors have played a disproportionately large part in producing major twentieth century inventions (Prakke, 1974).

Table 10.3 Research on the frequency of major inventions by small firms or independent inventors

Author	Type of inventions	Percentage of inventions by small firms or independent inventors
Jewkes, Sawers, Stillerman (1958)	61 important inventions and innovations of the twentieth century	(more than) 50
Hamberg (1963)	major inventions in the decade 1946–55	(more than) 67
Peck (1962)	149 inventions in aluminum welding, fabricating techniques and aluminium finishing	86
Hamberg (1963)	seven major innovations in the American steel industry	100
Enos (1962)	seven major inventions in the refining and cracking of petroleum	100

Source: Prakke (1974).

Reanalysis of the Jewkes, Sawers and Stillerman (1958) data showed, however, that while universities, independent inventors and small firms made the major contribution to the more radical type of twentieth century invention before 1930, since 1930 corporate R & D has played the dominant role (Freeman, 1967). It is also worth noting that at least half the inventions in the sample produced by small firms and independent inventors subsequently owed their successful commercial exploitation to the development work and innovative efforts of large firms.

Data from the United States show that smaller firms produce a much higher — although declining — number of patents per dollar of R & D expenditure than large firms (Table 10.4), which has been claimed as evidence of superior productivity of smaller firm R & D. However, one leading expert in the United States provides evidence that, contrary to general belief, large US firms have a *lower propensity* to patent than small firms (Schmookler 1966). In his view small firms cannot afford *not* to patent, and cannot afford to wait, so that patent statistics tend to exaggerate the contribution of small firms to innovative output. (Merely counting patents does not, anyway, give any indication of their relative importance.)

Table 10.4 Estimated innovation rate in major innovations per R & D dollar*

	Time interval	1–1000	1000–10 000	10 000 +
		Firm size (total number of employees)		
	1953–59	100.0	29.5	3.9
	1960–66	64.4	14.4	2.2
	1967–73	35.1	9.0	2.0
	1953–73 total	57.3	15.0	2.4

*Numbers are relative to the innovation rate for companies of 1 to 1000 employees in the 1953–59 period; this rate is assigned the value 100.
Source: Zegveld and Prakke (1978).

Firm Size and Innovation

Probably the most detailed data relating to firm size and innovation derives from the Bolton Committee of Inquiry on small firms in the United Kingdom (Freeman, 1971). The results in this study are shown in Table 10.5. The study reached the following conclusions:

— small firms contributed about 10 per cent of all industrial innovations made in the United Kingdom between 1945 and 1970. (This is greater than small firms share of R & D expenditure — about 5 per cent or less.) In 1958 (the median year), small firms accounted for 25 per cent of employment and 21 per cent of net output (including construction and utilities);
— the share of small firms in innovation has been more or less constant, while their share of employment and output has been falling — for example, in 1963 they accounted for only 22 per cent of employment and 19 per cent of output;
— very large firms (employment over 10 000) accounted for 54 per cent of all innovations; large firms (employment over 1000) accounted for 20 per cent of all innovations.

The share of small firms in innovation varied a great deal from industry sector to industry sector (Table 10.6). Generally speaking, in the capital-intensive industries, both product and process innovations were produced mainly by large

Table 10.5 Number and percentage share of innovations by size of firm in United Kingdom

Years	Small firms (1–199)		Medium firms (200–999)		Large firms (1000 +)		All firms	
	No.	% total	No.	% total	No.	% total	No.	% total
1945–53	17	9	25	12	160	79	202	100
1954–61	38	10	43	11	313	80	394	100
1962–70	54	11	53	10	399	79	506	100
Total 1945–70	109	10	121	11	872	79	1102	100

Table 10.6 Share of small firms in innovations and net output of industries surveyed in the United Kingdom

1958 SIC MLH Number	1958 SIC title of industry	Per cent share of innovations by small firms 1945-70	Number of innovations by small firms 1945-70	Number of innovations by all firms 1945-70	Per cent share of net output by small firms 1963	Value of net output by all firms 1963 (£ million)
471-3	Timber and furniture	39	7	18	49	220
351	Scientific instruments	28	23	84	23	154
431-3	Leather and footwear	26	5	19	32	157
450	Textile machinery	23	15	65	21	65
335	Paper and board	20	6	30	15	317
481-3	General machinery	17	18	108	14	409
339	Machine tools	11	4	38	18	100
332 411-15 417, 419 492	Textiles, carpets	10	6	63	18	670
364	Electronics	8	13	160	8	320
211-29	Food	8	3	38	16	814
381	Vehicles, tractors	4	3	64	5	733
276	Synthetic resins and plastic	4	2	52	12	77
370	Shipbuilding	2	1	59	10	215
271(1)	Dyes	0	0	22	7	35
272(1)	Pharmaceuticals	0	0	44	12	124
463	Glass	0	0	13	14	96
464	Cement	0	0	18	0*	41
383	Aircraft	0	0	52	2	185
321	Aluminium	0	0	16	10*	100*
311-13	Iron and steel	0	0	68	9	630
101	Coal	0	0	23	0	655
601	Gas	0	0	15	0	216
500, 336	Construction, earthmoving equipment and contractor's plant					
		12	4	33	53	1931

*Estimated.

Source: Freeman (1971).

firms. (The major exceptions are aerospace, shipbuilding and pharmaceuticals where, although capital-intensity is low, the development costs for most new products are very high). Small firms made their major contribution in machinery and instruments where both capital-intensity and development costs are low, and where entry costs for new firms are also low.

A second study, this time of 380 important* innovations produced in five countries, which were introduced onto the market between 1953 and 1973 looked, among other things, at the relative contributions made by firms of different sizes to the total number of innovations (National Science Foundation, 1976). The results of this study showed that:

— averaged over all countries, small firms contributed about one-third of all innovations (31 per cent), the majority share being taken by large firms (54 per cent);
— medium-sized firms played only a minor role, except in France where they contributed 26 per cent of innovations;
— small firms' contribution was highest in the United States (35 per cent) and France (31 per cent), followed by West Germany (26 per cent, and the United Kingdom (23 per cent);
— small (and medium) firms in Japan played a very minor role as producers of major innovations.

The study also looked at the comparison of firm size with the 'radicalness' of the innovation. The results of this comparison showed that:

— in the United States small firms produced a reasonably even distribution of 'radical breakthrough', 'major technological shift' and 'improvement' type innovations (27, 30 and 37 per cent respectively of all small firm innovations). A similar pattern was found for large firms;
— the output of small firms in the United Kingdom was entirely composed of radical breakthrough-type innovations. The emphasis in large firms was also on this type of innovation (56 per cent of all large firm innovations in the United Kingdom);
— in West Germany, Japan and France the emphasis for firms of all sizes was on the less radical types of innovations.

NEW TECHNOLOGY-BASED FIRMS (NTBFs)

NTBFs in the United States, the United Kingdom and West Germany

Many observers believed that a significant percentage of major technological innovations in the future will derive from new, entrepreneurial technology-based small firms, and that this will be an important spawning ground for new employment opportunities. At this point it is interesting to consider briefly a fairly recent and comprehensive report on NTBFs in the United States, the United Kingdom and West Germany, which was sponsored by the Anglo-German Foundation (Arthur D. Little, Inc., 1977). Some of the main conclusions of this report are:

---

*'Importance' was determined by an expert panel who chose the innovations out of an original total of 1310.

(1) While NTBFs have had a significant impact on the economy in the United States,* the number set up since 1950 and still in existence in the United Kingdom is only about 200, with total sales of about £200 million. In West Germany, the corresponding number of NTBFs is even less. The performance of NTBFs has been more impressive in the United States than in the United Kingdom and West Germany.

(2) Factors favouring the formation and growth of NTBFs in the United States are:

— a very large domestic market conducive to rapid growth and development;
— the availability of private wealth as a source of seed capital for the startup of new ventures;
— a fiscal framework which encourages the flow of private risk capital into new ventures;
— the existence of an active market for trading of shares in new ventures, that is, the over-the-counter (OTC) market;
— a prevailing attitude in society at large which encourages entrepreneurship;
— high mobility of individuals between academic institutions and private industry;
— the behavioural and attitudinal character of American scientists, many of whom are willing to establish their own business in order to exploit their technical knowledge;
— a large and active government expenditure programme which provides significant opportunities for NTBF endeavour, particularly through government procurement programmes.

(3) While the low level of investment and economic growth in the United Kingdom has had an adverse effect on the creation and growth of NTBFs, the much more favourable economic performance of West Germany has not led to the creation of large numbers of NTBFs. Therefore, while bad economic conditions can have negative impact on the number and performance of NTBFs, a favourable economic climate, *by itself*, is not sufficient to generate NTBFs.

(4) Three negative factors common to both the United Kingdom and West Germany are:

— cultural and attitudinal factors among academics, government scientists and research institutions that have been unfavourable towards technological entrepreneurship;
— in the United Kingdom, government R & D expenditure which has consistently neglected NTBFs — until recently the same was true in West Germany;
— the fragmentation of the European market which has restricted the growth of NTBFs in both countries.

(5) The total amount of corporation tax paid by a GmbH in West Germany which retains all its income can be as high as 62 per cent; the corresponding figure in the United Kingdom is 52 per cent.

This system disfavours NTBFs because they tend to retain most of their

---

*There are several thousand NTBFs in the United States; sales turn into billions of dollars and they probably employ in excess of two million. In the Silicon Valley area alone, for example, in 1974 there were 800 NTBFs with annual sales of $2.5 billion.

earnings. However, the system of capital allowances in the United Kingdom, whereby a NTBF need pay no corporation tax as long as its capital expenditure – on most types of assets – is greater than its pretax profit, is of real benefit to its cash flow. In contrast in West Germany, depreciation allowances, coupled to the 62 per cent tax on retained profits, have a very adverse effect on the cash-flow of a GmbH.

On the other hand higher rates of personal taxation in the United Kingdom pose a dual disincentive to private investment in new businesses; they make it difficult to accumulate private savings and do not favour the investing of savings in high risk, high return ventures (in 1979, the maximum personal level of taxation was reduced in the United Kingdom from 80 to 60 per cent). In West Germany income tax rates are much lower, and there is no charge on investment incomes.

Although in both the United Kingdom and West Germany there has been a token attempt to relieve the corporation tax burden on small companies, these special provisions have not been effective because the limits on the size of the company have been too low. (For example, in the United Kingdom companies whose pretax profits do not exceed £30 000 pay corporation tax at a reduced rate of 42 per cent.)

(6) Venture capital for NTBFs is more easily available in the United Kingdom than in West Germany, and there are more than a dozen UK institutions which provide venture and development capital for SMEs. However, NRDC and TDC are the only UK institutions which really focus on NTBFs. In general, traditional sources of finance in the United Kingdom are receptive towards new and developing ventures with high growth potential. In West Germany there are only a few institutions which provide venture capital. Traditional sources of finance are unreceptive to the needs of new firms for unsecured financing with the exception of short-term overdrafts.

(7) Many NTBFs are not based on patented inventions. Patents can, however, have both positive and negative effects on the formation and growth of NTBFs: they can hamper the spinoff process because employers are entitled to claim the right to inventions made by their employees; they can also offer security to the independent inventor and help NTBFs to attract outside capital.

While there are significant differences between the West Germany and UK patent systems, most of these differences have little effect on NTBFs. The major exception is the German Law of Employee Inventions whereby an employee inventor can claim the right to exploit his invention if his employer fails to do so. This law creates favourable spinoff conditions.

While, as stated above, venture capital has historically been more readily available in the United States than in Europe – there are now about 80 private venture capital companies in the United States – there is evidence to suggest that during the 1970s the financing of NTBFs has declined. This trend is illustrated in Table 10.7.

Morse (1976) also identified a distinct decline in venture capital investments in new projects in the United States for several years after 1974 as well as a general decline in the number of new small technical companies financed by public issues.

This decline in venture financing activity was attributed to an increase in capital gains tax in the United States from 25 to nearly 40 per cent in 1976, and to regulations concerning the use of pension funds. In 1979 the tax rate was lowered to

Table 10.7 NTBF financing in the United States, 1969–78

Year	Number of NTBFs financed by public issues on the US stock market	Funds invested ($ million)
1969	204	349
1971	73	138
1974	4	6
1978	37	—

Source: US Senate (1978)

30 per cent and pension fund managers were once again allowed to invest in innovative small firms.

The federal government in the United States has become increasingly involved in funding small firms via the Small Business Administration's Small Business Investment Companies, and has recently announced plans to establish regional corporations to finance innovation through equity funding along the lines of the NRDC in the United Kingdom. In fact, in general, governments have become increasingly involved in providing venture capital to fill the venture capital gap created by the reluctance of institutional investors to become involved in high-risk projects.

Finally, in the United Kingdom, historically high interest rates are currently posing a major disincentive to the establishment of NTBFs. This is also placing the cost of capital out of the reach of many existing, and would-be innovative, small companies.*

NTBFs and Radical Technology

It is relevant here to consider the role of NTBFs in advancing radical new technologies.† The question is, is such an advance best served by a few very big firms that possess large R & D, production and marketing resources, or by many small firms, or by some combination of both? Perhaps the leading example of the successful advancement of such a technology is the case of semiconductors in the United States, and an analysis of this might go some way towards providing an answer to the above question.

According to one commentator (Zegveld and Prakke, 1978):

... on Route 128 and in Silicon Valley Technology Oriented Complexes (TOCs) were created which consisted of a large number of entrepreneurial firms. These firms had strong relations with universities and government laboratories in the region, as well as with each other. Many of the firms were started by university graduates and as spin-offs from government laboratories. These institutions

*It is interesting to note, in this respect, that long-term, low interest loans by government and private banks in Japan and West Germany have played an important part in the funding activities of firms of all sizes in those countries.
†This does not refer to the production of a *specific* radical innovation, but rather to advance on a *broad technological and economic front* once a basic innovation such as electric power, polymerization or the semiconductor has been made.

also provided a continuous flow of highly specialised engineers. Moroever, communication between firms was guaranteed by that peculiarly American habit of job-hopping. *Fortune** at one time estimated the job turnover in Silicon Valley at 15% to 20% per annum. Risk capital was amply and expertly provided by local venture capitalists, many of whom were graduates of the small firm experience. Apart from the highly visible effects such as industrial parks and stock market values, these firms had a profound effect on the structure of the American electronics industry . . . none of the leading vacuum tube manufacturers in the US survived to similarly lead in the production of semiconductors. In Japan, however, the established firms were able to make the switch to semiconductors without interference from small firms. In Europe the traditional firms were also able to maintain their position.

It seems that two explanations are possible. They both throw a different light on the role of small firms as sources of technological change. The first explanation is that the success of the TOCs reflects a particularly American phenomenon. It is based on a culture that puts a low value on company loyalty and a high one on individual entrepreneurial activity. Innovation activity in large firms would be discouraged because of the threat technological change might present to individual job security. If this analysis is correct it would be unwise to expect much from recent European efforts to creat TOCs . . . It would then be wiser for Europe and Japan to concentrate their efforts on improving the performance of established firms.

The second explanation of the difference in the development of the US and non-US semiconductor industry lies in the fact that the US firms were at all times in the forefront of technological development in this area and that their European and Japanese counterparts can be said to have had the less risk-entailing task of following the leader.

A strategy of being second-to-market involves less uncertainty than being at the forefront. The question can be posed whether large firms in Europe and Japan would have been equally successful if US industry, characterised by the large role of small firms, had not paved the way. There is a proposition in general systems theory which says that 'only complexity can destroy complexity'.

Translated to our area this could mean that in an area of rapid technological change, of which the outstanding environmental property is complexity, the most successful organisational response will also be characterised by complexity. Such organisational complexity seems to be better provided by a system of many small firms than by a few large ones. The conclusion would be that Europe and Japan will not be able to compete successfully with the US in advanced technology by concentrating technological development in their established firms. These firms may be quite advanced scientifically through close co-operation with European university laboratories. They may be quite successful commercially through use of a second-to-market strategy . . . but if the above explanation of the small firm phenomenon is correct they will go on being dependent on technical know-how developed in a system which tends to assign a specific place to small firms as creators of new technology.

In the light of the above it might be possible to add to the current debate on the impact of microprocessors on the competitiveness of small firms *vis-à-vis* large firms. Microelectronics is, in a sense, phase two of the semiconductor revolution

Fortune (1975) 2, 27.

mentioned above; US firms are also in the forefront in the production of micro-processor units (in this case large firms). It seems feasible to postulate that in the United States small entrepreneurial firms might play a leading role in developing new 'smart' products, while in Europe and Japan they will in the main be produced, possibly at a later date, by established large firms.

GOVERNMENT POLICIES TOWARDS INNOVATION IN SMALL AND MEDIUM-SIZED MANUFACTURING ENTERPRISES

In all the advanced economies there exist a battery of measures to assist small and medium-sized manufacturing enterprises in the process of technologucal innovation. Measures common to most of these countries are (Rothwell and Zegveld, 1978):

— a network of cooperative research associations;
— provision of technical and market information services;
— provision of development credits;
— tax concessions to small and medium-sized firms;
— assistance with exports;
— government-funded R & D infrastructure (universities, government research laboratories and institutes).

Some recent internationally observable trends in the implementation of these measures are:

— the decentralization and regional administration of innovation assistance;
— encouragement of a variety of cooperative efforts among small and medium-sized firms;
— incentives for small and medium-sized firms to utilize the scientific and techno-logical infrastructure and contract-out R & D;
— some novel experiments to increase the utility of universities to smaller firms;
— increased involvement of research associations in problems of production, management and marketing, and not just R & D;
— a movement towards providing financial credits for complete innovation projects and not just R & D;
— increased involvement of industry in decision-making and the implementation of government measures.

While the above measures and trends are common to most of the advanced nations, the relative emphasis regarding the various measures varies a great deal from country to country. In the Netherlands, for example, the main thrusts of government policy towards small and medium-sized firms are technology transfer, assistance in product development — including the overall operation — and financial support through development credits. In Japan the main features of government aid are the encouragement of collaborative effort and the establishment of joint facili-ties for small firms, assistance with the establishment of cooperative associations of small firms, the provision of finance for small firms and the provision of manage-ment and technical manpower training and assistance. Innovation assistance in the United Kingdom includes a range of technical information services, management counselling, assistance with licensing, product development and productivity, and the encouragement of collaboration between small firms. In West Germany there is a marked emphasis on measures to promote technology transfer from various research institutes, the promotion of specific technologies (such as microprocessors), encouragement for small firms to contract-out R & D, the provision of venture-capital, and the regionalization of the whole range of policy measures.

These differences in emphasis mean that the focus of assistance according to the different phases of the innovation process (that is, basic research through to marketing) varies also from country to country. This is illustrated for France, West Germany, Italy, the Netherlands and the United Kingdom in Figure 10.1, which shows that for the first three countries aid is concentrated towards the earlier phases of innovation (fundamental research, applied research and development); in the Netherlands and the United Kingdom government assistance tends more towards the middle and latter phases of innovation, that is, development, prototype production and marketing.

In Japan the range of government measures to assist SMEs is comprehensive, and covers all the six phases shown in Figure 10.1. In the United States, where SMEs are regarded as a crucial cornerstone of the free enterprise capitalist system, there is a Small Business Administration to oversee their welfare. As well as having a wide range of measures on the supply side to the innovation process (financial assistance for R & D, technical assistance etc.), the SBA also offers assistance with demand factors, notably a scheme to assist small firms to obtain procurement contracts from the federal government. This scheme is probably unique.

It is not, of course, possible to offer here detailed descriptions, nor a complete inventory, of government measures to assist innovation in SMEs in all the advanced market economies. A number of the more generally adopted measures are, however, discussed below, with particular emphasis on recent and novel initiatives.

The Scientific and Technological Infrastructure

While the role of the scientific and technological infrastructure in innovation was described in some detail in the preceding chapter, it is worth while re-emphasizing here that it is increasingly being used as an arm of government policy towards SMEs. In the case of universities, the novel NSF Innovation Centre experiment in the United States was described; similar structures are currently being established in Canada and Ireland.

It is, perhaps, the collective industrial research organizations that have the greatest role to play in assisting SMEs, and the trend in all the advanced economies is, indeed, towards contract research assistance with special emphasis on SMEs. Certainly, there is a strong trend towards offering subsidies to encourage small firms to contract-out R & D to collective industrial research organizations (as well as to universities). In West Germany, for example, the subsidy rate is 30 per cent; in France it is 25 per cent; similar schemes also exist in the Netherlands and Switzerland. These schemes are designed not only to help would-be innovative small firms, but also to encourage SMEs which would otherwise not do so to become involved in R & D work.

Collective industrial research organizations are also generally adopting a more active stance towards assisting SMEs; they are more effectively marketing their services. Alongside this is the attempt to improve their speed of response to SMEs' requests for assistance, this being notably effective in Sweden. SMEs generally want solutions to their problems *now*; they cannot afford to wait months for decisions reached at a leisurely pace.

Collective industrial research organizations are increasingly offering a range of non-technical and training-services to SMEs. This is a recognition that SMEs often suffer from problems of management, financial control and marketing, especially during times of rapid technical and economic change.

Finally, collective industrial research organizations are the prime source of assistance to SMEs in the areas of testing, validation, standards, and problems of regulatory compliance. As seen earlier, problems of regulatory compliance can be particularly burdensome to SMEs.

Financial Assistance with R & D

In all the advanced market economies, schemes exist to offer direct financial assistance towards R & D in firms of all sizes. This was discussed in some detail in Chapter 6, which pointed out that only a small proportion of this aid had gone to SMEs. As a recent OECD study stated (OECD, 1979):

> In 1975 in the United States 80 per cent of funds went to firms with over 25 000 employees; in France, almost 90 per cent to the 20 largest firms; in the United Kingdom, 97 per cent to the 50 largest R & D spenders . . . in Sweden, 98 per cent to firms with over 1000 employees; and in Germany, 65 per cent to firms with over 10 000 employees.

Government financial support has been concentrated mainly in the high-technology industries, notably telecommunications, aerospace, computers and electronics, the very areas in which SMEs play a very minor role, if at all. The exceptions to this pattern are the Netherlands, Denmark and Ireland, where a substantial proportion of government financial aid has gone to SMEs.

According to Knox (1977), there are a number of reasons why SMEs have been very much neglected in the allocation of government R & D assistance. Allocation procedures are highly centralized and not very accessible to SMEs; application procedures are often complex; decision-making is often over-lengthy; decision-makers are often averse to funding risky, innovative projects in SMEs. More recently governments have instigated efforts to overcome a number of these problems, notably a general trend towards the decentralization and regionalization of measures, along with an increased allocation of funds earmarked specifically for SMEs.

An interesting recent experiment is the NSF Small Business Innovation Research Program. This is a three-phase programme in which the first two phases are funded by the NSF, while the third phase is intended for private industry venture capital funding.

Phase I solicits small feasibility research proposals from small firms to determine as closely as possible the feasibility of the idea, as well as the capabilities of the firm, within the limits of a $25 000, six-months' award. This phase acts as a screen to enable NSF to choose the most promising projects with, at the same time, only a small financial risk.

If phase I is successful, the firm moves to phase II, which covers the main research effort involving two to three professional person-years over one to two years. During phase II, the firm has to find a commitment for follow-on venture capital from a third party, at least equivalent to the amount of funds requested from the NSF; this represents an important coupling to the market place.

This scheme has the major advantage of providing funding for the early,

	Fundamental research	Applied research	Development	Production of 0-series	Marketing	Distribution
Italy						
Fund for Applied Research (FRA)	X	X	X			
Research centres		X				
Research centres for special branches		X				
CNR		X				
The Netherlands						
TNO		X	X			
Development credits		X	X	X		
Spearhead funds		X	X	X	X	
United Kingdom						
NRDC		X	X	X	X	X
Low cost automation centre (demonstration projects)				X		
Industrial liaison service centres			X			
Research associations	X	X				

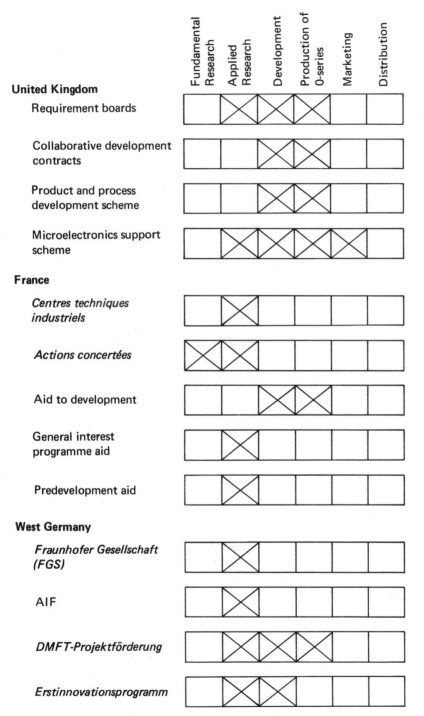

Fig. 10.1 Focus of government measures according to stage of project. Source: Hagedoorn and Prakke (1979)

high-uncertainty, high-risk phases of the project, which effectively lowers the risk for private venture capital. The awards are given to projects in certain specified areas of engineering and applied science that could have significant public benefit if the research is successful. Time between first application and grant is six months, and the amount of paperwork is kept to a minimum.

Interfirm Cooperation

One possible means that small and medium-sized firms might employ to gain the benefits of large scale in research and development, and also in production, finance and marketing, is the formation of loose groupings of firms. Firms belonging to these groupings could retain a high level of autonomy and the advantages of smallness, such as dynamism, flexibility and entrepreneurship.

A number of such groupings are already in existence, for instance OGEM in the Netherlands, which has about 200 small and medium-sized manufacturers and a central staff and other facilities. There have been similar developments in other countries, notably Sweden and Japan; and one way by which other governments could help technological innovation in small firms would be to provide financial and management assistance for such groupings. This has in fact happened in the United Kingdom, where since 1976 the government has been operating a scheme 'to encourage collaboration between small businesses over the provision of common services of a management, technical or commercial nature which individual businesses could not afford alone'. The government contributes up to half the cost, with a maximum of £5000, for approved studies to examine the feasibility of specific proposals. Up to 1978 at least, the response to this measure has been poor and only £20 000 of the £100 000 allocated for the scheme has been committed.

It is, perhaps, in Japan that the greatest emphasis is laid on encouraging collaborative efforts among small firms. The Small Business Promotion Corporation was founded by the Japanese government in 1967 to encourage SMEs to adopt concerted action through mutual cooperation in, for example, matters of production. The SBPC, in collaboration with prefectural governments, performs diagnoses of SMEs and offers management guidance; it formulates and implements programmes relating to structural strengthening activities. In addition it offers long-term, low-interest (or interest-free) loans through prefectural governments for implementing structural strengthening activities.

Some of the SBPC's structural strengthening activities relevant to SMEs in the manufacturing sector are for:

— the joint use of computer facilities;
— the leasing of anti-pollution equipment;
— the promotion of the establishment of joint facilities;
— the promotion of mergers;
— the promotion of joint small factories;
— the promotion of joint action against environmental pollution;
— the promotion of joint equipment scrapping;
— the promotion of joint knowledge intensification to enable SMEs to jointly carry out new product or design activities.

Finally, a number of private initiatives have been taken in the United States and Europe to create collaborative efforts between large and small firms. Here the large firms gain the benefits of dynamism and entrepreneurship while the small firms gain a number of benefits of scale in production, marketing, etc. In the United States a number of large firms have even attempted to create 'new ventures' completely within their own organizations (Rothwell, 1975). In the United Kingdom the London Chamber of Commerce and Industry has recently created, within the London Enterprise Agency, a 'marriage bureau' to bring together large and small firms, and to introduce small firms to a variety of potential backers. It will also seek to stimulate collaboration between small firms.

Innovation Assistance

Analysis of the areas of governmental innovation assistance in Figure 10.1 shows that of the 50 'crossed boxes', 35 (70 per cent of the total), lie in the area of research and development (fundamental research, applied research, development). Of the remainder, ten (20 per cent) relate to assistance with prototype development, three (6 per cent) are to do with marketing assistance and two (4 per cent) with assistance in distribution. In Italy, Germany and France, the measures cluster particularly markedly within the area of R & D.

There is little doubt that those government subsidies which have been made available to SMEs have generally concentrated on the R & D end of the innovation process and have, by and large, ignored production and marketing. In some areas, however, the major costs, and sometimes the highest risks, have occurred during these latter phases of innovation and, indeed, most innovations appear to fail for management and marketing reasons, rather than for technical ones (Rothwell, 1977). There is some evidence to suggest that a number of governments are becoming increasingly aware of this, and are now moving towards 'innovation', as opposed to 'R & D' assistance.

This process is probably most advanced in Canada where, indeed, a recent governmental initiative has taken matters one step further by backing firms, rather than individual innovation projects. This initiative — the Enterprise Development Program (EDP) — represents a significant step forward, and is described in some detail below.

This programme was introduced in April 1977 by the Canadian Department of Industry, Trade and Commerce and replaced a number of individual assistance programmes. This was done in order to overcome identified weaknesses in the previous programme structure. These weaknesses were:

— wide variety of highly specific programmes making it difficult for the SMEs to identify the programmes relevant to their needs;
— administration and approval procedures of previous programmes were centralized in Ottawa, with obvious communication problems for SMEs elsewhere;
— delays in obtaining project approval;
— focus on technical matters to the detriment of financial and management matters;
— larger firms gained the greatest share of project funds;
— too little involvement of the private sector in the decision-making process.

The EDP was designed to:

— decentralize administration for small projects and SMEs;
— involve the private sector in the project approval process;
— focus on overall firm performance rather than the specific innovation projects;

— ensure that innovation assistance is provided only if the project entails a real risk in relation to total firm resources.

The overall objective of the EDP is to enhance the growth in the manufacturing and processing sectors of the Canadian economy by providing assistance to selected firms to increase their international competitiveness and viability. The focus of the programme is on SMEs willing to undertake relatively high risk projects.

The EDP is administered by a Central Enterprise Development Board and by regional enterprise development boards in each province. It uses a corporate approach to analysis. It analyses the applicant firm and the proposed project to identify viable businesses with attractive future prospects. The firm is encouraged to outline its assistance requirements for current and future programmes. The assistance offered under EDP can then be tailored to meet the total requirements of the firm.

The key to this approach is flexibility. The EDP attempts to identify and structure sensible financial packages that will help the firm to realize its potential. Rather than simply supporting projects, this approach may be described as investing in the firm.

Under the EDP, all the resources of the firm are examined — human, financial physical and technological — along with market opportunities and constraints in a complete investment analysis that establishes the good business sense of the proposal and the ability of the company to exploit the results of the project within Canada and in export markets.

Industry, Trade and Commerce officers submit their evaluation and analysis of the projects and firm's potential to the EDP Board for a decision. If the decision is affirmative, a contract is signed which incorporates the commitments of both the Company and the EDP. In the case of shared cost programmes, the contract specifies the work which the company will undertake and procedures which the firm must follow to be reinbursed for eligible expenses. For term loan insurance, an agreement is prepared which the company can then use when negotiating the terms and conditions of a loan with an approved lender.

The EDP boards are composed of an equal number of prominent businessmen and senior civil servants who, as a group, are knowledgeable in all phases of product and market development. Strict confidentiality and conflict of interest guidelines protect the competitive interests of applicant firms. The use of regional boards, with their awareness of local business conditions, helps to ensure good decisions and to expedite the decision-making process.

There are two primary methods by which the EDP participates in projects with a firm: (a) through sharing of project costs, or (b) by providing insurance for a term loan which finances the project.

For the typical shared cost project, the EDP can make a contribution of *up to 50 per cent* of the eligible costs. Loan insurance, which helps to facilitate the availability of funds at reasonable terms and conditions, can be provided for 90 per cent of a term loan for a 1 per cent annual fee.

EDP projects generally include one or more of the following elements:

— proposal preparation:
  (a) shared cost of the development of relatively complex proposals which are expected to lead to a substantial EDP project;
  (b) shared costs for market studies which are part of or are expected to lead to a substantial EDP project;

— shared cost projects:
   (a) productivity improvement studies;
   (b) innovation projects for new or improved products or processes;
   (c) industrial design;
— term loan insurance for adjustment projects:
   (a) modernization or expansion of production systems including acquisition of plant and equipment;
   (b) working capital;
   (c) mergers and acquisition.

Productivity improvement studies are used to develop the detailed analysis and information required by the firm to make a decision on a major productivity improvement plan which the company has prepared. These plans often involve industrial engineering and improved financial controls for the revised operation.

Innovation projects incorporate new technology into the development of new or improved products or processes. The risk of failure due to technological problems is always an element in innovation projects. The EDP complements the Industrial Research Assistance Program, which the National Research Council operates, in that the EDP provides assistance for the development of projects which have passed the research stage.

Design projects generally entail less technological risk and focus on the process of integrating the needs of the user in Canada and elsewhere into the design of the product. Design projects normally relate to durable products which are mass-produced by industrial processes. The products are usually complete within themselves, as opposed to being a minor part of a larger product, and when in use the products normally involve extensive contact between the product and the user.

In general the costs that can be shared include: necessary professional and skilled labour; the purchase of special purpose equipment; materials for prototypes and models. The cost of general-purpose equipment cannot be shared, but lease costs of such equipment can be shared if it is used specifically for the project.

Loan insurance is normally used to raise funds for adjustment projects that help firms adapt to changing competitive circumstances by restructuring and rationalizing their operations. These projects often include working capital, plan expansion, or updating of machinery and equipment. In the case of mergers and acquisitions, term debt may be required as an integral part of the total financing package. Assistance is also available for special purposes such as insurance of surety bonds for offshore turnkey projects; and loans and shared-cost projects are available to encourage restructuring of the footwear or tanning industries.

Eligibility for the Enterprise Development Program varies somewhat depending on the project and the form of assistance required. But, generally, it will depend on three conditions:

— the viability of the project and the firm;
— the firm's need for EDP assistance; and,
— type of industry.

It is intended that the EDP should not support firms that have adequate financial resources to readily carry out the project on their own. For shared-cost projects, the project and its implementation generally must represent a significant burden on the resources of the firm. For loan insurance, the firm must be unable to obtain debt financing elsewhere on reasonable terms and conditions. Normally firms seeking loan insurance will have approached other lenders such as the Federal Business Development Bank, before applying to the EDP.

Recognizing the importance of exports to the growth of the economy and employment, manufacturing and processing firms are generally eligible for all aspects of the EDP. Firms in the service sector are not eligible for loan guarantees unless the proposed project will provide direct, tangible and significant benefit to firms engaged in manufacturing or processing.

Applicants for innovation or design assistance must be incorporated. It is not necessary to be incorporated to be eligible for other forms of assistance, although it is considered highly desirable.

Estimated expenditures under EDP in the fiscal year 1977–78 are:

Grants	— $26.0 million
Direct loans	— $ 6.0 million
Loan guarantees	— $35.0 million

Assistance with Regulatory Compliance

As suggested earlier, regulations can be particularly onerous to SMEs, and a number of governments have schemes to assist SMEs with regulatory compliance. In the United States there are two major provisions in the Revenue Code which attempt to reduce the cost of complying with pollution control regulations and which apply to firms of all sizes. These provisions grant deductions and credits for investments in pollution control hardware, and allow certain tax exemptions for municipal bond financing of pollution abatement facilities.

With regard to SMEs, the Small Business Administration in the United States makes, or guarantees, loans for pollution control-related investments precipitated by regulatory requirements. Recognizing the technical information problems of SMEs, the United States Food and Drug Administration has called for an office to be established to provide technical and other non-financial assistance to small firms to help them comply with the Medical Device Amendments Act of 1976.

Since 1970, the Japanese government has laid some stress on the implementation of anti-pollution measures. As a result, anti-pollution related investments undertaken by SMEs increased from 3 per cent of total investment in 1971 to about $6\frac{1}{2}$ per cent of total investment in 1974. To help alleviate this financial burden, the Small Business Finance Corporation and the People's Finance Corporation offer finance for pollution prevention equipment. The Environmental Pollution Control Corporation fosters the construction of joint anti-pollution facilities among SMEs, and there are anti-pollution equipment leasing schemes for smaller firms.

There are also tax-relief schemes and guidance, consultation and cash measures for firms carrying out anti-pollution development or pollution-related factory relocation projects.

Finally, in the United Kingdom a recent initiative has been undertaken to encourage small firms to set up in deprived inner-city areas, the creation of the so-called enterprise zones. As well as offering rate-free premises and capital allowances, the scheme is designed to streamline the planning process and do away with much of the red tape that small firms find so burdensome. It is an attempt to loosen regulatory constraints and create a freewheeling atmosphere in which small firm entrepreneurship might flourish.

Policy Implications

A number of government measures which might be expected to make some contribution to innovation in small and medium-sized manufacturing enterprises were outlined above. There does exist evidence, however, to suggest that in some countries many firms are unaware of the range of measures available to assist them (Rubenstein *et al.*, 1977). There seems little sense in governments having a battery of measures to assist industry if a large percentage of firms are unaware of their existence, and this precentage is almost certainly at its highest in the case of small and medium-sized companies. There is a need, therefore, for governments to take a more positive stance towards the dissemination of information describing the various available schemes, and to convince industry of their worth.

There is some evidence to suggest that many firms feel, because of bureaucratic application procedures and lengthy delays, and because of the need for accountability, the benefits gained from government aid are often outweighed by the costs incurred in applying and accounting for this aid (Allen *et al.*, 1978). The message for government here is clear; it is that application procedures should be considerably simplified and decision-making speeded up. This is particularly true for small firms which have little time or manpower resources to devote to these procedures, and which often, and especially during periods of high inflation, suffer severe, and immediate, liquidity problems.

There does appear to be a trend in government policy towards providing regionalized services for small firms, which should result in an increased awareness of available government measures. This trend is particularly strong in West Germany, France and Japan. It is an implicit recognition that innovation in SMEs is often a local phenomenon (Thwaites, 1978).

There exists convincing empirical data which strongly suggested that general measures (such as tax, safety legislation) have a greater impact on industrial innovation than R & D specific measures. It seems that, unless the general social and economic environment is favourable, specific R & D or innovation-related measures will only have a limited impact on entrepreneurship (generating new small firms) and on stimulating industrial innovation in existing small firms. Results of the few impact studies that have been undertaken indicate that innovation-specific government measures will only have the desired effect on innovation in industry when they complement, and not replace, or clash with, more general government measures.

By definition, innovation involves both technical novelty and economic utility. Every innovation must therefore rest on a new combination of a technical feasibility and an economic demand. To realize this combination some commitment of funds is needed, sometimes small, more often quite substantial. It is the unique characteristic of the successful innovator (whether he be an individual or an organization) that he (or it) is able to recognize both the technical feasibility and the demand, and is also willing to make an investment decision based on this insight. While the above follows directly from the broad definition of innovation using the concepts of technical novelty and economic utility, it is also the basis for a more detailed analysis of the innovation process and thereby of government measures to promote innovation. Even a preliminary analysis would tend to confirm the proposition that it is of little use to set up government programmes in isolation. Specifically it can be said that most programmes have only provided one of the three inputs defined in the above triple-input model of technological innovation (technical knowledge, finance, market knowledge). Success will then depend on whether the other two inputs are available within the firm.

Finally, most government schemes to assist innovation in SMEs — and in firms of all sizes for that matter — have concentrated mainly on supply factors, and these have been largely concentrated at the earlier phases of innovation, notably R & D. Considering the considerable purchasing power of governments and other public authorities, it would seem both feasible and desirable that greater efforts should be made to employ innovation-oriented public procurement as an important component of innovation policy towards SMEs.

References

Allen, T. J. *et al.* (1978), 'Government influence on the process of innovation in Europe and Japan', *Research Policy*, 7.

American Electronics Association (1978), *Capital Formation*, US Senate Select Committee on Small Business.

CBI (1979), *Innovation and Competitiveness in Smaller Companies*, London, October.

Echterhoff-Severit, H. (1977), *Forschung und Entwicklung in der Wirtschaft, 1973*, Essen, Stifterverband für die Deutsche Wissenschaft.

Enos, J. L. (1962), 'Invention and innovation in the petroleum refining industry' in National Bureau of Economic Research, *The Rate and Direction of Inventive Activity: Economic and Social Factors*, Washington, NBER.

Fothergill, S. and Gudgin, G. (1979), *The Job Generation Process in Britain*, Centre for Environmental Studies, Research Series, 32.

Freeman, C. (1967), 'Science and economy at the national level', *Problems of Science Policy*, OECD.

—— (1971), *The Role of Small Firms in Innovation in the United Kingdom Since 1945*, Report to the Bolton Committee of Inquiry on Small Firms, Research Report No. 6, London, HMSO.

—— (1974), *The Economics of Industrial Innovation*, Harmondsworth, Penguin Modern Economic Texts.

Gronhaug, K., Fredriksen, T. and Vatne, E. (1979), *Arbeidsplass, Lokalsamfunn og Bedriftsetablering*, Bergen, Industri Økonomisk Institutt.

Hagerdoorn, J. and Prakke, F. (1979), *An Expanded Inventory of Public Measures for Stimulating Innovation in the European Community with Emphasis on Small and Medium-sized Firms*, TN), PO Box 215, Delft, Netherlands.

Hamberg, D. (1963), 'Invention in the industrial research laboratory', *Journal of Political Economy*, 71, 2.

Jewkes, J., Sawers, D., and Stillerman, R. (1958). *The Sources of Invention*, London, Macmillan.

Kamien, M. I. and Schwartz, N. L. (1975), 'Market structure and innovation; a survey', *Journal of Economic Literature*, 13, 1, March.

Knox, J. (1977), *Government Aid to Industry*, Report to the Six Countries Programme on Innovation, TNO, PO Box 215 Delft, Netherlands, February.

Little, Arthur D., Inc. (1977), *New Technology-Based Firms in the United Kingdom and the Federal Republic of Germany*, Wilton House Publications Ltd.

Morse, R. S. (1976), *The Role of New Technical Enterprises in the U. S. Economy*, Report of the Commerce Technical Advisory Borad to the Secretary of Commerce, January.

National Science Foundation (1976), *Indicators of International Trends in Technological Innovation*, NSF–C889, Washington, DC, April.

Newmann, F. (1973), *Nutzung von Gesamtvirtschaftlichen Projectionen und Prognogen in der Industrie*, München, IFO.

OECD (1979), 'Science Resources', *Newsletter*, 4, Spring.

Oppenländer, K. H. (1976), 'Das Verhalten Kleiner und Mittlerer Unternehmen im Industriellen Innovatiosprosess', in K. H. Oppenländer (ed.), *Die Gesamtvirtschaftliche Function Kleiner unde Mittlerer Unternehmen*, München, IFO.

Peck, M. J. (1962), 'Invention in the postwar American aluminum industry' in National Bureau of Economic Research, *The Rate and Direction of Inventive Activity: Economic and Social Factors*, Washington, DC.

Prakke, F. (1974), *The Management of the R & D Interface*, doctoral dissertation, MIT.

Rothwell, R. (1975), 'From invention to new business via the new venture approach', *Management Decision*, **13**, 1.

— (1977), 'Characteristics of successful innovators and technically progressive firms', *R and D Management*, **7**, 3, June.

— (1980), *Industrial Innovation and Government Regulation*, Report to the Six Countries Programme on Innovation and the National Science Foundation, TNO, PO Box 215, Delft, Netherlands, March.

— and Zegveld, W. (1978), *Small and Medium-sized Manufacturing Firms: Their Role and Problems in Innovation-Government Policy in Europe, the USA, Canada, Japan and Israel*. Report to the *Six Countries Programme on Innovation*, TNO, PO Box 215, Delft, Netherlands, June.

Rubenstein, A. *et al.* (1977), 'Management perceptions of government incentives to technological innovation in England, France, West Germany and Japan', *Research Policy*, 6.

Schmookler, J. (1966), *Invention and Economic Growth*, Cambridge, Mass., Harvard University Press.

Soete, L. (1979), 'Firm size and inventive activity: the evidence reconsidered', *European Economic Review*, 12.

Stroetmann, K. (1979), 'Innovation in small and medium-sized firms — a German perspective', in Baker, M. J. (ed.), *Industrial Innovation: Technology, Policy, Diffusion*, London, Macmillan.

Thwaites, A. T. (1978), 'Technological change, mobile plants and regional development', *Regional Studies*, **12**.

Utterback, J. M. and Abernathy, W. J. (1978), 'Patterns of industrial innovation', *Technology Review*, **80**, 7, June/July.

Waite, D. (1973), 'The economic significance of small firms', *Journal of Industrial Economics*, **21**, 2, April.

Weidenbaum, M. L. (1978), *The Costs of Government Regulation of Business*, Washington, DC, US Government Printing Office.

Zegveld, W. and Prakke, F. (1978), *Government Policies and Factors Influencing the Innovative Capability of Small and Medium Enterprises*, paper prepared for the Committee for Scientific and Technological Policy, OECD, Paris.

11. TECHNOLOGY, STRUCTURAL CHANGE AND EMPLOYMENT: POLICY IMPLICATIONS

INTRODUCTION

Following the so-called energy crisis of 1974, unemployment increased significantly in most of the mature industrialized market economies. Moreover, the recovery of the world economy from the 1974–75 recession did not lead to a rapid fall in unemployment, which had been the pattern of all previous postwar recoveries (Rothwell and Zegveld, 1979). On the contrary, throughout Europe levels of unemployment have remained high by postwar standards, and in some countries rose even higher between 1976 and 1978. In the United Kingdom levels of unemployment are fluctuating but on an apparently rising trend. In the United States, although overall unemployment has remained higher than in the 1960s, there was nevertheless some reduction between 1976 and 1978, even though the labour force did increase fairly rapidly during this period. This was the result of active employment and expansionary economic policies through which a great many new jobs were generated primarily in the public sector. Unemployment levels during the 1970s for a number of countries are shown in Table 11.1.

During the 1950s unemployment in the United States was high relative to Europe, and there was considerable concern in American trade unions about the

Table 11.1 Levels of unemployment[a] (percentage of labour force)

	1962–73 (Average)	1974	1975	1976	1977	1978[b]	1979	1980[d]
Canada	5.3	5.4	7.1	7.2	8.1	8.4	7.4	7.4
United States	4.9	5.6	8.5	7.7	7.0	6.0	5.7	6.0
Japan	1.3	1.4	1.9	2.0	2.0	2.2	2.1	1.8
Australia	1.6	2.3	4.4	4.4	5.6	6.4	6.2	6.0
Belgium	2.1	2.6	4.5	5.8	6.6	7.1	–	–
Denmark	–	2.5	6.0	6.1	7.7	8.5	–	–
Finland	2.4	1.7	2.2	4.0	6.1	6.7	6.0	4.6
France	1.8	2.3	4.0	4.2	4.8	4.8	5.9	6.0
West Germany	1.3	2.7	4.8	4.7	4.6	4.3	3.2	2.8
Italy	3.6	2.9	3.3	3.7	7.2[c]	6.9	7.6	7.8
Netherlands	1.4	3.3	4.7	5.1	4.9	5.0	–	–
Norway	0.9	0.6	1.2	1.1	0.9	1.0	2.0	1.6
Spain	–	2.2	3.8	4.9	5.7	7.0	9.0	10.9
Sweden	2.1	2.0	1.6	1.6	1.8	2.2	2.1	1.8
United Kingdom	2.4	2.5	3.9	5.4	5.7	5.7	5.8	6.0
Ireland	–	7.9	12.2	12.3	11.9	11.8	–	–

Source: OECD *Economic Outlook* and *Selected Economic Indicators* – annual surveys for the years shown.

[a]National definitions, not adjusted for international comparability

[b]1978: latest three months available (usually second quarter)

[c]New survey definitions, not comparable with previous years

[d]First quarter

effects of automation and computerization on levels of employment. During the 1960s US policy became more expansionary and US growth rates were significantly higher than in the 1950s. Unemployment fell and there was a widespread feeling that the 'automation scare' had been a false alarm. It had proved possible to generate new jobs in sufficient numbers to offset any labour displacement involved in the adoption of new technology. It was thus concluded in the 1960s that the unemployment problem in the United States was overwhelmingly one of demand rather than one of structural or technical change, and it is probably true to say that today emphasis in the United States is primarily on the role of aggregate demand.

In Europe, on the other hand, there is greater interest in problems of structural and technical change, and it is increasingly being suggested that new features in the world economic situation and in world technology means that the employment problems of the 1980s will differ significantly from those encountered in the 1960s; that the high unemployment of the 1970s cannot be written off as due to a period of demand efficiency — a purely temporary aberration from a steady long-term growth pattern — but must be regarded as marking a transition to a rather different relationship between output and employment.

This chapter will present an argument for a 'structuralist' interpretation of the contemporary unemployment problem. It will argue that while aggregate demand is extremely important to maintaining employment, by itself it cannot explain current trends and that the rate and direction of technical change is one of the central issues involved. The discussion in this chapter will not, therefore, include an analysis of 'Keynesian' or 'monetarist' economics and their relationship with employment, but rather will focus on structural factors.

As stated above, this must not be taken to suggest that demand is unimportant, and indeed during the late 1970s employment increased in the United States as the result of expansionary policies. This was, however, accompanied by a rise in inflation, which appears to be the major barrier to the adoption of such policies in other countries during a period of slow productivity growth.

Nor are the dramatic increases in oil prices which took place during the 1970s regarded as an insignificant factor in the current employment crisis, since higher oil prices effectively lower domestic purchasing power and hence aggregate demand, as well as contributing to increases in inflation. The evidence presented in this chapter will, however, suggest that structural changes in the relationship between manufacturing output and employment occurred *before* the 1973–74 oil crisis. It will also suggest that, in the case of manufacturing employment at least, the level of output expansion required in order to maintain the current level of employment has been increasing during the 1970s, making manufacturing employment generation through demand stimulation progressively more difficult.

SHIFTS IN POSTWAR PATTERNS OF EMPLOYMENT

During the postwar era there have been a number of marked intersectoral shifts in labour in all the mature industrialized economies, and a number of common trends are clearly discernible (see Figure 11.1). It is an established fact that there has been a steady decline of employment in the primary sectors (agriculture and mining) between 1948 and 1975. The decline in agricultural employment has, moreover, been accompanied by a marked rise in agricultural output, and it is an

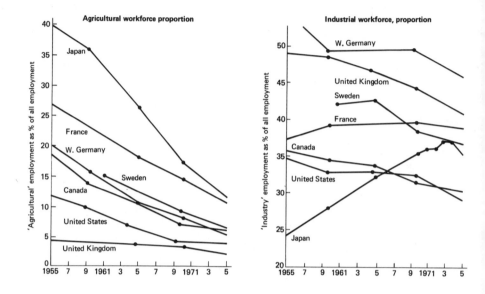

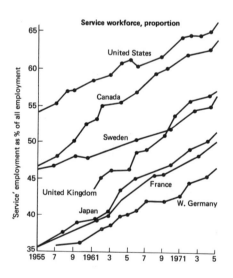

Fig. 11.1 Sectoral employment in seven economies. Source: Gershuny (1979)

important fact that a pattern of 'jobless growth' of output has been well established in a major economic sector for a long time.

The pattern of employment change in manufacturing is not as clear-cut or as consistent as in the primary sector. There are variations between countries and peculiarities in the direction and rate of change of employment growth over time. Nevertheless, one generalization can be made, and that is the rate of increase in manufacturing employment had already slowed down markedly in almost all mature industrialized countries well before 1973, which raises the question of whether the phenomenon of jobless growth has now become established in the secondary sector in the advanced economies.

A feature common to all the advanced western economies is the steady postwar growth in employment in the tertiary sector, both public and private, and for most, if not all, of the countries shown in Figure 11.1, the tertiary sector now employs more than either the primary or the secondary sectors. Two notable characteristics of the tertiary sector are that labour productivity and capital intensity are both relatively low. Now, while it is generally recognized that the marked shift of employment to the service sector is related to the increase in demand for commercial and public services by consumers and businesses, nevertheless the slow growth of labour productivity in this sector contributed to this shift. As Gershuny (1979) puts it:

> One condition for maintenance of full employment in an economy (holding relative wages constant) must be that the total product rises at the same rate as does the manpower productivity across the economy. Over the past two decades, throughout OECD, manpower productivity in manufacturing industry has risen faster than GNP [see Figure 11.2]. Employment can only be maintained under such conditions by passing labour into the relatively low productivity, low productivity growth, service sector.

Thus, an important question to ask here is 'are there developments in technology which are liable to cause a dramatic increase in labour productivity in the service sector, with its consequences for employment growth in this sector?' The current debate concerning microelectronics very much revolves around this question.

THEORIES OF MANUFACTURING EMPLOYMENT/UNEMPLOYMENT

Aggregate Demand Theory

Table 11.2 shows production and employment in the manufacturing industries of twenty OECD member countries between 1973 and 1978 (Soete, 1978). It shows that, with the exception of the United States, the industrial recovery from the 1975 depression has not been accompanied in any of the 'rich' OECD countries by a similar recovery in employment. On the contrary — again with the exception of the United States — in all the rich OECD countries employment has declined during the 1975–78 period, despite some growth in industrial output. These figures question the ability of the western economies to solve their employment problems using purely neoclassical or Keynesian demand stimulation measures.

Figure 11.3 plots industrial output and employment in the nine EEC member countries during the period 1950–78. It shows three very distinct periods in the relationship between output and employment (Soete, 1978):

	1	2	3
	GNP growth	*Manufacturing productivity growth*	*1-2*
Canada	3.6	3.7	−0.1
United States	2.5	3.6	−1.1
France	4.4	4.8	−0.4
W. Germany	3.5	4.9	−1.4
Sweden	3.3	5.9	−2.6
United States	2.2	3.6	−1.4

Fig. 11.2   Gap between manufacturing productivity growth and GNP growth, 1960–74

- the period 1950–65, which is characterized by high growth in industrial output (7 per cent annual average rate) accompanied by an important creation of employment (1 per cent annual average growth rate);
- the period 1965–73, characterized by high growth in industrial output (6 per cent annual average rate) and employment stagnation;
- the period 1973–78, characterized by low and stagnant growth in industrial output (1 per cent annual average rate) accompanied by 'deployment' (−1.8 per cent annual average rate).

Between 1950 and 1978 the relationship between output and employment has clearly altered. Underlying structural change in this relationship appears to have become established during the mid to late 1960s, and has intensified following the so-called energy crisis of 1974. Thus, while the aggregate demand theory of industrial employment would appear to have been valid between 1950 and 1965, its validity for the period 1965–78 is highly questionable, at least for the nine members of the EEC. Under these circumstances demand stimulation measures aimed at generating employment through growth in industrial output would seem to stand little chance of more than only limited success. This is not to suggest that levels of aggregate demand are unimportant, but rather that prescriptions and explanations couched solely in terms of aggregate demand are insufficient. What Table 11.2 and Figure 11.3 suggest is that the phenomenon of jobless growth is now firmly established in the manufacturing sector of a number of advanced western economies.

Table 11.2 Production and employment in manufacturing industry 1973-78 (OECD) (1973 = 100)

OECD countries	Industrial output						Employment in industry					
	1973	1974	1975	1976	1977	1978*	1973	1974	1975	1976	1977	1978*
Canada	100	103.2	98.2	103.2	106.6	107.8	100	103.0	97.3	98.6	97.3	97.4
United States	100	99.6	90.8	100.0	105.6	110.9	100	99.9	91.4	94.5	97.4	100.8
Japan	100	96.2	86.0	95.5	99.5	104.9	100	99.4	94.1	91.6	90.0	87.5
Australia	100	102.6	94.8	100.0	98.3	100.0	100	100.5	92.9	94.5	88.9	86.6
Austria	100	105.0	98.5	104.7	108.3	110.4	100	99.6	94.5	93.0	93.8	92.6
Belgium	100	103.4	94.0	101.7	100.9	102.6	100	101.1	85.6	85.6	80.0	77.8
Denmark	100	95.7	89.6	100.0	100.9	107.8	100	95.6	85.4	86.3	84.4	81.9
Finland	100	105.0	100.8	101.7	98.3	102.5	100	105.0	104.3	100.5	99.0	96.7
France	100	102.5	95.0	103.3	105.0	105.8	100	100.8	98.2	97.1	96.4	92.5
W. Germany	100	98.6	93.0	99.8	102.8	102.7	100	97.3	90.8	88.6	88.8	88.3
Italy	100	103.9	94.8	105.8	105.8	108.4	100	104.0	104.2	103.0	97.0	95.5
The Netherlands	100	105.0	100.0	105.9	106.7	105.9	100	98.9	95.7	91.4	89.2	NA
Norway	100	104.3	111.3	119.1	120.0	101.7	100	100.8	105.7	106.9	105.1	100.8
Sweden	100	105.4	103.6	102.7	100.0	95.5	100	105.4	107.1	103.9	104.3	96.5
Switzerland	100	100.9	88.2	89.1	93.6	93.6	100	99.8	90.7	84.3	84.1	84.8
United Kingdom	100	98.2	92.8	93.7	95.5	97.3	100	100.5	95.7	92.6	93.9	93.7
Greece	100	98.4	102.7	113.6	115.9	123.1	100	100.9	101.7	108.5	112.8	113.7
Ireland	100	102.5	95.8	105.0	113.4	121.8	100	100.9	93.9	93.7	96.4	96.6
Spain	100	109.5	102.2	108.8	121.9	127.7	100	103.5	103.8	104.4	NA	NA
Yugoslavia	100	112.0	117.6	121.6	133.6	144.0	100	105.5	108.5	112.1	117.3	120.5

*First six months only

Sources: OECD (1976, 1978), UN (1978)

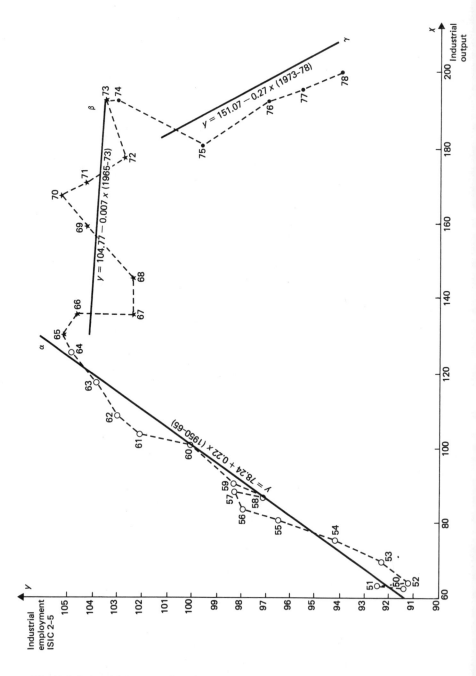

Fig. 11.3 Industrial output and employment in the EEC nine (1950–78); 1960 = 100.
Sources: EEC (1978), ILO (1977), OECD (1976, 1977, 1978), 1950–59 estimated

But what about the situation in the United States, where industrial employment increased consistently between 1975 and 1978 as industrial output increased? The answer might lie, at least in part, in differences in the structure of US industry compared to industries in Western Europe.

A recent report commissioned by the Anglo-German Foundation (Little, 1977) showed that *new* technology based firms have played a major role in the US economy, while their role in the United Kingdom, and West Germany has been only small. (There are several thousand NTBFs in the United States employing in excess of two million. In the Silicon Valley area alone, in 1974 there were 800 NTBFs with annual sales of $2.5 billion. In the United Kingdom the number of NTBFs currently in existence is only about 200 with total sales of £200 million. In West Germany the number of NTBFs is even less.) Although the regenerative capacity of small and medium-sized firms in Europe may be higher than in the United States, trade statistics also show that US exports are more technology-intensive than those from other major OECD exporters (Kelly, 1978). Now, it is well known that the United States led the world in the production of semiconductors and semiconductor devices. A similar pattern is being established in the production of microelectronic circuits and devices. In both instances, initially small, but fast-growing high-technology firms played a major role in the production of these new technologies and devices. It might be, therefore, that the recent development of microelectronics in the United States has played an important role in the generation of new jobs via the creation of many new, fast-growing high-technology firms. (Between 1963 and 1973, the growth of the US semiconductor industry was five times that of the US GNP; growth of the integrated circuit segment was about 80 times that of the US GNP.)

The results of a recent study by the US Department of Commerce would appear to lend some support to this 'new small firm' argument. The study looked at six 'mature' corporations (including General Motors and Bethlehem Steel), five 'innovative' companies (including Polaroid and IBM) and five young 'high-technology' firms (such as Marion Labs. and Digital Equipment). The mature firms, which had combined annual sales of $36 billion, added only 25 000 workers between 1973 and 1978; the innovative companies, with combined annual sales of $21 billion, added 106 000 workers; the high-technology companies, with total sales of 857 million, created 35 000 new jobs. In terms of workers created/$ million of turnover, this yields the figures: mature corporations 0.7, innovative companies 5, young high-technology companies 41. In the 1950s and 1960s the semiconductor and computer hardware industries were generating a lot of new employment. In the 1970s the main growth in employment has not derived from the hardware side, but from the software side, for example, computer bureaux, and information services, where small new firms have proliferated (the role of small firms in employment is discussed later in this chapter, page 230).

In contrast to the United States, semiconductors in Europe were developed and exploited by existing large electronics firms. It seems reasonable to suppose that a similar pattern is occurring with the development and exploitation of micro-electronics. This could mean that while the information technology has generated many new jobs in the United States, this may not be true in Europe.

Thus, it might be that in an economy whose industry is characterized to a significant extent by the rapid growth of many *new* firms based on the emergence of new technological opportunities, the relationship between output and employment is positive. In an economy based more on mature industries and in which *existing* large firms largely exploit the same new technologies, the relationship between output and employment is much weaker.

It is not being claimed here that the apparently greater success of US manufacturing in generating new jobs during the 1970s is due to the semiconductor industry in which, indeed, many new jobs were generated during the 1950s and 1960s. Rather, it is being suggested that the phenomenon of the creation and growth of new firms is more prevalent in the United States than elsewhere, especially in areas of high technology. Certainly small and medium-sized manufacturing firms in the United States appear to play a very significant role in manufacturing employment; the percentage of all workers in firms employing between 50 and 400 increased in the United States from 40.7 per cent in 1961–62 to 43.2 per cent in 1971–72. In West Germany, the United Kingdom, Italy and the Netherlands, the percentage of employment in such firms fell in each case.

International Comparative Advantage Theory

According to the theory of international comparative advantage structural unemployment in the advanced economies is due primarily to shifts in stagnant, labour-intensive industries from high-labour-cost developed countries to less developed countries where labour costs are much lower. At the same time labour in the developed world shifts to capital-intensive sectors with potential for growth. The final result of this process is one of national specialization in relative factor-abundant industries or products, and all countries end up being better off. According to this interpretation, unemployment in the developed world is only temporary and is due more often to past unwillingness to adjust under trade liberalization.

If a significant percentage of employment in the labour-intensive industries in the western economies has moved to the less developed, low-wage-cost countries (LDCs), then this might be expected to be reflected in a significant level of imports from LDCs to the developed nations. Further, if this factor has grown in importance, and is making a major contribution to recent high levels of unemployment, then the percentage of imports from the LDCs would be expected to be significantly higher today, than, say, twenty or so years ago. Thus, by separating imports originating from LDCs from those originating from the advanced economies, it should be possible to separate international competition based largely on comparative advantage (that is, low wage competition) and competition based largely on non-price factors (that is technical change).

Soete (1978) has produced data which show that international competition from developed countries is a more significant factor of domestic consumption – 4.31 per cent (1959–60) to 7.35 per cent (1973–74) – than international competition from LDCs (less than 2 per cent of domestic consumption in the western world). Further, the evolution over time indicates that developed country competition has grown more rapidly than low-wage competition. Other data broken down for eleven broad industry groups showed that:

— in most industries foreign penetration of western domestic markets is relatively high, and in the first place the result of competition from developed countries;
— in terms of 'low-wage' competition, market penetration is weak in all industrial sectors, except in clothing, petroleum products and ferrous and non-ferrous metal products (two natural resource-intensive industries). Only in the food industry, textiles but also chemicals, LDCs' imports represent more than 1 per cent of domestic apparent consumption;

— in terms of growth, import competition has increased in all industrial sectors, especially in clothing (mainly low-wage competition), but also in textiles, rubber, transport equipment and machinery.

The natural conclusion to draw from these figures is that, contrary to 'pure' trade theory, and the concept of the international division of labour, low-wage-cost foreign competition has, directly, played only a minor role in the structural employment crisis in the western economies. However, it might be that competition from low-wage-cost countries has accelerated the scrapping of old vintages, and also resulted in some product and process innovation, thereby having an indirect effect on structural change.

The Technology Gap and Rationalization Technical Change Theories

According to the technology-gap theory jobs can be lost because of lack of competitiveness in the face of technically advanced imports. In the second place, jobs are lost through rationalization by the home industry in attempting to increase its production efficiency to match that in major competitor countries, as well as attempting to overcome the price advantage enjoyed by traditional goods produced in the LDCs.

In order to provide a rigorous verification of the importance of technical change on the export performance in manufactured goods of OECD member countries (Iceland and New Zealand being excluded), Soete (1978) investigated the relationship between patents granted to those countries by the US patents office between 1963 and 1976 in 40 industrial sectors with, for these same countries, the 1974 exports of the 40 industries. It was assumed in this analysis that the United States is the leading inventive activity country and market, and will thus attract most of the important patents from other OECD countries (this issue is discussed in greater detail in Chapter 3). The results of this analysis are:

— for most capital goods industries, significant results are obtained;
— for most consumer goods (just as intermediate goods and materials where technical change is weak) where technical change is more based on the diffusion of innovations that have occurred in the capital goods sector, non-significant results were obtained.

In interpreting his results, Soete assumed that most technical change in capital goods is of the cost-reducing, continuous type. He therefore concluded that while technical change *per se* is important to competitiveness, cost-reducing technical change in particular is the crucial factor in international competition in capital goods; as a result, in the western economies between 1963 and 1976, competition mainly from other developed countries has been the crucial factor in inducing industries into, in the first instance, job-displacing, labour-saving technical change.

While much technical change is undoubtedly of the cost-reduction type, nevertheless a number of detailed studies of specific industry sectors, have highlighted the importance of 'product performance' technical change in international competitiveness. Examples are agricultural machinery (Rothwell, 1979) and portable power tools (Walker, 1978). Several studies have also emphasized this aspect of competitiveness over a wide range of industrial products (NEDO, 1977; Corfield Report, 1979). Two studies of machine-building industries have explicitly linked job loss in the United Kingdom to lack of performance-orientated technical change. The first of these (Rothwell, 1980) showed that during the postwar period the position of the UK textile machinery industry has been one of decline and that this decline was primarily the result of the failure of many UK firms to undertake programmes of technical development. As a result the United Kingdom's share of world trade in textile machinery declined from 30 per cent in 1954 to 11 per cent in 1975. At the same time, employment in the industry dropped from 75 000 in 1951 to 35 000 in 1973. This fall in level of employment was the result mainly of loss of market share due to a decline in 'product performance' international competitiveness rather than the rationalization of manufacturing processes. According to the second of these studies (Swords-Isherwood and Senker, 1978):

> There has been a trend towards reduction in employment in the British engineering industry. Automation has played some part in causing this. But it has been the result to a greater extent of the failure of British management to invest sufficiently in research and development and production facilities to make products which would be more competitive on international markets. If management in the British engineering industry fails to remedy these deficiencies, the consequences in terms of job loss could be considerable because of the impact of overseas competition. If the industry does modernise, this could result in pressure to continue to reduce job opportunities. But the industry would be creating resources which collective bargaining can ensure are used to alleviate these effects by securing benefits such as shorter working weeks and better working conditions.

So, there exists evidence to suggest that both rationalization and international competitiveness technical change have resulted in the loss of significant numbers of jobs in some western economies especially, in the case of the United Kingdom, the latter. Now, while steps can be taken to reverse lack of international competitiveness through vigorous programmes of product development, jobs lost through rationalization can only be recouped via the growth of new businesses or through significant business expansion. The recent development of microprocessor controlled production systems however, makes it likely that many firms can significantly expand output with the same, or even reduced, manpower, which would place the burden of new job creation on the growth of new manufacturing firms and on the service sector of the economy.

Finally, Cox (1978) has looked in some detail at the relationship between employment costs, sales receipts and rationalization and has presented extremely convincing data from the United Kingdom and West German mechanical engineering industries to show that where there is a mismatch between sales receipts and employment costs, firms shed labour and rationalization investment replaces growth or replacement investment. The process of employment loss through wage cost inflation is illustrated in Table 11.3. Cox concludes:

> . . . in current output technological development is responsible for maintaining and increasing sales and, potentially, the numbers employed. If however unions negotiate an average cost per employee that is out of line with increase in sales receipts, then technical development comes to play an additional role that of substituting machine effort for human effort, which has become too expensive.

Thus, wage push and social security push have reduced employment and favoured rationalization investment.

Table 11.3 The relationship between costs per employee, sales and employment in the United Kingdom and West German mechanical engineering industries

	Percentage increase per year		*Actual change in employment*
	Costs per employee %	*Sales* %	
United Kingdom			
1958–63	3	6	+56 000
1963–67	7	9	+33 000
1967–71	12	14	+54 000
1971–75	23	19	−77 000
West Germany			
1967–71	15	16	+143 900
1971–75	9	7	−96 100

The above explanations are not, of course, mutually exclusive and can act concurrently to reduce levels of employment in the advanced economies. This is illustrated in Table 11.4 for the United Kingdom, which shows the reasons for jobs lost in the 24 industries most affected by Third World competition between 1970 and 1975. It can be seen that 12.3 per cent of jobs lost were due to falling demand at home (aggregate demand) 50 per cent were due to rising productivity at home (rationalization technical change), 26 per cent because of trade with non-Third World countries (technical change competitiveness) and 9 per cent as a result of trade with Third World countries (low-cost competitiveness). In the area of textiles, in which Third World countries probably enjoy their greatest success in trade in manufactured goods, only 25 per cent of UK imports derived from these countries. This suggests that current demands for stringent controls on UK textile imports from the LDCs are largely misdirected.

Table 11.4 Reasons for jobs lost in 24 industries most affected by Third World competition in the United Kingdom between 1970 and 1975

Reasons	*Number*	*Percentage*
Falling home demand	52 800	12.3
Rising productivity at home	214 300	50.0
Trade with non-third world counties	113 400	26.5
Trade with Third World countries	47 800	11.2
	428 300	10.0

Source: *Sunday Times*, 10 February 1980, 'Mythical threats of Third World imports'

STRUCTURAL CHANGES IN THE RELATIONSHIP BETWEEN MANUFACTURING OUTPUT AND EMPLOYMENT

Figure 11.3 presented data which strongly suggest that, within the nine countries of the EEC, the relationship between manufacturing output and manufacturing employment has undergone a number of marked structural changes during the

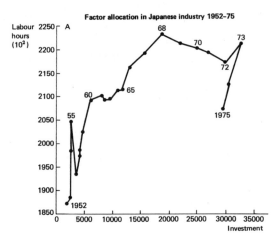

Factor allocation in Japanese industry 1952–75

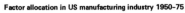

Factor allocation in US manufacturing industry 1950–75

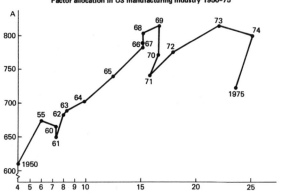

Legend: A = labour input indicator (Bill. weekly man-hours)
I = capital input (Bill. of current dollars)

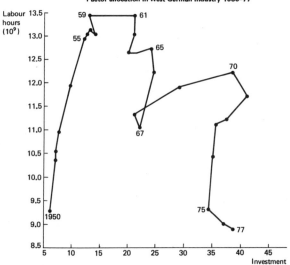

Factor allocation in West German industry 1950–77

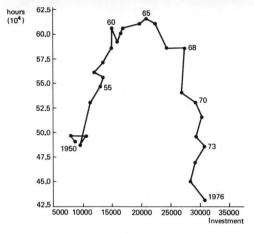

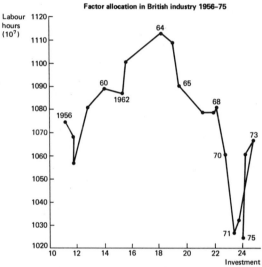

Factor allocation in British industry 1956-75

Fig. 11.4 Investment and employment in West Germany, the Netherlands, the United Kingdom, Japan and the United States, 1950–75. Source: Mensch (1979)

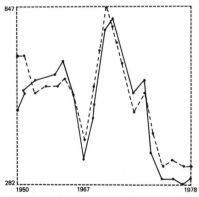

Fig. 11.5 Ratio of Expansionary to Rationalization Investment in West German Manufacturing, 1950 to 1978. Source: Mensch (1980). ○——○ S from official statistics; - - - - - estimates: S = bE/R; S = number of 'open' position in industry; E = expansionary investment; R = rationalization investment.

postwar era. Figure 11.4 presents similar data for three EEC countries separately, and for Japan and the United States (Mensch 1979).* It shows that the general pattern indicated in Figure 11.3 generally holds true for the five countries separately — although there are obvious differences of detail and timing — which suggests that the phenomenon of structural change in the output–employment relationship is common to all the major advanced market economics.

In interpreting these results, Mensch *et al.* (1980) point to changing patterns of investment in industry. Utilizing data from West Germany, he has shown that the relationship between *expansionary* investment (E) and *rationalization* investment (R) has altered during the postwar era. During the 1950s and early 1960s, investment aimed at expansion was sufficiently high in relation to that aimed towards rationalization that job generation was greater than job displacement. In the mid-1960s the productivity effects of rationalization investment began to dominate and increased industrial output could be attained with no increase in employment. A period of jobless growth was thus established. From the beginning of the 1970s rationalization investment effects swamped expansionary investment effects, and increased output was achieved with a reduced labour force. The pattern of change in the E/R ratio for West German industry is shown in Figure 11.5, which indicates that from the late 1960s on E/R dropped rapidly and reached a fairly stable 'low' in about 1975–76.

On the basis of these data, Mensch suggests a 'threshold theory' for the structural changes in the output–employment relationship. Thus, when E/R fell to a particular level (Mensch calculates this at approximately 0.5 for West Germany — point α on Figure 11.3), the output–employment relationship switched from a net 'job-expansion' phase into an 'employment neutral' phase in which it continued until E/R reached a second threshold (approximately 0.25 — point β on Figure 11.3) when labour substitution effects became dominant. E/R then fell to a fairly stable value (approximately 0.23) when a lower level 'underemployment' equilibrium was reached.† According to Mensch, only when E/R increases to a certain threshold (point γ on Figure 11.3), the value of which is unspecified, will employment in manufacturing once again increase as output increases.

It is interesting to compare Figure 11.5 with the West German data in Figure 11.4. As E/R dropped rapidly in 1965, so did employment; when E/R increased rapidly after 1967, employment increased too. In this case, however, the fall in E/R was the result of a rapid cutback in 'E' — associated with government action during a period of relatively high inflation in West Germany — rather than with a large and sudden, increase in 'R'.‡ Indeed, as Figure 11.4 indicates, between 1965 and 1967, West German industrial output remained more or less constant, and even declined slightly in 1967. Similarly, the rapid fall in E/R between 1973 and 1975 was the result of 'E' declining rather than 'R' increasing significantly.§

*Mensch has, for convenience, substituted input data (investment) for output in these figure. He found a consistently high correlation (better than 90 per cent) between the two quantities.

†Mensch's investment data are based on an IFO survey of 6000 West Germany manufacturing companies only. Given the difficulties in accurately specifying the amount of investment aimed purely at expansion and that aimed purely at rationalization, the validity of quantifying the 'turning-points' must be seriously questioned, and Mensch himself acknowledged this. Nevertheless, the concept is an interesting one.

‡Between 1965 and 1967, 'R' remained more or less constant, while 'E' fell by nearly 40 per cent.

§Between 1973 and 1975 'R' remained almost constant, while 'E' fell by about 50 per cent.

Recent research at the Science Policy Research Unit has investigated the relation-ship between annual changes in manufacturing employment and annual investment in UK manufacturing. It shows that the ratio $\Delta E/I$, which is the annual change of employment per unit of investment, has varied in a cyclical manner during the past 60 years or so. These data are interpreted (see Figure 11.6) as suggesting that changes in the relationship between expansionary investment and rationalization investment also vary in a cyclical manner.

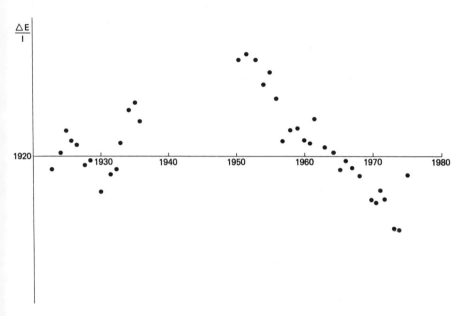

Fig. 11.6 Employment change per unit of investment (smoothed), UK manufacturing.
Source: Clark (1979)

The question now is, what relationship do the above sets of data have with technical change? If expansionary investment can, in general, be associated with the development of new products, and new production systems for manufacturing them, then the employment expansion phase in the output–employment relation-ship can be associated with a period of new product development and the rapid growth of new markets. The 'employment neutral' phase can be associated with a period of market expansion, mainly with the improvement of existing products, but also with some new product development for existing markets; in particular, it is a period of consolidation and rapid improvement to the production system, in parallel with increase in industry concentration and growing economies of scale*. The final phase — in which labour is rapidly shed — is associated with lack of new market opportunities, demand stagnation in existing markets, and continuing high levels of expenditure on production and organizational rationalization — including increased automaticity. In this phase productivity growth, albeit small

*Mensch (1977) has analysed 342 major innovations in West German industry between 1952 and 1973 that were identified by an NSF Science Indicators Project. He showed that the ratio of 'expansionary' innovations to 'rationalization' innovations changed from 53 per cent for the period 1952–59 to 28 per cent for the period 1960–73.

in relation to the second phase, nevertheless outstrips growth in output (demand), and employment thus falls.

This sequence can be linked to the concept of long waves discussed in Chapter 3, and to the change in the nature of innovation — from a focus on new product innovations to one of process optimization innovations — described by Utterback and Abernathy (1978).

Finally Maier and Haustein (1980) have also discussed the way in which industries change structurally over time. They have extended Utterback's work and developed a five-stage model of this ageing process (Table 11.5). According to this model (as with Utterback's) as an industry ages, so the underlying nature of technology changes from mainly new product development to mainly process change: at the same time the substitution of capital for labour increases progressively until the industry reaches a crisis stage when all types of investment generally decrease. (According to Maier and Haustein it might be possible to avoid decline in the saturation stage, which results in crisis, if the industry adopts a vigorous policy of innovation, to regenerate demand in existing markets, as well as a policy of diversification into new market areas.) Thus the process of capital–labour substitution is closely associated with the underlying nature of innovation.

THE ROLE OF THE SERVICE SECTOR AND THE FUTURE IMPACT OF MICROELECTRONICS

The data presented above support the contention that fundamental structural changes are taking place in the relationship between industrial output and employment, resulting in the establishment of the phenomenon of jobless growth in the secondary sector of the economy. This means — in the absence of a relatively massive increase in world demand for manufactured goods — that any significant number of new jobs must come from the generation of new firms (which is a very marked phenomena in the United States) or the expansion of the tertiary sector of the economy. On past evidence, the former seems unlikely to occur to any marked degree in Western Europe at least in the medium term (Rothwell and Zegveld, 1978); a number of factors — economic, political and technical — make the latter expansion unlikely in the advanced western economies.

Taking, first, *public* sector service employment. There are acute problems of measurement but it is commonly agreed that labour productivity increases in this sector (and to a lesser extent also in the private service sector) have been a good deal lower than in agriculture or in manufacturing. Yet they are very labour-intensive activities and wage and salary pressures for parity with other workers in percentage increases in incomes have been strong. This has two consequences. On the one hand, it is clearly a major source of wage cost inflationary pressure. On the other hand, it generates problems of the scale and control of public expenditure where these services are financed primarily through central and local government budgets and taxes. The 1978 Californian Referendum 13 is only one extreme example of what has become a widespread political tendency to resist further increases in taxation, and further increases in public expenditure on service employment. It is difficult to be sanguine about the probability of a reversal of this trend when the political pressures to reduce taxation have become so powerful, both in Europe and in the United States, where counterinflationary policies to reduce budget deficits and curb public expenditures have also become strong (especially in the United Kingdom).

Table 11.5 Stages in the development of industrial organizations, creating and adopting innovations. Source: Maier and Haustein (1980)

No.	Characteristic		Takeoff	Rapid growth	Maturation	Saturation	Crisis
1.	Example		solar energy	microelectronics	chemistry	synthetic fibre industry	steel industry
2.	Predominant type of change in production units		new establishments	enlargements	total modernization	rationalization	rationalization
3.	Degree of technology change	product	very high	high	medium	low	very low
		process	low	medium	high	low	low
4.	Technological policy for growth mainly oriented towards		push	push and compensation	compensation	compensation and continuation	compensation and continuation
5.	Relative efficiency*		low	very high	high	middle	very low
6.	Total benefits		negative	low	very high	high	low or negative
7.	Substitution of labour by capital		negative	low (high demand for qualified personnel)	high (high demand for less qualified personnel)	very high	low
8.	Firm strategy		creative push	offensive long-term oriented	market-oriented	defensive or pseudo-offensive	defensive
9.	Management		flexible risk-taking creative	flexible risk-taking entrepreneurship	less flexible rigid organization	risk-avoiding rigid organization	preference of strong leadership

*Incremental efficiency increase in relation to total industry increase.

For economical and political reasons, it would, therefore, seem to be rather unwise to pin great hopes on the expansion of public sector service employment in the 1980s.

Thus, it is on *private* sector service employment that the main hopes must be based for future employment expansion. The question is, in view of recent advances in technology pertaining to work in the service sector (such as word processors, electronic communications), and especially office work, is this expansion likely to occur? It might first be useful, before attempting to answer the above question, to try to explain why employment in the service sector has grown so much more rapidly than in manufacturing industry. Fuchs (1978) explained patterns of employment change in the United States over the period 1929–65 and suggested four possible reasons for the more rapid growth of employment in services there:

— the *quality* of labour increased faster in industry than in service activities: 'of all the variables identified, labour quality is probably the most important one in explaining the differential trend in employment';
— hours of work declined faster in service industries and institutions than in goods-producing industries;
— capital per worker increased faster in goods-producing industries than in service activities;
— goods-producing industries have experienced a faster rate of technological change than service industries and institutions.

Now, while it is generally recognized that the marked shift of employment to the service sector is related to the increase in demand for commercial and public services by consumers and businesses, nevertheless as described above the slow growth in labour productivity in this sector made a major contribution to this shift.

This again raises the question of the future ability of the service sector to continue to generate large numbers of jobs. In attempting to answer this question, Peitchinis (1978) looked at current trends in the four variables identified by Fuchs:

. . . in relation to the quality of labour, the general level of education increased substantially over the past two decades. To the extent that quality is measured in terms of the average level of education possessed by the labour force, it is doubtful that there remains any difference on the average between the level of those in goods-producing industries and the level of those in service industries and institutions. Indeed, considering the very substantial increase in the numbers of teachers, nurses, all categories of professionals, public service administrators and scores of other high quality occupations over the past two decades, it is conceivable that the average level of education of the labour force engaged in service activities now exceeds the average level of those engaged in goods-producing activities.

Regarding the hours of work in services and industry, statistical evidence suggests that while the standard hours are still lower in service industries and institutions than in goods-producing industries, the gap is not as wide on the average as it was ten or more years ago. The evidence suggests perhaps that the standard hours of work in service activities reached a level of downward resistance, whereas those prevailing in goods-producing industries are still at levels which have downward flexibility.

In relation to the third variable, i.e. capital investment, service industries have lagged substantially behind goods-producing industries on the average, *largely because of a lack of appropriate technology.* In recent years some significant changes have been recorded: the advent of electronic data processing has been rapidly transforming labour-intensive processes into capital-intensive electronic processes; as a result, substantial increases in capital investment are being recorded in service industries and institutions, as well as in the service areas of goods-producing industries, such as marketing, warehousing, planning, finance, and other office and administrative activity areas.

In relation to the fourth variable, i.e. the rate of technological change, it is not surprising that goods-producing industries should have recorded a faster rate than service industries, since in many service activities there has been relatively limited deployment of technology. But, significant changes have been recorded in recent years: the transformation of labour intensive processes has been accompanied by an acceleration in the rate of technological change.

Now if the more rapid growth of employment in the tertiary sector can be explained largely by the four variables forwarded by Fuchs (1978) (lower quality of labour, shorter working week, lower per capita capital investment, slower rate of technological change), then the significant recent improvements in all these variables described by Peitchinis (1978) can be expected to reduce the future rate of growth in employment. As Peitchinis puts it:

The question now arises whether the widespread application of electronic technology in service activities will reduce the rate of increase in employment in the (service) sector in the way that mechanical technology reduced the rate of increase in employment in goods-producing processes. There is no apparent reason for the employment effects of technology to be different in service activities from those in goods-producing activities.

In relation to this crucial point, Peitchinis goes on to state:

Heretofore, changes in technology entailed, for the most part, increases in the speed of equipment and improvements in materials. In most activities, particularly in the service sector, *the worker-machine ratio remained unchanged.* For example, scores of improvements have been introduced to the typewriter and to activities and materials relating to the typing function (paper, erasers, etc.) but the typist-typewriter ratio remained unchanged — the operation of each typewriter requires a typist. To the extent that the increase in speed in typing activity could not satisfy the increase in demand for typing services, and more typewriters had to be added, for each additional typewriter a typist had to be employed. This provides a basic general explanation for the rapid increase of employment in the service sector: demand for services increased faster than the increase of productivity in the sector.

The application of electronic technology to service sector processes facilitates a change in the worker–machine ratio that was not possible to the same extent under mechanical technology: a number of typewriters can now be linked to a computer and can perform the typing function without the participation of typists. The need for another typewriter does not generate demand for another typist. This capacity to link production processes to electronic systems, and thereby reduce the worker–machine ratio, has very significant implications for the future labour absorptive capacity of the service sector, and that of the economy at large. Developed economies are confronted with a critical problem.

The Central Policy Review Staff (ACARD, 1978) has also commented on this last point:

Word processors are microprocessor-based typing systems. Work measurement experiments seem to point fairly consistently to productivity gains something in excess of 100 per cent, comparing word processors with conventional type-writers. Thus, in theory they should make it possible for organisations which employ them to reduce their employment of typists by more than 50%.

However, the report goes on to state:

In practice, this has not occurred. Many organisations have invested in word-processors in order to assist them in overcoming shortages of typists, and organisations often discover that word processors make possible new ranges of services — the use of standard letters as prestige forms of advertising — to which they attach more value than they do as potential staff saving. Thus, in a way which is in some way analogous to the experience of the Civil Service with computers, the potential productivity does not translate at all directly into actual job loss.

It seems probable, therefore, that while word processors — and parallel developments in office and communications technology — will have only a marginal impact on *current* levels of office employment (at least in the short-term) their greater productivities will enable firms to increase office workloads with existing staff. Thus, it is *future* employment prospects that are mainly affected, *and a pattern of jobless growth seems likely to become established in this important aspect of the service sector.* Indeed, this is already apparent in banking. For example, mainly due to the use of electronics technology by the National Westminster Bank, while the volume of business increased between 1970 and 1979 by 7 per cent per annum, employment increased during the same period by a *total* of only 7 per cent (Haslam, 1979).

It also seems probable that microprocessor-based office systems will be less labour-intensive in maintenance, thus potentially reducing the labour requirement in this field. The same is true for home-based electrical devices which will increasingly employ microprocessor controls (such as washing machines, automatic dish-washers).

A marked postwar phenomenon has been the growth in the 'self-service' economy. For example, television has largely replaced cinema-going as a form of visual enter-tainment and the automatic washing machine has largely substituted for external laundry services. With the advent of cheap microprocessor controls, this trend is likely to intensify. Some examples of the potential impact of microelectronics devices on services in the home are:

— the use of television to provide a variety of information services:
— remote reading of gas and electricity meters;
— direct access to libraries;
— remote shopping and ordering;
— home electronics mail.

These will all tend to reduce overall service sector employment.

Finally, another important area in which microelectronic devices seem likely to intensify the trend towards self-service is medicine, and there is evidence that this is already occurring in the United States (Martin, 1978).

THE IMPACT OF MICROELECTRONICS ON EMPLOYMENT IN MANUFACTURING

The impact of microelectronics on employment in manufacturing will vary considerably with the nature of the production process (such as batch, continuous flow), with current levels of usage of existing electronics devices (for example Numerically Controlled (NC) machine tools) and with potential for substitution for mechanical devices. Where microelectronics does have potential for employment displacement, the rate of displacement will vary according to the speed of adoption of microelectronics systems; it is thus likely to be relatively high in the United States and relatively low in the United Kingdom.

In the continuous process industries (such as the chemical industry), where high levels of automation already exist, and where electronics controls are commonplace, it is difficult to imagine how microelectronics can have a significant impact on employment levels. Microelectronics systems should, however, be more versatile and reliable, and capable of producing a higher quality product.

With production-line systems as, for example, in the automobile industry, the potential for labour displacement by complex microelectronics devices – notably robots – is relatively high. The same is true of discontinuous flow systems – batch production – where 'smart' robots giving increased flexibility, linked to electronics data handling and production scheduling, will enable semicontinuous systems to be established with a much reduced direct labour requirement.

Robots and other electronically controlled assembly machinery will have an employment-destroying impact in all areas of assembly work. According to a recent article in *Business Week*,* General Electric Company is about to launch a sweeping automation programme that may eventually replace nearly half of its 37 000 assembly workers with robots. The same article goes on to state the opinions of some automation experts who believe that the next generation of 'smart' robots could displace 65 to 75 per cent of today's factory force.

Where microelectronics substitute for mechanical, or electromechanical systems, the potential for employment displacement is very great and, indeed, examples can be offered where this process is already well advanced. Because of the adoption of integrated circuits, manufacturing employment in the National Cash Register Company fell by 50 per cent between 1970 and 1975, from 37 000 to 18 000. In Western Electric, employment in the switching equipment division fell, as the result of the shift from electromechanical to electronics technology, from 39 200 direct employees in 1970 to 19 000 in 1976. Similar effects are occurring in Western Europe (although more slowly), and in the United Kingdom employment in telecommunications equipment manufacture fell between 1973 and 1978 by as much as 30 per cent as companies switched to the newer electronics systems.

A further area of labour displacement is within the semiconductor manufacturers themselves. Because microelectronics circuits are very much more powerful than

*9 June 1980

the components they replace for equivalent output, fewer manufacturing workers are required. Since the substituting circuits are less material-intensive and less energy-intensive, they are also less handling, machining, forming and fabrication-intensive, and there is a corresponding reduction in the need for equipment to perform these functions, with a concomitant reduction in labour required to produce such equipment.

If demand for microelectronics-based devices, such as robots or smart toys, grows rapidly, then this will of course generate new manufacturing employment opportunities. This new employment, however, might be rather less than the assembly employment displaced by robots and the employment displaced in 'conventional' toy manufacturing. Perhaps the area which offers the greatest employment generation opportunities is that of informatics. If the information society develops as rapidly as many pundits suggest (wired cities by the end of the decade), then very many new jobs will be generated in the manufacture, installation and maintenance of the new information systems. Whether this employment generation will be sufficient to offset microelectronics-induced employment displacement is, of course, a matter for conjecture.

Finally, while the adoption of microelectronics devices will undoubtedly result in manufacturing job loss, failure to take up the new technology will result in greater loss of jobs in the longer term, due to lack of technical change competitiveness. In this regard, Japanese robot manufacturers are showing a marked reluctance to sell robots abroad; the Japanese philosophy appears to be to offer home manufacturers the maximum advantage in terms of productivity increase before looking for export sales of the new devices.

QUALITATIVE EFFECTS OF TECHNOLOGY ON EMPLOYMENT

Table 11.6 summarizes the various impacts of technical change on employment in a number of industries and for several technologies; it can be seen that a large proportion of these changes are qualitative rather than simply dealing with levels of employment.

It is interesting to consider the last three columns, all of which concern the impacts of electronics-based technologies, and in which qualitative effects dominate. (As the previous section suggested, however, the next generation of microelectronics devices used in manufacturing will have a definite quantitative impact on employment as well.) Consideration of these technologies might provide a pointer to possible future effects (qualitative) of microelectronics-based production systems.

In the first case, there seems little doubt that the trend towards de-skilling, or rendering redundant certain craft skills will be intensified with the adoption of microelectronics-controlled manufacturing systems. At the same time, however, there will be an increase in demand for new, higher-level skills in the area of electronics maintenance and computer software design. This trend seems likely to result in a bifocation effect, where the manufacturing workforce consists of mainly unskilled workers (machine-minders) on the one hand and of white-collar workers possessing the 'new' skills on the other; the intermediate range of skills (semi-skilled workers, craftsmen) will largely disappear. One regrettable result of this will be a marked reduction in possibilities for the upward mobility of the unskilled workers.

In the past (and increasingly in the future) the trend towards replacing human

Table 11.6 Summary of the quantitative and qualitative impacts of technical change on employment in a number of industries

	Agriculture	Coalmining	Canadian railways	Textile machinery	Textile industry	Cement industry	Steel industry	Metalworking industry	NC machine tools	Computer-aided design	Automation
Reduction in labour force	✓	✓			✓		✓	✓			✓
Increased output with same or reduced labour force (jobless growth)	✓	✓	✓		✓		✓	✓	✓	✓	
De-skilling or making certain skills redundant	✓				✓	✓			✓	✓	✓
Generated the need for new skills	✓	✓	✓	✓	✓	✓			✓	✓	✓
Reduction in job satisfaction	✓		✓					✓	✓		✓
Required higher level management skills		✓		✓	✓	✓		✓	✓	✓	✓
Displacement of specialist skills outside the factory					✓	✓				✓	✓
Job loss due to lack of technical change competitiveness.				✓			✓		✓		

Source: Rothwell and Zegveld (1979)

skills with electronics controls resulted in job dissatisfaction on the part of skilled and semi-skilled workers. On the other hand, increased versatility of machinery, and improved (electronics) communications within the factory will provide an opportunity for greater decision-making on the part of machine operatives. Whether or not this occurs is, however, more a function of management attitudes rather than one of technical feasibility and, indeed, the additional production information more easily available from machines linked to computers will increasingly enhance management control. These factors might result in vigorous worker and trade-union resistance to the adoption of microprocessor-controlled production systems. The optimum usage of electronics-based production systems also places greater demands on the skills of management, and demands a broader range of management skills. There exists some evidence to suggest that, in fact, in the past, management resistance in several European countries has been a more important factor in retarding rates of adoption of NC production systems than has worker or trade-union resistance (Swords-Isherwood and Senker, 1978).

Finally, the adoption of electronics devices in manufacturing can result in the displacement of certain skills outside the factory. Indeed, a number of NC manufacturers have already developed computer-based diagnostic skills (some operated remotely by datalink over telephone lines, others installed at plant location) which can reduce the requirement for in-house electronic skills. Other examples are the use of external software specialists, and computer-aided design bureaux which will reduce the requirement for in-house design skills.

THE ROLE OF SMALL FIRMS IN EMPLOYMENT GENERATION

It was suggested earlier that an important contributing factor in the relatively successful performance of US manufacturing industry in holding down levels of unemployment during the 1974–78 period was the relatively large number of new small firm start-ups in the United States. The question is, is there convincing evidence to suggest that small firms make a greater net contribution to job generation than their larger counterparts?

The study quoted earlier in this chapter (page 213) suggested that *younger* US companies are rather more effective in creating new jobs than are mature companies*. It is, however, difficult to generalize from the result of this study since it dealt with only sixteen highly successful, leading US companies. What is, perhaps, significant is the concern expressed by the same study over the sharp reduction in new small company public underwritings of equity securities of less than $5 million, for companies with a prior net worth of less than $5 million, from 409 in 1972 to only 29 in 1976.

A study by the American Electronics Association (1978) also emphasized that 'younger' companies generated jobs at a greater rate than mature firms. Companies were divided into four age categories: mature (more than twenty years old); teenage (ten to twenty years old); developing (five to ten years old); start-up (less than five years old). This survey showed:

*Between 1969 and 1974, young technology companies with sales totalling only 2 per cent of those of the mature industry leaders created 34 per cent more new jobs than did the mature firms. The younger innovative companies with sales of 58 per cent of those of the mature companies created over four times as many new jobs as the mature companies. Total employment in the mature firms increased by only 3.2 per cent over the five years compared with 23.7 per cent for the younger innovative companies.

- the employment growth in start-up companies was 115 times greater than for mature companies in 1976;
- it was 55 times higher in developing companies than in mature companies;
- it was about 30 times higher in teenage companies than in mature companies;
- although the mature companies had on average 27 times more employees than the average of all firms founded since 1955, in 1976 the newer companies generated an average of 89 new jobs per company — while mature companies created an average of only 69 new jobs per company.

These results might be taken to offer some support to the earlier discussion on the relationship between the firm's age, technical change and capital–labour substitution.

Probably the greatest contribution to the debate on firm size and job generation is the work of Birch (1979) who examined employment change in 5.6 million business establishments (but rather fewer firms or companies) in the manufacturing and private service sectors in the United States between 1969 and 1976. Adopting a dynamic approach, he looked at new openings plus expansions (equals gross new jobs) and closures plus contractions (equal gross job losses) from which he computed net job change. Birch's main conclusions were:

- gross job loss through contraction and closure was about 8 per cent per annum;
- of gross job gains, approximately 50 per cent derived from expansions of existing companies and about 50 per cent from new openings;
- of the 50 per cent of jobs created by new openings, half were produced by independent, free-standing entrepreneurs, and half by multiplant corporations.

Table 11.7 summarizes Birch's results regarding the contribution to *net* job generation by firms/establishments of different sizes. It shows that 66 per cent of net new jobs were created by firms/establishments employing less than twenty people, of which 51.8 per cent were created in independent firms. The most startling results are for the US manufacturing sector, in which firms/establishments employing fewer than 50 people showed large net job creation, while the larger firms, especially those in the largest size category, showed a substantial net job loss.

Table 11.7 Percentages of net new jobs generated by size in the United States

Firm/establishment size	0–20	21–50	51–100	101–500	500+	Total
All	66.0	11.2	4.3	5.2	13.3	100
All independent Firms	51.8	4.4	0.0	−1.5	3.1	57.8
Manufacturing	360.0	61.7	−27.3	−163.4	−326.7	−100

Source: Birch (1979)

Storey (1980) has presented data comparing employment change by size of firm/establishment in both the United States and the United Kingdom over roughly comparable periods (Table 11.8). If the UK data, which are taken from the East Midlands, are at all representative of the country as a whole then there is a remarkable similarity in terms of manufacturing industry job-generation by size between the United States and the United Kingdom.

Comparable data from other countries are currently not available. However, the Canadian Federation of Independent Business showed that businesses with twenty or less employees created 72 per cent of all new jobs in Canada between

Table 11.8. Manufacturing employment change by size in Britain (East Midlands) and United States, as a percentage of total manufacturing employment in base year

	Size					
	0–20	*21–50*	*51–100*	*101–500*	*500+*	*Total*
United States 1969–76	+3.2	+0.5	−0.2	−1.5	−2.9	−0.9
East Midlands 1968–75*	+2.7	+2.3	+1.5	−2.2	−5.9	−1.5

*Openings for East Midlands are placed in 1975 size band, but *in situ* plants and closures are according to 1968 size. The procedure is assumed to be identical to that adopted by Birch.

Data derived from: East Midlands: Fothergill and Gudgin (1979); United States: Birch (1979). Source: Storey (1980)

1969 and 1977 and that, during this period, these small firms in manufacturing created 317 000 jobs, while those employing more than twenty showed a loss of 124 000 jobs. Thus, there exists rather convincing evidence to suggest that small companies do play an important role in generating new jobs. This has clear implications for government policy during a period of high (and growing) unemployment.

POLICY IMPLICATIONS

To increase employment opportunities in mature industries, where the thrust of technical change is currently very much one of manufacturing process rationalization, and in which productivity growth appears to be outstripping demand growth in stagnant markets, companies would need to adopt a policy of vigorous product diversification into new market areas, or one of significant market regeneration. An example of the latter would be the planned expenditure in the US automobile industry of $70 billion over the next five years to produce a small, energy-efficient motorcar. It is unlikely that this will be achieved without considerable government backing and, indeed, US federal government regulations have played a significant part in forcing these changes. A second such area would be the development of more efficient public transport systems in which governmental regulations, financial backing and innovation-oriented procurement, could play a major role.

Mature industries could also look more to the capital-rich developing countries as sources of rapid market growth for existing products (although, as Iran showed, there can be major problems caused by political instability). In other developing countries, where capital shortages are acute, long-term, low-interest government credit might be offered to stimulate demand and to facilitate subsequent economic growth. This appears to be a major tool of the Comecon countries to aid exports to the third world. There also exists a great need in developing countries for the agricultural regeneration and reclamation of vast areas of marginal and non-productive land. This would appear to present potentially very large opportunities for western companies involved in agricultural chemicals and soil-based biological products.

If, as Mensch suggests, a new push of 'basic' innovations is needed to form the basis of the next Kondratiev upswing, then government might look increasingly towards the stimulation and support of radical innovations in promising areas (such as biotechnology, coal products). The government-supported scientific and technological infrastructure could also play a key role in identifying and developing radical new technologies, and in transferring their result to industry.

Governments might help to accelerate the formation of new industries through the process of innovative procurement in the public sector. For example, the French government is sponsoring a number of 'wired' villages in order to stimulate the development and adoption of new microelectronics telecommunications systems, which is part of a strong French interest in the general area of *télématique.*

Although the evidence is not conclusive, it is probably safe to say that new small firms do play a very significant role in the generation of new manufacturing employment opportunities and, indeed, governments in most of the advanced market economies are currently taking steps to facilitate manufacturing start-ups. It seems, however, that the general climate — social, cultural and regulatory, as well as economic — is crucial to the stimulation of entrepreneurship, and specific government measures (reduced corporate tax, cash credits) appear to have met with only limited success in this respect.

A number of recent initiatives in the United Kingdom have shown that it is possible to establish new small firms, and new branches of existing firms (in both services and manufacturing), in areas of high unemployment. For example, the Community of St Helen's Trust, established in St Helens, Lancashire, which was created on the initiative of Pilkington Bros. (the largest local employer), the local authorities, industry, Chamber of Commerce, unions and banks (and which has the support of the Department of Industry), has successfully attracted new firms and branch establishments into the area. A second example is BSC Industries, a company established by the British Steel Corporation to fill the gaps left by closing British Steel Works in company towns in Scotland, Wales and the North of England; it helped to create 3000 jobs in 1978 and a further 6000 in 1979.

In terms of future industrial competitiveness, upon which many jobs hinge, a number of governments are attempting to stimulate the production, and especially the widespread adoption into industrial use, of microelectronic components and devices. Schemes to this end exist in the United Kingdom, West Germany, France and Japan.

Since the design, use and maintenance of microelectronics systems and devices requires the application of specialist skills, governments have a key role to play in the areas of education and training. In particular, a great deal of effort needs to be put into the retraining of displaced workers. Already, some major companies are experiencing a severe shortage of microelectronics skills (Siemens, for example, has reported a shortage of 2500 in this area), and the situation is likely to be much worse in small and medium-sized firms; such shortages appear to be widespread in the United Kingdom. Clearly, at a time when unemployment is increasing, these shortfalls in human capital are untenable, and vigorous governmental action is called for to greatly reduce this mismatch in skill supply and demand. In general terms, the situation existing in most advanced economies in which high unemployment coexists with often large numbers of vacancies, but for workers of different skills to those unemployed, calls for comprehensive retraining policies.

Finally, if existing industries are to cope successfully with increased demand during the next upswing, then they would do well to ensure that they possess sufficient productive capacity to accommodate increased output, otherwise capital shortage unemployment could occur. Such a situation, if sufficiently widespread, could significantly retard the economic recovery, and governments could play a key role here by making investment grants and low-cost loans available for building new factories and for purchasing new capital equipment.

234 Technology, Structural Change and Employment

References

ACARD (1978), Central Policy Review Staff, *Social Implications of Micro Electronics*, London, Cabinet Office, November.

American Electronics Association (1978), *Capital Formation*, US Senate, Select Committee on Small Business.

Birch, D. L. (1979), *The Job Generation Process*, Cambridge, Mass. MIT, Center for Policy Alternatives.

Clark, J. A. (1979), *A Model of Embodied Technical Change and Employment*, Science Policy Research Unit (mimeo).

Corfield Report (1979), *Product Design*, London, National Economic Development Office.

Cox, J. (1978), *Technical Development and Employment — Problems of Keynesian Economics*, Six Countries Programme on Innovation Workshop, Paris, November.

Fothergill, S. and Gudgin, G. (1979), *The Job Generation Process in Britain*, Centre for Environmental Studies, Research Series, **32**.

Fuchs, W. R. (1978), *The Service Economy*, New York, National Bureau of Economic Research Inc.

Gershuny, J. I. (1979), 'The informal economy: its role in the post-industrial society', *Futures*, February.

Haslam, J. (1979), 'An appraisal of microelectronic technology', *National Westminster Bank Quarterly Review*, May.

Kelly, R. (1978), 'Technological innovation and international trade patterns', in Gerstenfeld, A. and Brainard, R. (eds.), *Technological Innovation: Government/Industry Co-operation*, New York, Wiley Interscience, John Wiley and Sons.

Little, Arthur D., Inc. (1977), *New Technology-based Firms in the United Kingdom and the Federal Republic of Germany*, London, Wilton House Publication.

Maier, H. and Haustein, H. D. (1980), *Innovation, Efficiency Cycle and Strategy Implications*, IIASA, Schloss Laxenburg, Austria, January (mimeo).

Martin, J. (1978), *The Wired Society*, London, Prentice Hall.

Mensch, G. (1977), 'Indizien für eine Innovationstuecke', *Wirtschaftsdienst*, **7**, 350.

——(1979), *Stalemate in Technology*, Cambridge, Mass., Ballinger.

—— Kaasch, K., Kleinknecht, A., and Schnapp, R. (1979), *Innovation Trends and Switching Between Full- and Under-Employment Equilibrium, 1950–1978*, Berlin, International Institute of Management, Discussion Paper Series, January.

National Economic Development Office (1977), *International Price Competitiveness, Non-Price Factors and Export Performance*, London, April.

Peitchinis, S. G. (1978), *Technology and Employment in Industry and Services*, Six Countries Programme Workshop, Paris, November.

Rothwell, R. (1979), *Technical Change and Competitiveness in Agricultural Engineering Products: The Performance of the U.K. Industry*, Science Policy Research Unit, Occasional Paper Series No. 9, September.

—— (1980), 'The textile machinery industry', in Pavitt, K. (ed.), *Technical Innovation and British Economic Performance*, London, Macmillan.

—— and Zegveld, W. (1978), *Small and Medium-Sized Manufacturing Firms: Their Role and Problems in Innovation — Government Policy in Europe, the USA, Canada, Japan and Israel*, Report to the Six Countries Programme on Innovation, TNO, P.O. Box 214, Delft, Netherlands, June.

—— and Zegveld, W. (1979), *Technical Change and Employment*, London, Frances Pinter.

Soete, L. (1978), 'International Competition, Innovation and Employment', paper to the Six Countries Programme on Innovation Workshop, Paris, November.

Storey, D. (1980), *Job Generation and Small Firms Policy in Britain*, Series 11, London, Centre for Environment Studies.

Swords-Isherwood, N. and Senker, P. (1978), 'Automation in the engineering industry', *Labour Research*, November.

Utterback, J. M. and Abernathy, W. J. (1978), 'Patterns of industrial innovation', *Technology Review*, **80**, 7, June/July.

Walker, W. (1978), 'The portable power tool industry: a study of international industrial development', Science Policy Research Unit (mimeo).

12. POLICIES AND STRUCTURES APPROPRIATE TO THE 1980s AND 1990s

The benefits currently accepted to be associated with industrial innovation are such that governments in most industrialized countries feel that they cannot do without explicit innovation policies. The pressures to construct such policies have grown as a result of a number of factors, including the worldwide deterioration of the economic climate during the 1970s, changes in the international economic order, competitiveness of national industry, balance-of-payment problems, and, last but not least, by the general acceptance of the case long argued by many economists that innovation plays a key role in stimulating economic development.

Innovation policies are becoming a point of convergence between industrial policy and science and technology policy, containing elements of both, but at the same time opening up totally new perspectives and avenues of policy. Innovation policies are also attracting more attention now in view of the fact that traditional economic policies are seen by many not to be capable alone of forming an effective response to the current economic stagnation. On the other hand traditional science and technology policy is seen not to provide sufficient impulse and direction to technical change.

The knowlege of why, where and how governments should intervene in the process of industrial innovation currently stems largely from empirical studies of the nature and the extent of the hindrances to economically and socially desirable innovations, and on the effectiveness of alternative government policies to remove these hindrances.

Little is as yet known about the true effects of government innovation policies on individual industrial firms. Such economic indicators of output like return on investment, as can be constructed for individual cases, seldom tell most or even a significant part of the story. They become increasingly insufficient when one takes into account the fact that innovation instruments often serve several objectives. Furthermore, international comparison is complicated by the different weights given to objectives in different countries. Innovation policies, however great may be their theoretical problems, have one important feature derived from experiences in several countries including West Germany, Sweden and Japan: they work!

Contemporary innovation policies may be interpreted as an attempt to achieve simultaneously diverse social technological and economic goals which cannot always be easily reconciled. On the one hand there is the widespread desire to sustain an improvement in living standards. On the other hand, there are increasing pressures to discriminate between various alternative new technologies and to mitigate many of the injurious external and long-term effects of technical change. The daunting but socially indispensable task of those concerned with policies in this area is to achieve a constructive synthesis of these objectives.

We will now compare European innovation policies with those in the United States. Before this, however, it is worth commenting briefly on innovation policies in two major Western European countries, West Germany and France.

In the former, the federal government is continually adding to an existing and comprehensive set of innovation measures. There has been an awareness of the crucial importance of technical change for industrial performance, and for many years this has been an integrated component of governmental philosophy. Therefore, there already exists in West Germany good government–industry–university relationships. To a great extent, government innovation policy has focused on the development and the successful use of the infrastructure essential for providing the conditions under which innovation can flourish, particularly in small and medium-sized firms. The measures employed by the government are constantly changing and being improved, giving a continuously developing innovation policy. Given the existence of this well-established and successful government innovation policy, it is perhaps not surprising that the German government has not felt it necessary to draw up a report on future policy similar to those produced by other western nations.

In France, a white paper on innovation policy for the first half of the 1980s is currently under preparation. It is based on a number of background papers on such areas as microelectronics, biotechnology and communications. The overall philosophy behind the measures described in the white paper has been developed from an initial set of broad aims drawn up by the National Planning Commission and further elaborated following discussion by the Economic and Social Council. The French plan is based on 'strategic thinking', concentrating on support for strategic growth sectors. For each strategic industry, there will be specific objectives and a set of measures designed to ensure that industry will achieve these objectives. In this respect, there would appear to be certain similarities between France and Sweden, Japan, and Canada, in that all are attempting to identify potentially important *new* industrial sectors. These countries seem to have accepted that fundamental structural change in their economies is to be actively pursued, reasoning that greater advantage is to be gained from exploiting changes in the new world economic order rather than steadfastly resisting those changes through measures seeking to protect ailing industries.

It is certainly worth while contrasting European innovation policies with the debate in the United States, and comparison can best be made in three areas: public awareness, the traditions in economic policy and the actual measures that have been or will be taken.

With respect to public awareness it can be said that innovation is now a major issue in Europe as well as in the United States. There are, however, two major differences. First, in the United States, the debate on innovation has a longer history, with broad policy reviews dating back to efforts at the Commerce Department in the 1960s. In Europe innovation has only recently emerged as an issue from a traditionally much more narrow discussion of R & D policy. The broader American awareness leads to greater attention being paid to not strictly R & D-related issues such as taxation, patents, public procurement, regulation and the role of small firms. Secondly, it can be said that the awareness has become particularly intense because of President Carter's eighteen-month Domestic Policy Review, with truly large-scale participation by public groups and large numbers of government departments and agencies. In comparison, the European efforts have been limited to small circles of officials and experts. Moreover, the US awareness is fed considerably by the acute realization by Americans of their loss of primacy on the world scene and their poor performance in the areas of productivity and inflation. With only slight exaggeration it might be said that the Americans have now woken up to the fact that in order to sustain their welfare and position in the world, they must actively develop a national policy to compete with other nations on world markets.

The Domestic Policy Review on Innovation is a first implementation of such a policy.

To understand the debate on industrial innovation in the United States, it is necessary to first understand the differences in tradition in economic policy between that country and Europe. Without going into an in-depth analysis, a few major differences can be sketched.

Most importantly, because the United States traditionally exports only some 5 per cent of its GNP, US economic policy has been very little export-oriented. Contrary to the debate in Europe, international competitiveness has rarely been used as an argument for policy measures. Unemployment is related to deficient macro-economic demand in the home market rather than to international trade. The typical American response to balance-of-trade problems in mature industries has been the imposition of import quotas. This is a defensive policy, with little effect on the productivity or long-term strength of the industry concerned. On the other hand, the typical European responses to decline in a particular industry have been measures to promote investment, an offensive strategy, improving (in principle at least) the competitiveness on international markets.

A second result of the large home market for US economic policy has been a relative absence (outside the military sector) of selectivity with respect to certain technologies or firms. For that reason much attention is given to tax measures and other non-specific instruments. There has been a strong preference to let competition, however imperfect, be the regulating force and even to design policy measures that work through market forces. A similar free market policy has been much more difficult for European governments, because there were rarely more than two major firms in a particular industry or technology. It was therefore logical in Europe to develop government–firm partnerships, especially in areas of 'big science' or national prestige.

The related anti-trust tradition has kept the United States from establishing institutions of collective research, as are common in European countries. It is still an obstacle to the US proposed generic technology centres, but there seems sufficient political force behind them to overrule the anti-trust objections. 'Basic technology' centres in such areas as corrosion prevention, lubrication and welding, appear to be a major change in US policy and signal a readiness to pull together for greater international competitiveness.

Whereas in Europe industrial policy has tended to be a large firm policy, in the United States small firms have always received strong political support, as well as having their own agency, the Small Business Administration. Japan has even more comprehensive aid programmes for small firms, but Europe seems to lag behind in this area. An exemplary programme to aid innovation in small firms, and one based on a thorough understanding of the innovation process, seems to be the US National Science Foundation's Small Business Innovation Research Program. The programme forces a certain portion of departmental funds for applied research to contractors who can establish a potential link (in the first phase) and a real link (in the second phase) with venture capitalists or industrial users.

A final difference between US and European views on economic policy, again based on the relative lack of concern in the United States for international price competition on export markets, is the traditional emphasis placed on public welfare rather than industrial competitiveness. Although the latter issue is now finally emerging, the basic goal behind US innovation policy is still seen to be public welfare, that is, environmental protection, health, safety, inflation, and energy conservation. This means that regulation is an integral part of innovation policy, whereas in Europe innovation policy is all-too-often a narrow search for support measures for industrial firms. Typical of the isolationist view taken by the Americans is perhaps that productivity-increasing measures are more often supported on grounds of fighting inflation than on grounds of improving the balance of trade.

One of the main difficulties in formulating and in executing innovation policies is that responsibility for policies which affect technical innovation is normally divided between several different government departments. Some have a direct responsibility for stimulating, encouraging and supporting invention and innovation in agriculture, industry and services. Others have responsibility for safety, employment, consumer protection, education, the urban environment, international trade, health and so forth. They are often only imperfectly aware of the implications of their departmental policies for innovation elsewhere in the economy. Even when they are aware of these indirect connections, they will not usually attach any great weight to them, being preoccupied with their primary mission.

A further complication arises from the perfectly understandable desire of those working in industry and services to participate in decision-making which affects their conditions of employment, including of course, changes in techniques. Thus, the attainment of satisfactory policies for technical innovation is by no means easy. Apparently clumsy methods of interdepartmental coordination have to replace the deceptively simple invisible hand of Adam Smith.

In addition to the requirements of coordination there is the necessity for consistency in innovation policy and for effective government–industry relationships. Countries having reportedly effective innovation policies, such as West Germany, Japan and Sweden, have succeeded in developing structures to meet these two basic requirements.

The new aspirations of society have been accompanied by a more critical assessment of science and technology. Technological *laissez-faire* is presently as much a thing of the past as is economic *laissez-faire*. These changes in approach are reflected politically in the establishment in most countries of machinery for the social assessment of technology, and in requirements for greater public participation in decision-making with regard to science and technology.

Governments thus play a role in a rather broad way and have a task of both advancing and directing science and technology. Of the innumerable ways in which governments may affect technical innovation some of the most important are demand, subsidies to firms, regulation, the technical and scientific infrastructure, the support of small and medium-sized manufacturing firms and through a banking system well adapted to the need of innovative industry.

Whereas before the Second World War government policy for invention and innovation rested on three main pillars – the patent system, technical education, and the promotion of basic science – now a whole new array of government measures and instruments have been introduced to try and accelerate technical progress. Unfortunately, many of these measures were deployed hastily with very little regard for any theoretical understanding of the system which was being manipulated. Often they were based on simplistic but false analogies with the military system, or on a desire to maintain employment in design and development departments no longer required for military purposes, or on the primitive tendency to equate accelerated technical change with a simple increase in R & D expenditure.

None the less, some theoretical arguments have been advanced to justify government subsidies. Galbraith has argued that the growing scale imperatives of modern technology are such that governments increasingly have to intervene financially to underwrite technical and market risks. Although based on observation of American experience, Galbraith's justification for government intervention had already been put forward by practitioners in Western Europe, in order to justify increasing government expenditures in aircraft and computer industries.

Although studies show the dangers and difficulties of large-scale government intervention in commercial development activities without sufficient regard to cost and market realities, it would be illusory to conclude that trust can always be put in the market, or that government need finance only basic research and the development of skills. Such an approach neglects three important and interrelated problems: market imperfections, dynamic comparative advantage, and the problems of adjustment.

Market imperfections do exist, especially in the high-technology sectors, where there is considerable monopoly power and barriers to entry, and where lead times for the development of new technologies are long. For example, in the 1960s, falling real energy prices led to the neglect in the market sector of R & D on coal-related and new and unconventional energy technologies and of energy conservation technology. Governments did not compensate for these deficiencies, but instead concentrated most of their energy R & D resources on nuclear energy development and, within nuclear energy, on fast-breeder reactors: in other words, a 'narrow front' approach.

Second, there remains the problem of dynamic comparative advantage, or how to sustain infant industries in an internationally free trade world. Europe has been at a comparative disadvantage in some high-technology sectors, given the US government's stimulus through their military and space programme. The original French *Plan Calcul* may have failed to produce a viable computer industry, but perhaps the UK government expenditures, coupled with management and marketing changes, may ultimately lead to a viable self-sustaining industry.

Finally, there is the problem of adjustment. In an open world, with rapid technical, competitive and political change, how can firms and the labour forces adjust? In this context, the aircraft industry is not really different from shipbuilding. Government responsibility to tackle the social costs of transition cannot be escaped, but manpower training policy may be more helpful than subsidies to redundant R & D groups.

Taking into account the existence of these three problems, the notion of government responsibility cannot simply be banished. In such a context the institutional setup can be considered very important. Attitudes and habits, born of military relationships, have carried over into civilian areas where they do not work (Concorde, for example). In addition, as can be argued, the system of obtaining and repaying launching aid is perverse: there is little or no financial penalty for failure, and the greater the commercial success, the harder the terms of repayment become.

Despite past problems, it is probably true to say that the main form of government assistance towards innovation in industry continues to be cash credits for R & D, and from previous experience a number of recommendations can be made. First, and bearing in mind the causes of the current economic crisis, R & D assistance must clearly be directed towards certain strategic technologies, in other words, those which are likely to result in the new industries of the future (biotechnology, energy technology, communications technology) or which might regenerate existing industries (high-density fuel cell for the long-distance electric automobile). At the same time the rapid development and diffusion of certain key existing technologies, notably microelectronics, must be catered for. *In other words, R & D subsidies should be linked to an overall strategy of technological and industrial development along the lines of those being developed in Japan and France.*

Second, R & D subsidies should be more equitably distributed. While it is recognized that governments must intervene in areas where the costs of development are very high — as per Galbraith — nevertheless large firms have, for a variety of reasons, taken more than their fair share of the cake to subsidize often minor projects of dubious quality. Projects should only be subsidized that represent a significant risk to the firm. This would result in a greater percentage of funds going towards assisting innovation in SMEs.

Third, it should be explicitly recognized that innovation does not just involve R & D. It includes prototype production, production start-up and learning, and marketing as well. These latter aspects of innovation often are more costly, and can involve greater uncertainties, than R & D. Cash credits should, therefore, take these post-R & D costs and uncertainties into account, and *governments should offer 'innovation', as opposed to 'R & D', subsidies.* This trend is already apparent in Canada.

Both engineers and economists have always recognized the importance of demand in stimulating invention, innovation and the diffusion of innovation. Ordinary common sense has summed up this stimulus in the terse proverb: 'Necessity is the mother of invention'. Unfortunately, as so often occurs, this perfectly reasonable proposition is sometimes exaggerated in a onesided way so as to imply that no father would be needed. However, the history of technical innovation amply demonstrates that the process is one of a continuous interaction between 'demand' and 'supply' — 'supply' in this context meaning the advance of scientific knowledge and technology and the creative work of researchers, inventors and engineers. Government itself is heavily involved in setting the rules of the marketplace in general and is for many particular market segments a major customer. Government influences demand through *regulation* and *procurement.* In fact, a variety of studies that stress the importance of 'demand pull' as the critical input in the process of innovation support this standpoint. If innovation policy is to become more than the traditional science and technology policy, governments cannot neglect the manner in which they influence demand. This contention was born out in the joint SPRU–TNO report to the Six Countries Programme (1977) which gave a number of cases of procurement leading to innovation: the empirical evidence presented supported the conclusion that 'the most important way that governments have influenced technical innovation is through demand' (see Chapter 7).

There is also a different ground on which the need to study government demand can be argued, namely the present stage of technological development and the economic stagnation in the industrialized world. It can be argued that the present economic crisis has underlying causes related to the *type of technological change* that has characterized the latter part of the third quarter of the twentieth century. The spectacular increase in personal income in this period and the development of a number of technologies based on major innovations of the 1930s, has led to a situation in which many individual needs are now much better fulfilled by industry than ever before. In fact a certain saturation of the market for many consumer goods can be pointed to, as well as a lack of recent major innovations in this area. On the other hand, many public or collective needs go unfulfilled and the impact of innovation in this area seems to be much less. The modern industrial corporation, one might conclude, has found it much easier to respond innovatively to private than to public sector demand.

As mentioned previously, with the exception of military hardware, the public sector has lagged behind technologically. Public transportation technology has developed much slower than the automobile. The telephone system lags behind development of computer terminals and other non-collective communication equipment. Block heating has lost out to the one-household central heating unit. Developments in preventive medicine and productivity in the health system look pale when compared to innovation in the pharmaceutical industry. Thus there is clearly considerable scope for stimulating public sector technology through innovation-oriented procurement.

Having argued the need and potential benefits of studying an innovation-oriented procurement policy, this leaves us with the problem of how best to go about it. Only in a limited number of countries is such a policy seriously being implemented, and it is probably true to say that insufficient results are available from these initiatives to be able to offer definitive guidelines. Nevertheless we believe that innovation-oriented procurement has great potential for significantly affecting both the rate and direction of technological innovation. In particular it might be used to reduce the market entry risks for would-be innovative SMEs.

While a large number of forms of governmental intervention in industry are essentially a recognition of a failure of the market mechanism, which gives rise to various externalities of industrial production, this is most explicitly the case with government regulations. Here, the stated objective is to minimize externalities by controlling environmental impact, improving worker health and safety, minimizing the danger sometimes inherent in the use of new products, etc. While the satisfaction of regulatory requirements might itself require some product or process innovations, regulations are rarely, if at all, formulated with the stimulation of business innovation as a primary objective.

Society's norms and values determine the rate and direction of regulation. At the same time the need for growth and/or change might well demand technological innovations. The direction of innovation (and to some extent its rate) is in turn at least partially determined by government regulations, but also by the structure of industry, society and the marketplace. The question is, of course, just what impact does regulation have on determining the rate and direction of innovation? How important is regulation in relation to a myriad other factors affecting the technological innovation process? If regulation is important, what can governments do to mitigate possible adverse impacts and to encourage potentially positive ones?

The data presented in Chapter 8 indicate, for the United States at least, that regulation can have a marked effect on the firm's propensity to undertake risky technological innovation endeavours. The effect of regulation on the rate and direction of industrial innovation is less clear, and it seems likely that the impact, where it exists, is most often an indirect one. Nevertheless, a number of useful observations can be made.

First, the major impacts appear to be associated with the regulation formulation and implementation process, which adds a considerable element of uncertainty to an already uncertain endeavour. Clearly governments should take steps to reduce this regulation-induced uncertainty. These would result in reducing interagency ambiguities and the formulation of clear and precise regulations. Such steps would include closer interaction between regulatory agencies and industry during regulation formulation, and better coordination between the various government agencies involved in the formulation and implementation of regulations. More meaningful standards might be promulgated if the regulatory agencies possessed greater technical expertise, which might be supplemented by the greater use of external experts in the formulation process.

In terms of the impact on technical change of the *nature* of the regulation, then performance standards appear to be preferable to specification standards or design characteristics as a spur to compliance innovation. There are, however, situations where the level of risk is so great, that specification standards are necessary (in, for example, the nuclear power industry). 'Best available' or 'best practicable' technology standards also appear preferable to specification standards from the point of view of stimulating innovation in that they are clearly highly sensitive to technological development and to variations in local conditions. *Thus governments have, given the right approach, the possibility for using regulations as a means of directing technology along certain preferred paths.*

Finally, it seems clear that regulations can have a relatively much greater negative impact on small firms than on their larger counterparts. In areas where small firms play a significant role as generators of technological innovations, governments might instigate measures to alleviate regulatory impacts so that high rates of innovation can be maintained across firms of all sizes. Possible measures are tax credits and compliance grants.

In most of the advanced market economies the scientific and technological infrastructure plays an important role in the performance of national research and development work, although the significance of the infrastructure varies considerably between countries, being relatively high in Israel, Ireland and Denmark and relatively low in the United States. Despite national differences, however, indications are that governments in the advanced economies are laying increasing emphasis on utilizing the infrastructure as an adjunct to national innovation policies. This is evident even in the United States, where President Carter's Domestic Policy Review included statements concerning the need to improve university–industry inter-actions and the intention to establish government-funded collective industrial research organizations.

Certainly the establishment and maintenance of a strong and comprehensive science and technology infrastructure would appear to be eminently sensible during an era that has been characterized by high rates of technological change. It should be well suited to assist innovation in SMEs, to develop generic technologies and to create new technologies as the basis for future industrial development and economic growth. The mere establishment of a science and technology infrastructure by itself is not enough, however, and vigorous steps must be taken to encourage and facilitate interaction between the infrastructure and its main potential users, that is, industry. Steps currently being taken in this respect are the use of university industrial liaison officers, information brokers for small firms and the regionalization of services.

Now, while the collective industrial research organizations must be allowed to continue to perform some long-term research, at the same time the direct economic relevance of their work must be increased. This might be achieved via a greater emphasis on contract research, and the more widespread application of the customer–contractor principle for projects involving direct government funding. Finally a notable, and laudable, trend in collective industrial research institutes in a number of countries is the provision of a wide range of non-technical services (technological forecasting, management training, marketing, for example). This is an explicit recognition on the part of the institutes that they are in the business of innovation assistance and not just R & D assistance.

Support for small and medium-sized firms comes from many and diverse quarters. Historically we find two rather different approaches to the problem: the first approach, which has generally prevailed in most European countries and in Japan, takes as its starting-point overall economic, social and political considerations concerning the place of small firms, and considers a large range of measures aimed at strengthening their productivity and competitiveness. Among these measures we generally find some which are more specifically aimed at strengthening the technological capacity of the firms concerned and improving their position as utilizers of modern technologies. The second approach, which is based to a high degree on American experience, centres its interest mainly on the problem of the growth and existence of the small innovative firms active in industrial branches generally characterized by science-intensive technologies, fluid industrial structures and rapid growth rates. Some countries have begun to develop a two-tier policy and build-up measures directed specially at the small innovative firms alongside the wider measures aimed at the overall population of small firms. This development, however, is by no means general yet, or complete.

We can say with some confidence that the peculiar problems of small firms in innovation have become increasingly recognized and accepted by most western governments who are, accordingly, formulating and implementing an increasing number of measures for their assistance. The most important of these measures were described in Chapter 10 and will not be repeated here. The fact that these measures are increasingly being implemented on a regional basis is an explicit, if somewhat belated (in most countries), recognition that innovation in small firms is very often a regional phenomenon; this represents an important step forward.

It is possible to state quite succinctly the prime needs of would-be innovative small firms. First, and perhaps most important, they require risk capital. Second, they often need high-level technical assistance. Third, they sometimes need market information, especially export market information. In all three areas they suffer, generally, a severe disadvantage *vis-à-vis* their larger counterparts. It is also possible to state that the prime requirement of any government scheme to assist small firms in any or all these areas is *speed*. Thus, in the case of small firms, application procedures should be straightforward and decision-making quick. This is particularly important during periods of high inflation (especially, as in the United Kingdom, where this is coupled to historically high commercial rates of interest) when problems of liquidity in small firms are severe.

One factor that has played a crucial role in Japanese industrial development has been the availability of long-term, low-interest rate loans to Japanese industry to fund developments in strategic areas from the government-backed Japan Development Bank. Following the recent MITI white paper (see Chapter 5), for example, which has identified a number of advanced high-technology industries suitable for exploitation by Japanese companies, the Japan Development Bank will lend $4.5 billion in the 1980 fiscal year to fund developments in these designated strategic areas. This, in turn, will trigger a spate of lending for parallel projects by the commercial banks.

This long-term view taken by the Japan Development Bank, and which is closely followed by the commercial banks, allows Japanese managers in turn to take a long-term view concerning technological development and market exploitation. This is also true of managers in West Germany, where traditionally close and stable links between companies and banks encourages managers to take a long-term view of technology and growth.

In the United States and the United Kingdom, however, the situation is rather different. In both countries financing is largely dependent on commercial capital markets and managers are thus forced to emphasize short-term profitability, often to the detriment of long-term technical developments and market growth. Thus, a strong case can be made for the greater involvement of commercial banks to participate on a long-term basis in industrial development along the lines of Japan and West Germany.

Similarly, a strong case can be forwarded for the establishment of a *government industrial development bank* in most countries, whose aim would be to offer *long-term loans*, perhaps at preferable rates of interest, to fund *strategic developments* in industry. In the case of loans to small firms, they would need to be made rather quickly, involving the minimum of red tape.

Discussion of the need for long-term industry finance leads to consideration of the prime necessity for *long-term governmental industrial innovation policies*. Governments should formulate strategies based on a careful assessment of current and future technological, economic and social needs and problems, and on an awareness of technological trends and associated commercial possibilities. These policies must therefore be the result of consensus, and not dictated by the whim of party politics (which generally has a four to five year cycle) or the influence of powerful, but minority, pressure groups. The combination of consensus and long-term perspective has clearly paid high dividends in Japan.

Now, while governments need long-term strategies towards technological and industrial development, that is not to say such strategies should be completely rigid. They must be amenable to change in response to economic and technological change. In other words they should be flexible with respect to changing needs, threats and opportunities, but not to the often cynical, and almost always short-term, dictates of party politics. Nor must their implementation become overbureaucratized.

Two other important issues are the *level* of government involvement in the implementation of policy, and the *competence* of government policy-makers In the first case, in deciding which innovation measures to take, and in expediting them, there are considerable advantages to be gained from involving the industries concerned. This would go some way towards bridging the communications gap (and sometimes the credibility gap) that often exists between industry and government; it could improve both the quality of the measures taken and the degree to which they are taken up by companies. Certainly very close industry–government collaboration has paid handsome dividends in Japan. On the other hand, care must be taken by governments over their level of involvement in the day-to-day implementation of policy measures. While governments must be the prime movers in establishing the technological and economic targets and priorities their measures are designed to meet, too much involvement at the level of the firm might be seen by managers and especially small firm managers — a normally fiercely independent breed — as unwarranted interference.

In the second case it might be doubted whether most government decision-makers — or their bureaucratic advisers — possess the full competence to properly assess technological and market opportunities and threats during an era of rapid technological, and dramatic economic, change. This would again support our plea for a *collaborative approach to strategy formulation* involving governmental, industrial, academic, infrastructural, and other representatives.

A notable feature of past innovation policies has been a marked lack of assessment regarding their efficacy. Because of the cost — both direct and potential opportunity cost — of implementing innovation measures, it would seem sensible that governments should establish mechanisms to monitor their performance objectively (such as is currently happening at the Frauhofer–ISI institute in Karlsruhe). Perhaps the major problem here is that of timing, and assessment should not take place until the measures have been given a fair chance to prove themselves, or otherwise.

Perhaps the most suitable — and innovative — approach is that adopted in the United States where initiatives are taken on an *experimental* basis. Examples of this are the Department of Commerce's Experimental Technology Incentives Programme which experimented with, among other things, innovation-oriented procurement; the National Science Foundation's innovation centres experiment, which attempted to stimulate entrepreneurship in several US universities; the recently proposed generic technology centres programme, which will establish centres in a variety of insitutional settings. On the basis of the results of these experiments, the initiatives are continued, discontinued, or continued with modifications.

As a final point there is, as touched upon earlier, the key issue of the vital role of government as a *coordinator of policies*. Indeed we saw earlier that even in a single area of government intervention — regulation — industry can suffer severe problems as a result of interagency ambiguities. In other instances, policies from different government agencies can appear to be diametrically opposed. The point can be well illustrated by considering the policies of a number of different agencies in the United States. The US Energy Department is encouraging firms to change from the use of imported oil to dirtier-burning coal, while the EPA is pressing for more stringent air pollution standards; the EPA restricts the use of pesticides, while the Department of Agriculture actively promotes their use; the Transport Department in attempting to maintain high rail transportation costs for coal to aid US railways, while the Energy Department is attempting to lower these to encourage plant conversions from oil; the Transport Department is mandating for lighter vehicles as part of their energy conservation programme, while the National Highway Traffic Safety Administration is legislating safety features for cars which *add* weight. These apparently conflicting policies add significantly to industrial uncertainties, and clearly greater coordination between the various agencies could resolve, or find compromise solutions to, a number of the apparent contradictions that currently exist. *This can only be achieved under the aegis of central government and following guidelines laid down by a clear strategic policy statement.*

Finally, in relation to this issue, the latest report by ACARD in the United Kingdom on information technology strongly underlines the need for government to play a strong coordinating role concerning politices towards the development and procurement of this key technology; it emphasizes the need for *integrating* a highly fragmented and largely uncoordinated set of measures spread across a range of ministries and trade and regulatory bodies. Such an approach already exists in France and Japan.

To conclude, experiences and developments in government innovation policy measures have been described in the preceding chapters. Government policy in itself has to be innovative in order to cope with the complexity of the problem. It is certain that new structures and institutions have to be devised to deal effectively with the problems of innovation. It has been the intention of the authors of this book to put forward the results of empirical research and of tendencies that show that devising effective government innovation policies is both feasible and acceptable.

INDEX

Aggregate demand theory, 209-14
Aggregate production function, 23-4
Agricultural machinery, export competitiveness, 35, 36
Agriculture, employment pattern changes, 207; incomes, 3-4
Alienation of the individual, 10

Banks, providing finance for industry, 89
Belgium, collective research, 167
Biotechnologies, 15, 43
Brooks Report, 11
Bundesministerium für Forschung und Technologie (BMFT) (W. Germany), 103-5

'Call off' contracts, 94
Canada, Department of Supply and Services, and Science Centre, 106-8; Enterprise Development Program (EDP), 199-202
Capital accumulation, 18; cyclical nature, 38-9
Chemical industry, changes in source of research, 148-9
Collective research, 157-73; attitudes to small firms, 194-5; funding, 160-1; government policy, 161-2; increasing economic relevance, 242; international trends, 172-3; national trends, 167-70; programme selection, 162-3; range of services, 166-7; staff quality and mobility, 166; US antitrust legislation preventing, 237
Communication systems, 15; external, of small firms compared with large, 181; informal channels, 152; internal in small firms, 180; slow technical development, 90
Competition, to encourage technological development, 98-9
Competitiveness, related to technical change, 29-30, 34-6
Computers, affecting US employment, 207; computer-aided manufacturing programmes, 113; development, 111; French government intervention, 113
Confidentiality, 138
Construction industry, effect of regulation, 122; indicating economic change, 5
Corporatism, 18
Costs, changing pattern, 12-14; reduction through technical change, 215

Decision-making, by centralized governments, 97; by collective research organizations, 162-3; changes of emphasis, 21
Demand, government influence, 90; shifting patterns, 14; stimulating invention, 240; see also Aggregate demand theory
Democratic movements, 21
Developing countries, industrial competition from, 7; relationships with OECD countries, 7

Economic forecasting, multiple scenarios, 8-9
Economic growth, between 1948-73, 3; effects, 8; global trends, 28; interwar period, 3; necessity for technical change, 23-9; relationship of R & D expenditure, 26-9; slowdown, 11, 63
Economic theory, attacks on, 7
Economies of scale, 176-7; effects on US national income, 25
Economy, informal, 19-20; long wave theory, 36, 38-9; problems of recovery, 6; structural change related to technology, 36, 38-44
Education, comparative levels in producing and service industries, 224
Electronics industry, 11, 15; influenced by US military procurement, 110-13
Employment, aggregate demand theory, 209-14; conditions in large and small firms compared, 177; international comparative advantage theory, 214-15; lack of challenging jobs, 16; mobility factor, 17; policy implications of innovation, 232-3; qualitative effects of technology, 228-30; role of small firms, 230-2; shifts in postwar patterns, 207-9; structural changes in relationship with output, 217-22; supported by small firms, 177; technology gap theory, 215; see also Unemployment
Energy, increasing costs, 6; new technologies, 15, 43
Energy conservation, proposed ETIP experiment, 101-2; solar and heatpump technology, 104, 105
Energy crisis (1973-4), economic effects, 1; subsequent unemployment, 206; triggering change in economic climate, 5, 36
Enterprise Development Program (EDP), 199-202
Environmental awareness, 116-17, 130; disclosure of information, 138
European Economic Community (EEC), industrial output and employment (1950-